RECRUIT
The Savage Way

Skills, attitudes and tactics to be an outstanding recruiter

GREG SAVAGE

MACMILLAN

Praise for *RECRUIT – The Savage Way*

'Another masterpiece from the master of the recruitment sector! *RECRUIT – The Savage Way* is a comprehensive toolkit for every recruiter, no matter how long you have been in the business – a cradle-to-grave tutorial of "best in class" tips and tactics.'

Geraldine King, CEO, Employment & Recruitment Federation (ERF), Ireland

'This book is your best bet to ensure your recruitment consulting skills lead you to success. If you want to be better, earn more and succeed in recruitment, leverage Greg's knowledge and expertise. The power is in your hands!'

Angela Cameron, CEO, Consult Recruitment, New Zealand

'Greg's passion for the recruitment industry, wisdom and knowledge jump off every page.'

Simon Hair, Managing Director, Precision Sourcing Australia, Australia

'This book is a superb reminder of the importance of self-belief and the impact that YOU can have on people and organisations. The book is packed with actionable tips, thought-provoking commentary – and inspiration! A must-read for every recruiting professional.'

Simon Lusty, Chief Marketing Officer, Aquent, USA

'This book is a must-read for every recruiter, non-negotiable – it's brilliant! Greg's no-nonsense style, with plenty of humour, keeps you turning those pages. There is no other book like this. It's what the recruitment industry has been waiting for. Thank you, Greg. I can't wait to share it with everyone in my team.'

Nikki Beaumont, CEO/Founder, Beaumont People, Australia

'As a rookie recruiter in 1983, I would have been far more productive MUCH sooner if I had read this book. *RECRUIT – The Savage Way* is a must-read for any career recruiter who wants to be the best version of themselves! Greg Savage, you have done the profession I love a great service!'

Andrew Banks, Founder/CEO, Morgan & Banks and Talent2, Australia

'Greg is always an inspiration. He puts things in a simple, blunt and unapologetic way that every recruiter needs to hear. *RECRUIT – The Savage Way* only galvanised my pride in this job and the industry I love. Whether you're a rookie, new to the industry, a manager, owner or CEO, it's a great read, and there's much to take away.'

Jeremy Sampson, CEO, North East Asia, Robert Walters Group, Japan

'*RECRUIT – The Savage Way* is the go-to for rookies and experienced recruiters to hone these skills or refresh their experience. It should be part of your onboarding kit for all your new recruiters and on the desk of those who have been with you forever.'

Mark Smith, Group CEO, people2people, Australia

'*RECRUIT – The Savage Way* is a mini library of recruitment nuggets and ideas. They are as easy to digest as they are to implement, making this an absolute must for new and experienced recruiters who want to learn new ways of working, refresh old ways of thinking and put ideas into action.'

James Osborne, Chairman, The Recruitment Network, UK

'Greg writes as he talks – with honesty, directness, intelligence, humour, passion, and care. In reading *RECRUIT – The Savage Way*, you will come away with a new respect for the character strengths, human skills and technical proficiency the best recruiters possess – and the inspiration to be one.'

Ross Clennett, FRCSA, High-performance recruitment coach, Australia

'Greg is an industry leader with decades of experience but a modern approach, and this book is filled with tips, tricks and strategies for people to thrive. If you're looking for a comprehensive guide to modern recruitment practices, I highly recommend *RECRUIT – The Savage Way*.'

Paul Hallam, Founder and Director, Six Degrees Executive, Australia

I dedicate this book to Ron Savage and Deb Savage:
two outstanding human beings who gave me so much more
than I thanked them for while they were here.

First published in 2023 by Major Street Publishing Pty Ltd

First published in India 2024 by Macmillan
an imprint of Pan Macmillan Publishing India Private Limited
707 Kailash Building
26 K. G. Marg, New Delhi 110001
www.panmacmillan.co.in

Pan Macmillan, The Smithson, 6 Briset Street, Farringdon, London EC1M 5NR
Associated companies throughout the world
www.panmacmillan.com

ISBN 978-93-6113-539-2

1 3 5 7 9 8 6 4 2

Internal design by Production Works
Printed and bound by Gopsons Papers Pvt. Ltd., Noida

Contents

About the Author

Greg started his career in executive search in Australia before he went on to manage the London office of the United Kingdom's largest accounting recruiter for two years. Then, in the early 1980s, he returned to Australia to run the Sydney office of Accountancy Placements (now Hays), where he was invited to join the board of directors at age 27.

With two others, Greg founded Recruitment Solutions in 1987. He rapidly built the start-up across Australia and New Zealand, culminating in its successful listing on the Australian Securities Exchange, with Greg as Executive Director and COO.

In April 2001 Greg joined Aquent and, as International CEO, assumed responsibility for all Aquent businesses outside of North America, comprising 25 offices in 17 countries across Europe, Asia, and Australia and New Zealand.

In 2010 Greg acquired Aquent's Permanent and Search business in a management buyout and founded Firebrand Talent Search. He quickly created a global brand for this specialist digital and marketing recruiter and successfully sold the company, in seven countries, in January 2013.

In recognition of his contribution to the Australian recruitment industry, Greg was named an Honorary Life Member of the Recruitment and Consulting Services Association (RCSA) in 2004.

In 2011 he was awarded a special commendation by the RCSA for 'Outstanding Contribution to the Recruitment Industry'. In addition, he was named the most influential Australian businessperson on Twitter in 2016 and the most influential recruiter in Australia in the past 60 years in 2015.

In 2018 Greg was inducted into the Recruiter International Hall of Fame.

In November 2018, he was named one of LinkedIn's 'Top Voices'.

An early adopter of social media for recruiting, Greg's industry blog, 'The Savage Truth', attracts more than 1 million visitors annually and is a must-read for the recruitment industry.

Greg's first book, *The Savage Truth*, was instantly successful, selling over 10,000 copies. As a result, the book was made mandatory reading for the first recruitment degree in the world at the National College of Ireland, which now offers a BA (Honours) in Recruitment Practice.

In 2021 Greg founded the Savage Recruitment Academy, a niche learning management system for the recruitment industry. It has seen outstanding success and growth, with thousands of subscribers worldwide.

Greg now acts as a non-executive director and advisor for 16 recruitment and HR tech companies in Australia, the United Kingdom, Singapore and New Zealand.

Greg still takes an active interest in founding and growing recruitment businesses, investing in recruitment start-ups in Australia and the UK.

Foreword

In my line of work – advocacy for businesses that are making a difference – there is a truism that has emerged over the past few years: it's about *the stories you tell*, not *the facts you have*. Indeed, this book is full of great stories – my favourite is about the human skills of David, the Pitt Street coffee shop owner. These examples are a treasure trove of experience from decades in our industry worldwide.

But facts also matter. For an industry so visible in people's daily lives – here in the UK, recruiters are heavily represented among the winners of *The Apprentice*, and people deal with us every day – the value of our work is often underappreciated. I have a nice line in facts that counteract this: a million temps in the workplace every day, a new permanent job every 21 seconds, a sector more significant in value added than law or accountancy (often seen as professional services powerhouses).

Given this vast impact now, our productivity matters. Our professionalism matters. Greg identifies tangible signs of increased professionalisation across our industry in this book. As a career, recruitment is exciting and meaningful.

But we also need to step up. Clients face fast-changing product markets, labour and skills shortages, and hugely different employee expectations post-pandemic. CEOs have always claimed talent as their number-one priority – now they are acting like it.

What will set a recruiter apart in this world? Human skills. Professionalism. The ability to advise and guide both the client and the candidate. When the tech stack – an essential part of every business – is a leveler, it is the people who make the difference.

There is no one better to guide us through this challenge than Greg Savage. For decades, across multiple continents, Greg has recruited, built businesses and guided recruitment leaders. He has worked with us at the REC to support the UK industry for many years. Now, he returns to the basics: building great recruiters. It could not be timelier: when I ask REC members what keeps them up at night, the first answer more often than not is developing their team.

We are on a treadmill of 'technology will disrupt recruitment' right now. It will. It has. We adapt. But, as Greg points out, some of these tools have allowed recruiters to hide behind the technology. He notes how 'it has weakened the human skills that made great recruiters so special'.

This isn't back to the future; it's the behaviour we always needed to make a difference as professional consultants. But we are heading towards a time when recruiters won't just be less productive if they get this wrong – their market will go away. With that in mind, this book is a great guide – from the tips on the human skills that retain and guide candidates (up to and including coaching them for resignation meetings and preparing their letters!) to how you can offer easier, quicker and more productive solutions to clients.

It's a human business. We need to compete on value, on professionalism. No one hires the cheapest lawyer or the lowest-cost strategy consultant. We win with high standards of service to clients and candidates, swift processing and strong delivery – with strong career paths built on insight, experience and effort. There is no better guide to getting there in your career than Greg.

Enjoy the journey!

Neil Carberry
Chief Executive, Recruitment and Employment Confederation, UK

Preface

Welcome to *RECRUIT – The Savage Way*.

Gleaned from 44 years in recruitment, this book is based on a key premise: success in recruitment is determined by your ability to master human influencing skills for the greater good.

Of course, the process is critical too, and only a fool would deny the impact of technology, especially the emergence of AI tools. However, the recruiter's value is determined by their ability to create excellent outcomes through managing the key 'moments of truth' in recruitment.

You have no real future in agency recruitment unless you can build relationships, become authentically consultative and earn what I call in this book 'recruiter equity'. Recruitment comprises a series of critical interactions between people, the outcome of which can be impacted by an intelligent question, a piece of advice or an injection of encouragement. Of course, great recruiters own these moments of truth.

The moments of truth in recruitment are when the magic happens. If you hide behind digital technology, you will fail as a recruiter. Of course, you must be excellent at using technology, but the differentiator is in building relationships, garnering trust and influencing outcomes. Agency recruiters must master the 'craft' of recruitment.

There are lessons in this book for anyone involved in recruitment and sales. However, it is written for agency recruiters: an often maligned, poorly acknowledged group of people who deserve much more credit than they ever get.

I have based these 128 chapters firstly on my own experience as a recruiter. I was a good recruiter but I was not truly great. So, I have built in the lessons I learned from the many great recruiters I worked with and against, managed and mentored.

The danger is to chase the recruiting pack to the bottom, ending up as no more than a résumé-racing, inbox-spamming, cold-calling, transactional recruiting hack: harsh words, perhaps, but used with intent because they are accurate, and I wish you to choose the right path.

Recruitment is the most wonderful of careers if you can develop the nuanced consultative skills I share in this book. Like any career, it will be a journey of constant improvement, learning, upskilling, growth and evolution. But, unfortunately, many recruiters stagnate; when they do, it is the beginning of the end. *RECRUIT – The Savage Way* invites you to restock your 'skills briefcase' and be dexterous and nimble in a rapidly evolving world.

The skills I share here are crucial to your success, but even mastery of those will not compensate for a poor attitude or a flawed mindset. If any job needs enormous mental strength and a positive mental attitude, it is agency recruitment. Unfortunately, I have seen many otherwise capable people fall by the wayside because of a lack thereof.

The sections on candidate skills and client skills are micro in their advice, including scripts you might use for the best outcomes. This is intentional, as I have learned that getting 5% better at those interactions can lead to a 50% increase in revenues.

Unsurprisingly, *RECRUIT – The Savage Way* covers a great deal on 'selling', but it mainly focuses on how selling is built on questioning, listening and understanding needs. I expand my selling advice to include digital brand-building and social selling tactics, which are so essential in the modern era but so poorly understood or implemented by most agency recruiters.

Finally, this book leaves you with thoughts on how to prolong your recruitment career and maximise the fun and money this great profession can offer.

Agency recruitment is challenging. Few survive two years in the business, and fewer still turn it into a lifelong career. However, if you do the work, develop the skills and hone the attitude, success will come and self-esteem will soar. When that happens, recruitment truly rocks.

I trust that you will enjoy *RECRUIT – The Savage Way*. I hope it helps you to be the most outstanding recruiter you can be.

PART I

ATTITUDE AND MINDSET

It is hard to imagine a professional career in which attitude and mindset play a more significant role than recruitment. Too many to count are the recruiters I have known who had excellent skills, high intelligence and great potential but just lacked the grit and the optimism to succeed in a job that will taunt you with failure and success in equal measure but without pattern. Equally, so many recruiters who are modest in their natural talents but who bring determination, coachability and fortitude to their work over time learn the skills, thrive and then excel.

Later in this book, I will share the core tactics and strategies to improve your skills in every step of the agency recruitment process. However, all of them need to be built on some fundamental approaches to your work, which I have found to be non-negotiable. Great agency recruiters are competitive. They love the hunt. But, equally, they never forget that recruiting is all about people and that mutually positive outcomes are the road to long-term success.

You must have the mindset of learning and growth coupled with the courage to do difficult things. I will talk a lot about resilience and what it really means in this role, because you will have no long-term future without it.

If I were to sum up the attitude of a great career recruiter, it would be that they understand their job is to make things happen for the greater good. They impose themselves on the process and use their sophisticated influencing skills during the key 'moments of truth' in recruitment, creating outcomes that enhance the chances of a successful match. But they always do that with the interests of candidates, clients and themselves finely balanced, reaching outcomes with empathy.

1 | Recruitment is not rocket science

Recruitment starts with a deep understanding of the value, complexity and integrity of what we recruiters do.

Often, people outside recruitment like to mock the recruitment profession. You will see it on LinkedIn daily. As a recruiter you will hear it over drinks and at the dinner table. This is usually deeply ill-informed, but it's still not fun to be on the receiving end as a recruiter fighting your daily battles.

However, there is a widespread phrase used by many *inside* recruitment that undermines everything we do. It fuels the fire for the profession-criticisers and eats away at our self-image. It's a throwaway line, breezy and easy and, on the surface, not offensive or controversial. I have used it myself.

But not anymore. Ever.

Recruiters who say it are foolish because it belittles their job and diminishes the value of what they do. It reinforces a false stereotype, and it feeds the fire of disrespect for an honourable and important profession. It goes to the heart of an underlying lack of self-belief, which hinders growth and maturity, and even careers. The recruiter who spouts this phrase does not know what a complex, nuanced and hard-to-master career they have chosen.

So, it's an ignorant thing to say: 'Recruitment. It's not rocket science.'

Of course, that statement is true. Recruitment is, indeed, not rocket science. *But we are not building effing rockets, are we?* So, who cares if it's 'not rocket science'?

Writing a rock song people love and that sells millions is not rocket science. Making a hundred runs before lunch at the Sydney Cricket Ground in a test match is not rocket science. Giving a compelling speech in front of 1000 people and holding their attention for two hours is not rocket science. But you haven't done any of those things, have you?

Raising children is not rocket science. Overcoming addiction is not rocket science. Plenty of you are struggling with those challenges right now. Easy, is it?

Blithely dismissing recruitment as 'not rocket science' is banal and profoundly ignorant. It suggests that being a recruiter is straightforward, that it's child's play. Anyone can do it. It requires no skills or intelligence.

Really?

It misses the all-too-obvious point that being a recruiter, especially an agency recruiter, is relentlessly demanding. Doing this job well requires an intricate blend of art and science. It requires the highest level of emotional intelligence and demands the most evolved questioning, consulting and advising skills. Furthermore, you must deliver highly sophisticated human influencing skills, essentially the most challenging skills to master.

If recruitment is so easy, why do such a depressingly high percentage of new entrants to our profession fail and leave within two years?

So, it's a silly thing to say, but it's also profoundly self-sabotaging. Why? Because it damages self-belief, and from self-belief flows credibility – and these two qualities are the foundation upon which any consultative recruiter builds their expertise and career.

So, stand proud, my recruiting friends! Being a recruiter rocks (see chapter 3). Don't mock your own chosen path.

Go the other way. Treat recruitment as the fantastic career it is. Strive for continuous learning that increases the value you bring to candidates and clients and delivers you the self-esteem, fun and money that hard work in an important job deserves. (See Part VI for more on this.)

Stare down your gloating lawyer and banker mates in the pub who seek to belittle what you do. Remind them that some lawyers take money to defend criminals they know are guilty of heinous crimes, and that, in the case of the bankers, they might actually be criminals themselves as far as we know! (No one in finance ever broke the law, right?)

What recruiters do is inherently good. We find people jobs that enhance their careers and support companies as they search for skills that drive their growth and progress. Also, it's an exceptionally challenging job requiring a heady mix of hard work, subtle influencing skills and incredible logistical mastery.

Think about this. You have ten experienced recruiters in a room. In the room next door, you have ten experienced rocket scientists. With your life at stake, you must choose one group to recruit for you against the other (in a sort of recruiter-versus-rocket-scientist version of *Squid Game*!). Which group would you choose to represent you in these fatal recruitment 'hunger games'? Are you really going to choose the rocket scientists to recruit for your life? Or the recruiters?

I think I know your answer.

2 | The best recruiter ever

Graham Whelan is the best recruiter I've ever met, and he has been that way since before most of you reading this book were even born. (He started in recruitment in the 1970s.)

Prior to writing this book, I went to lunch with Graham, and he was so excited he could not contain himself. Graham had just come from a client meeting at which three of his candidates had been selected for final interviews for a CFO job. It was so refreshing: his energy and sincere enthusiasm for the looming placement were as vigorous and heartfelt as in many similar conversations we have had over the previous 35 years. No matter that he had been placing people in finance jobs since 1978. No worn-out apathy or cynicism here. His love of the chase, his desire to make the match and his interest in the welfare of his client and the candidates have not waned in five decades.

I worked with Graham for over 15 years, including 12 as partners in building a business called Recruitment Solutions, which went from start-up to an IPO on the Australian Securities Exchange. (For that story, read my first book: *The Savage Truth*.)

Graham epitomises what a great recruiter should be. I am in awe of his longevity in this most demanding of businesses and his passion and commitment to service.

What is it that makes Graham special? He has all the technical recruiting skills, of course. But he has more too. Let me count the ways.

He cares

He cares about his clients, of course, but also about every candidate he deals with. Sure, he is looking to make the placement and the fee, but Graham has never lost sight of the human element of our business, and every person he deals with he treats with kindness and attention to detail (chapter 79).

He has incredible energy

I don't want to break any privacy laws, but even post-60, he worked at the pace of the Energizer Bunny. Graham is a shorter man than I am but, when we went on client visits together, I almost had to run to keep up with him. He strides around the office and often stands when speaking on the phone during important conversations. He moves quickly from one call or meeting to the next. He is a little whirlwind of activity and inspires action around him. Typically, he works from 8 a.m. to 6 p.m., starting with a booming *'bore da'* (Welsh for 'good morning') across the office as he strides in. Lunch is a sandwich at the desk. Every other minute is spent conversing with clients, candidates and colleagues. So many recruiters today could learn from this 'activity ethos'. It is not blind 'busyness'; it's all quality and it's all with care. And he gets things done!

He is honest

Of course, he has impeccable business integrity, but he is honest at a deeper level. He tells clients when he can't help. He advises candidates on their exact status. If the news is bad, he gives it directly but with compassion. He is one of the 'honest recruiters' described in chapter 15.

He does what he says he is going to do

This alone separates Graham from most other recruiters: if he says he will call you back, he does. If he tells you that you are on his shortlist, you are. If he tells you that he will keep you in mind for a specific role, he will and you can expect a call, even if it is four months later.

He listens

Again, so many recruiters can learn from this: Graham asks many questions, digs, hears and is purposely 'slow to understand' (chapters 28 and 37). He does not make assumptions (chapter 27). As a result, he inevitably develops a better search brief with the client than anyone else. He always gets to the core reason a candidate is looking to move jobs, which every good recruiter knows is often not the reason they initially give (chapter 70).

He has an elephant-like memory

If he interviewed you as an accounts clerk 20 years ago, Graham would remember not only you but also your company and probably your salary and the person you reported to. There is a good chance he would remember your family, too. Seriously. Sit in a restaurant with Graham and he will be nodding to, and shaking hands with, every second person, not only because of his longevity as a recruiter but also because he remembers everybody and has never burned anyone in business. He has no enemies that I could imagine. None. (See chapter 35 for another example of this.)

He is the embodiment of PMA

PMA stands for 'positive mental attitude' (chapter 20). Graham believes and behaves as though good things will happen, then he works hard to make sure they do. I believe so much in this trait. To Graham, his candidates *will* get the job, which makes them think they will and, as a result, they usually do.

He makes you feel special

Graham makes you feel special without even knowing or trying. He is interested in you. You are his focus when you are talking to him. He remembers your spouse's name, your kids' names. He asks how they are and you can tell he is interested. He sends handwritten thank you notes and he calls on your birthday. He cries when a friend is having a bad time or is seriously ill.

*

What a great man.

Don't get me wrong; the man is not perfect. He endlessly talks about the Welsh rugby team of the 1970s (he is Welsh). He is not the quickest on the technology uptake, and he just smiles and pours another glass of pinot when I talk about social media (as I do in chapter 58). But he is the best hardcore recruiter I have ever worked with or against, and he has made an immeasurable contribution to countless lives and our profession.

The truth is that Graham has inspired me for decades, and I know for a fact he has inspired many others because so many have told me so.

3 | Being a recruiter rocks!

I love being in recruitment. Seriously, I think it's the best job in the world.

It is *tough* being a recruiter, and I believe it's getting even more challenging in the modern era. During the COVID-19 downturn, it got worse. We all worked harder and harder and earned less and less.

But the tide has turned and, after the next downturn, it will turn again. Skills shortages mean we have never been more relevant. Clients and candidates alike are sick and tired of the transactional recruiting model and want to engage again with professional, credible advisors.

If you can master the influencing skills of a great recruiter, this job will be intensely satisfying and rewarding in years to come.

I know many recruiters have doubts. I know plenty of recruiters feel slammed. You may be feeling like that right now! It is usual for recruiters to wobble. I am not going to gild the lily: it's a tough gig. Being a long-term success won't be easy. But name me anything genuinely worthwhile that is. (More on that in chapter 13.)

It will be worth it! Here's why.

Recruiting is a win-win-win

Unlike most commercial transactions, recruiting is not a win-lose scenario. If I sell you a car, I aim for the highest price and you push for the lowest: one of us will feel we 'won', the other will feel a bit despondent that we 'lost'. It might even get a little acrimonious. However, in the perfect recruitment scenario, *everybody* wins. Happy client, happy candidate, happy you. This is not as trivial as it seems. There is something intensely rewarding about doing a job where everyone is grateful and excited about the outcome – and then you get paid.

You create excellent outcomes

Maybe the coolest thing about being a recruiter is that this is a job where you literally *make good things happen.* Well, good recruiters who can influence the key 'moments of truth' do (chapter 24). The candidate is reluctant to go on an interview but, through your influencing skills, they reluctantly go along, do exceptionally well, love the job *and get hired*! Or the client won't see your top candidate because of something they spotted in the résumé, but you persist, explaining the person is better than the paper; the client relents and your candidate gets the job, gets promoted and in time becomes your client! For me, when I recruited, this was the real buzz. Making things happen. Controlling the process. I would crack open a beer on Friday and reflect: *That would not have happened if I had not seen the opportunity and influenced the outcome.* Not with arrogance; with gratitude. Beyond cool.

What we do matters

And, of course, that leads us to another reason why recruiting rocks: I mean, it *really* matters. Recruiters get a horrific reputation sometimes, and occasionally it's deserved, but hey, at the end of the day, *we find people jobs*! And that's a good thing, right? It's something to be proud of. It makes an impact. We change people's lives. We solve companies' staffing issues. We help people further their career ambitions. Fantastic!

Our business is so measurable

One of the beautiful things about our business is that it is so measurable. Of course, this does not suit everybody, but there is nowhere to hide in recruiting, and I like that. If you have the right temperament, you will thrive in this competitive environment, love that you can measure yourself against your competitors and colleagues, and revel in the transparency of fee tables and pay by results. You could probably be an average accountant or teacher and no one would really know or remark on it. In recruitment, though, you know when you are good. You know when you are mediocre. You know when you are underperforming. And so does everybody else. There is nowhere to hide (chapter 12).

You can 'own' your market

If you have longevity, maintain integrity and deliver service and outcomes that your customers want, you can elevate yourself to the position of trusted advisor, and then recruitment becomes a beautiful thing. All your work is exclusive, all your candidates come via referrals and recommendations, and clients treat you with respect, seek your advice and bring you 'into the tent'. You 'own' your patch, and that is a wonderful place to be! Graham Whelan, who I referred to as the greatest recruiter ever in chapter 2, could walk into any board room in Sydney or Melbourne to be greeted with handshakes and hugs, because he probably placed half the people around the table, and the rest he has helped in some other way, quite likely finding a job for one of their children. Literally.

*

So, if you are having a down day, never forget: recruitment rocks!

4 | TrReCo

If there was a positive to come out of COVID-19 regarding the dynamic between agency recruiters and clients, it was most definitely the opportunity to shift the way we work together.

Many clients reviewed how they had been working with recruiters and recognised how transactional and commoditised the arrangement had become, primarily to their *own* detriment. There emerged a desire to get closer to service providers, build partnerships and look for real value.

But it won't 'just happen' for agency recruiters. It will be the making of some individual recruiters, but the opportunity will pass many others by. In fact, at time of writing, I see it already has. Many recruiters are cascading back to their transactional, résumé-spamming ways, dropping fees at the first sign of a slowdown.

There are others thinking differently, however. All recruiters, even those working in a highly transactional environment, should grab the chance to strengthen relationships, select clients who think in this collaborative way and move from primarily transactional recruiting to building relationships and, ultimately, to consulting (TrReCo).

To shift the dynamic is a conscious decision and a considered strategy by the recruiter. You need to choose clients who want to work this way and move away from those who don't. Learn how to ask great questions, develop the subtle art of pushback, hone your influencing skills and, imperatively, look for opportunities to advise, offer insights and consult.

Rapport can be built in moments of disappointment and failure, too. Authenticity, transparency and sound advice when things have gone wrong can be the making of a business relationship (chapter 44). I have seen excellent examples of this among my clients who used the post-COVID-19 talent-short dynamic to reinvent their relationships with their clients.

One of my clients now only takes exclusive, retained and fully qualified permanent recruitment assignments. Before COVID-19, her company accepted contingent job orders in competition with multiple agencies, like all the rest. Now, politely and with the door left open, she turns away clients who are not ready to work that way. And she works in high-end business support, placing executive assistants and the like. As a result, all her work is retained, and her client relationships and productivity are stronger than ever.

Another client, who runs a 30-recruiter IT business, led the charge to shift the dynamic in the highly transactional IT recruitment world from 'spray and pray' to exclusivity and order qualification, both of which require clients to buy into a consultative approach. They measure job-fill ratios religiously, and they have dropped to better than one in two – down from one in three (and sometimes worse than that). Everybody wins!

I have long believed that clients *want* an excellent recruiter to control the process, and we've never had a better opportunity to do that. But the recruiter must step up and make it happen.

5 | 'Recruiter equity'

Why do some recruiters forge long, successful careers while others struggle and fade away? It is a mystery to many.

How can a handful of recruiters survive, even thrive, during a downturn and generate more significant returns in the good times? Why do some love this profession and turn it into a meaningful career, while others leave bitter and damaged? How do you follow the TrReCo path and evolve your dynamic with clients and candidates?

All your training as a recruiter is a total waste of time unless the skills and techniques you learn are built on a platform of self-belief.

In business, as in life, you get treated the way you *allow* yourself to be treated. We all know individuals who are always 'the victim'. Bad things are always happening to them. If something could go wrong with a client or candidate, it will. It's all so unfair! But the reality is that their behaviour, demeanour and attitude are the problem. They are failure magnets.

I believe that self-belief is the foundation point for a great recruiter. You are the expert. Your client may be an Executive Director of a listed company or the CEO of a multinational conglomerate, but who knows more about the permanent recruiting market – you or them? Who interviews hundreds of candidates each year? Who negotiates salaries every day? Who negotiates temp rates? Who knows what motivates candidates in today's marketplace? Who knows permanent market-rate salaries or how to handle a counteroffer situation? You do! *You* are the expert. Believe in that and behave as though you believe that. If you do, your client will believe in you. But if you act like a processor of résumés or a clerical resource, that is how you will be treated.

It's not arrogance. Being cocky will not fly, and you must walk before you try to run. But you can set the tone of the relationship with your client. Too many of us are forever apologising for our profession and trying to justify our role. I have even heard consultants say that our fees are expensive, and they find it hard to justify our service. Nonsense! We must put that behind us. We must be proud of what we do and fiercely protective of our value. Any other way means we lose respect – and, therefore, control.

Your relationship with your client is one of equality. It is not a master-servant relationship. Instead, through your credibility, communication skills and self-belief, you impress upon your client a process that you know will benefit them. Approach all contact with clients respectfully but always on a professional-to-professional basis. If you are subservient, apologetic or lacking in confidence, the client automatically takes control, and you will be lost.

To be a winner in the recruitment business, you must have the attitude of a winner. You need the skills, of course, but only through the right attitude can you grow your 'recruiter equity'.

Recruiter equity is the trust, buy-in and belief your clients have in your ability and judgement. It combines your experience and knowledge, but also the personal confidence you show in delivering that expertise. It gives you the power to advise clients and truly impact the outcomes of your interactions with them.

Equity means ownership, or a share of ownership. In the case of recruiter equity, I mean the joint ownership of the *problem* and the *solution*. Recruiter equity is the key difference between winners and also-rans in this business. Do your clients trust your judgement? Do they interview every candidate you refer? Do they build questions into their recruitment process based on your advice? Do they adjust their hiring process, refine their offer letters and add extra benefits because you counsel them that this is the way to attract better talent?

No? Then your recruiter equity is low – maybe non-existent. It takes hard work to build up your equity. It takes determination, study, courage and practice. (We talk about this courage in chapter 19.) But it all stems from your attitude. Think about the best recruiters you know. The relationships they have with clients amount to shared equity.

Sharing the problem. Sharing the solution. Sharing the rewards.

If you want to build recruiter equity, your service needs to be consultative rather than transactional, as discussed in the previous chapter. In other words, do you provide résumés, or do you provide expertise? Is following a process the extent of your service, or do you offer insights? Because your survival depends on your ability to provide something your clients currently *lack*.

Does your client value your counsel in hiring trends, candidate mindset, salary movement and interview techniques, for example? You see, you are the expert – yet, for some crazy reason, many recruiters do not act like that in front of their clients. Well, I know the reason. It's not that they're crazy. It's just that they lack self-belief.

You have the knowledge and expertise, and the contacts clients desperately need if they are going to hire the best people available. Likewise, hiring managers need your wisdom. It's just that you may have not yet learned how to communicate that fact to them.

Deep down, I believe the client *wants* you to control the process. Do you go to your doctor and tell her what tests to run and what drugs to prescribe? No. Do you go to your lawyer and tell him what words to use in your legal documents? No. You trust and expect them to drive the solution to your medical or legal issues, advise and lead.

This is how great recruiters succeed in our business: belief in their value and their ability to control client and candidate interaction.

6 | Do not use 'tentative language'

If we lack recruiter equity, there is a good chance we will lack conviction in our stakeholder communications.

We don't mean to be hesitant, do we? We want to be bold, believable and confident when dealing with clients. We want to leave candidates impressed and trusting our advice and expertise. Yet, time and again, we use words that are stumbling blocks. Our insecurity takes over.

And we use *tentative language*. Words that offer the client or candidate a reason to doubt us. Phrases that reduce our credibility.

Do you use words like 'normally'? If the client asks you, 'How much do you charge?', do you start by saying, 'Oh, normally…'?

Disaster! Right there, the battle is lost. You've stepped onto a landmine.

When you say 'normally', the client knows at once that your price is negotiable. They know you are not sure of your worth. You may not even believe in your value (chapter 52). And, hey presto, the client is in the driver's seat.

Recruiters need to evolve into true advisors. Even if you don't see it right now, you have vast insight to offer your clients. After all, who knows more about salaries, talent motivation and skills availability – and so much more – than you (chapter 45)? But you can only 'advise' if you have credibility. And you can only be credible if you have the knowledge to share.

But it's also crucial how you deliver it! We all use words that prevent us from being in the driver's seat: 'approximately'; 'usually'; 'I feel that…'; 'sometimes'; 'our average price'; 'ballpark figure'; 'maybe'; 'probably'; 'I will check with my manager'. These words are not evil in themselves, and there are times when they should be used. But often, combined with a hesitant tone, these words send an instant message to the client that you're a bit unsure – just a little insecure. Tentative. Guessing. Bluffing, even.

When the client – or the candidate, for that matter – hears insecurity in your words, they cannot help but simultaneously hear the insecurity in your work and your service.

Think about your conversation with a doctor, hairdresser or house painter. They say, 'We could try this because sometimes it can work'. Are you going with that plan? Are you filled with confidence?

Don't say, 'GS Recruiting is *one of* the leading marketing, creative and digital search companies in Sydney'. Instead, say, 'GS Recruiting *is* the leading marketing, creative and digital search company in Sydney'. Who is going to argue? What defines 'leading'? Claim it!

I am not advocating hubris, BS or senseless bravado. But say what you believe with pride, and then follow through.

When a recruiter says to a client, 'For this job, we charge $20,000, and we deliver an outcome in one week or less', the client is instantly impressed. There was no tentativeness regarding price or ability.

Candidates are sensitive to tentativeness, too. Don't say, 'This job might have some of the things you are looking for in a new role', or, 'This job is probably worth looking at'. Why would that compel the candidate to go to see that client, especially when (at the time of writing) candidates have so many choices?

Instead, say, 'This is an excellent company with a great client list and a fantastic culture. What's more, it fits all the criteria you outlined for a job move, including more client-facing time and the international travel you are looking for'. (This is an example, of course. What you say must be true!)

Specifics impress. Remember, it's not just you who feels uncertainty in the sales situation; the client is in unknown territory as well.

So, as a client, what would you prefer to hear: 'The job will be advertised tomorrow, my database will be fully searched by Friday night, my research team will map the market in a week and I will have a shortlist in one week or less', or, 'We'll start soon and do our best in a tough market'?

As a candidate, would you rather hear, 'You have great skills, and I am going to market your résumé to clients A, B and C by Tuesday. We will have feedback by that night', or, 'I will do my best to get you interviews with suitable companies, and we might have feedback soon'?

Think about your words. Think about your tone of voice. Consider your body language. It can make all the difference.

One thing is sure: stop using tentative language, because it is holding you back.

7 | Your 'skills briefcase'

This chapter is for every recruiter everywhere, but especially those recruiters with a couple of years of experience who think they are good. You may think you are outstanding!

Well, there is a considerable threat facing you, and it's not AI, automation, the economy, RPO (recruitment process outsourcing) or the rise of in-house recruiters. It's *you*.

To be more specific, it's your attitude. To be even more precise, it's your *complacency*. I can't tell you how many promising recruiters have fallen off the rails because of early success, which they mistakenly understood to mean they 'know it all'.

Complacency does not mean laziness. It means being too easily satisfied with the status quo (chapter 123).

One of the things I always look for when hiring new recruiters is 'coachability'. I don't even know if that's a word, but I know what it means: the ability to learn new skills, the willingness to change, the mindset to seek improvement and the ego to accept that there may be a 'better way'.

I see it all the time and have done for decades: a new recruiter has raw potential, works hard, gets some basic skills and has some early success. Then, usually after about two years, complacency emerges. The barriers to learning go up. The 'gun recruiter' plateaus, stagnates and, unbeknown to them, starts to wither!

Of course, we all love recognition, but why is it in this business that prima donnas bloom so early and with so little reason? Actually, I know why. We all worship at the altar of 'fees' in this profession, and some companies will excuse ignorance, arrogance and a lack of real understanding of client and candidate need as long as a recruiter bills. In fact, they reward it. And so, a recruiter with early success – maybe off the back of a booming market, or inherited clients, or a company with a great brand, and probably because of a combination of those things – thinks they know it all (chapter 15)!

That is the danger period for you. Give me a dollar for every recruiter who told me, 'We always do it this way', 'This works for me', 'I know what I am doing', 'Have you seen my numbers?' or, heaven save me, 'That won't work in this market!'

Even worse is the 'silent antediluvian', who does not voice disagreement but just avoids or ignores any new tactic or advice, any technological advance. It's not that they *want* to sabotage. They are just closed to any new ideas whatsoever – dinosaurs who are always looking backwards, scoffing at training sessions and doing things 'the way that has always worked for me'.

Slowly, these people start to fail. And the more they fail, the more they blame it on their employer, on the economy, on the market, on the technology, on their colleagues, on their clients and even on their admin support! Anyone, anywhere, but the real culprit: themselves.

Do you want to be great at this job? To forge a real career? Then you must understand the concept of your 'skills briefcase'.

Imagine all your skills, capabilities, competencies and knowledge, and then place them in your imaginary skills briefcase. The question is simply this: what skills, knowledge, tactics, relationships and competencies will be in your skills briefcase one year from now that are *not* in there today? And what is in there now that was not there 12 months ago?

Nothing? Hmm.

Tackle skills you are not good at and perfect them. Look for a mentor. Seek training and coaching. Tune into professional trends and changes, and grab what you need.

Above all, be open to learning the *nuances* of this demanding job. Anyone can match a résumé with a job description; that takes a week to learn, and you may even make some placements. But it's the *craft* of recruiting I am talking about. The art. The skill of it. That takes years. Decades. Forever.

Great recruiters are sponges for life. In this business, you are never totally 'on top of your game'. You can always get better. And if you don't, others around you most certainly will.

And then, for you, it's welcome to the massive cohort of recruiters who enter our profession… and fail.

8 | There is no 'luck'

I hear these remarks often: 'I had another unlucky quarter'; 'That placement was pure luck'; 'You are so unlucky to have three offers turned down this week'.

With apologies to Oscar Wilde, to have one offer turned down may be regarded as a misfortune; to have three looks like carelessness.

Let me be clear: *There is no luck in recruitment.* No good luck, no bad luck.

Of course, I know that things go well and badly for the most bizarre and uncontrollable reasons. Sometimes everything you touch turns to gold, and sometimes it turns to mud.

It's the same with life. If a meteorite lands on your head, that is poor fortune. But you can't factor that possibility into your life and behave differently, can you? You would live in a bunker underground forever.

I was 'lucky' to be offered a job in recruitment when I was 21 – very fortunate, because it worked out great for me. It is a profession that suits my temperament and my competencies. I am forever grateful.

But my honours degree in psychology and my dozens of cold-call approaches to any business in the 'personnel' profession ('HR' was not even a thing back then) looking for my first job didn't do any harm. I would not have received my 'lucky offer' if I hadn't worked hard to get noticed and get a few interviews.

Over time, luck is not a factor in your success. *Hard work* and *fundamental skills* are what create excellent outcomes.

That recruiter who was 'so lucky' to secure the right candidate for that hard-to-fill job? Yes, because she built up an online brand, approached the candidate via LinkedIn and interviewed them at 7 p.m. That is why, not luck.

That really 'unlucky' colleague who always seems to have offers turned down and candidate counteroffers? Yes, that's not luck, either. That's a lack of process and influencing skills.

When you have a good day, week or even year, soak it up, be grateful and ride it for all it's worth. When going through a shocking patch, bear it with courage and work your way out of it through *effort* and *process analysis*. (The survival process is detailed in chapter 13, and the solution in chapter 23.)

It's not luck. The 'god of recruitment' is not frowning on you. In fact, she always smiles on the hardworking and consistent learners. Always.

Focus on the things you can control: Skills. Learning. Attitude. Relationships. Reputation. Hard work. You will be amazed how 'lucky' you become if you do.

9 | The great recruiter iceberg

We all want to be successful. And most people who enter recruitment are ambitious and driven.

It is also true that modern life encourages many to seek (and expect) instant gratification. We want it all, now!

Well, recruitment will not give you that. Worse still, recruitment might taunt you with some early success and then smash you with lengthy periods in the doldrums.

All this is exacerbated by the mindlessly banal observation that 'recruitment is not rocket science', leading many recruiters to expect quick and relatively easy results. Recruitment is clearly *not* rocket science, but it most definitely is not easy, as we learned in chapter 1.

Strangely enough, we can look to the iceberg for a lesson on recruitment success. What do we know about looking at an iceberg? *Most of it is hidden.* The part under the water, the unseen part, supports and holds up the part you *can* see. And 90% of an iceberg is underwater!

When you see a highly successful recruiter who seems to sail through life with everything falling into place, don't believe that for one second. It took work and sacrifice to get there!

Have a look at figure 1.

You see the success, money and status, But really, what you need to look at to understand that recruiter is the journey – what went before, the 90%. The rejection. The long hours. The fear. The hard work. The courage. The sacrifices. The focus on activity. The stress. The discipline. The huge learning curve. The many failures and disappointments.

Don't focus on the part of the iceberg you can see. What you see there is the end game – the result.

Focus on the part you don't immediately see. Then, *replicate that behaviour.* Work on the part of your skills portfolio iceberg that is underwater.

Figure 1: The recruitment iceberg

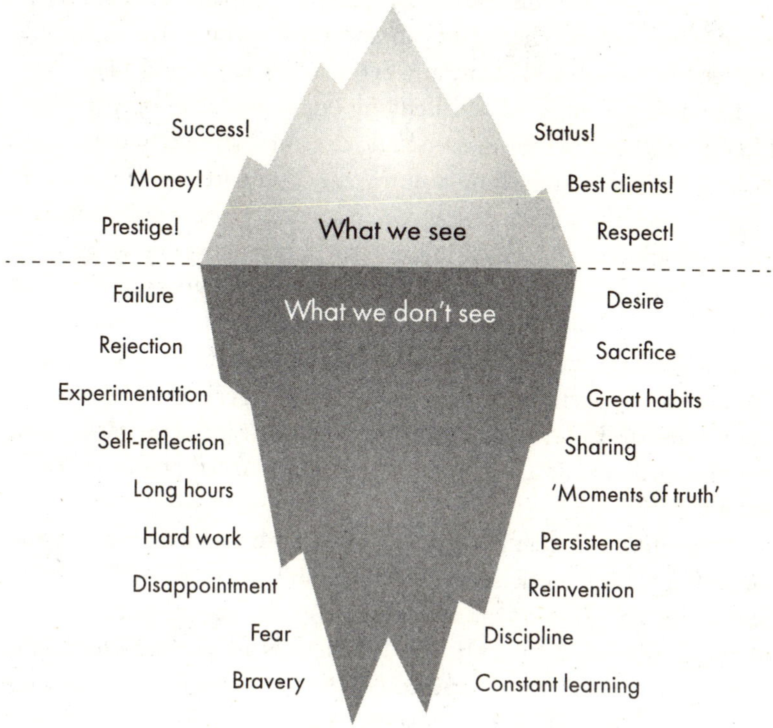

10 | Time to toughen up!

Most recruiters do not last.

There are many reasons for that. Poor hiring decisions and inadequate training are high on the list. But there is another critical reason why so few people last in the hurly-burly world of agency recruiting: *it's a frigging hard job!*

So, I know that sometimes you question why you do it. There are times when you hate what you do. There are days you go home feeling deflated, worn out and, frankly, useless.

I doubt there is a recruiter on the planet who has not felt that way at times, so do not despair.

Being a recruiter can be the most fabulous job of all (chapter 3) but, to survive, you must know the pitfalls, prepare for them, minimise their impact where you can and push through the inevitable challenges this job will throw at you (chapters 12, 13 and 14).

Recruiting is uniquely challenging because it's the only job that I know of where *what you are selling* can turn around and say 'no'. Think about it. I am selling you my car. You agree to buy the car. I agree to sell the vehicle. We agree on a price. The car does not then jump up and say, 'Hey, you know what, I am not going to go with this new guy'. Don't laugh; that happens to recruiters every day. We do everything right – take an excellent job brief, impress the client, recruit great talent, make the match, manage the process, architect a fair deal for all parties, secure a great offer and get everything agreed upon – and at the last minute our product, the candidate, says, 'Nah, I've changed my mind. I will stay where I am'. And that is it. All over, red rover!

Recruiting is a killer because it is all or nothing for us. Sure, a tiny percentage of our work is retained, but mainly recruiting is first prize or nothing ('dosh or doughnut', as my cockney colleague in London in the 1980s used to say). Our business is unlike the Olympics, where you can pick up a respectable silver or bronze for competing well. For us, it's gold, or it's 'loser'! We do all the work, spend vast amounts of time and expertise, and manage the process with skill and diligence – but if our four great candidates get pipped by a late runner from another recruiter, or an internal candidate, then it is a big fat zero for us. That's tough. That's hard to take. Especially when it happens often (and it does).

Recruiting grinds you down because you do so much work you don't get paid for. When you hear the words 'I am feeling burned out' from a recruiter, what that actually means is 'I just can't stand doing so much work for so little return'. To be a little blunter, it means, 'I cannot take this relentless failure any longer'. Contingent recruiters are lucky to fill one job out of every four they take, and to place one candidate out of every ten they meet. Combined with the 'all or nothing' fee model most work on, this means lots and lots of hours for which they don't get paid and, equally importantly, see no tangible success. And success, in the form of happy clients and talent, is the bedrock upon which self-esteem is built (chapter 120). Once that crumbles, it is the beginning of the end.

So, what to do?

Firstly, recognise that if you are going to be a recruiter, these challenges come with the job. So, in the memorable words of my under-18s rugby coach, 'Toughen the fuck up' and prepare yourself for plenty of disappointment. That was excellent advice – an unpopular sentiment these days, no doubt, but pure gold for both rugby and recruitment.

Secondly, work hard to mitigate the risk of these things happening to you. Hone your recruitment skills, talent management skills and job qualification ability. Build trusted advisor relationships and work to get exclusivity on orders to increase your job-fill ratios. Great recruiters, who move from transacting to consulting, start to win more than they lose (chapters 1 through 128).

Finally, never forget that, if you choose to be a recruiter, you have made a high-stakes bargain. You have selected a career fraught with pitfalls, and sometimes it feels like a living hell, but do it right and the fun and money you need for a great job are within your grasp. Being a recruiter can really rock, too (chapter 120)!

11 | Running the recruiter marathon

The theme of 'resilience' being a vital attribute of a career recruiter runs through this book, especially where I define it my way in chapter 13. But the very closely aligned trait of 'determination' ranks highly too. This short anecdote shows how I nearly failed the 'determination test', and you must make sure you don't when it comes to your recruitment career.

It's a while ago now, but I am proud to say I ran the Sydney Half Marathon. That's 21.1 km around the streets of Sydney. It took just over two hours for me to do it, too.

But running a half marathon is no big deal, even at my age, with my extra weight and my drinking habits. Thousands do it regularly. So, why tell you this?

Well, running this half marathon reminded me of a fundamental life lesson. It's a lesson that has enormous significance for anyone who wants to be a great recruiter and make a long-term career in this profession.

The story goes like this.

I suspected I might be a little unfit, so I went for a jog around my neighbourhood. After 3 km, I had to stop as I was out of breath and felt dizzy. Bad news. I was seriously unfit! As I hobbled home, I made a rash promise to myself. It was nine weeks until the Sydney Half Marathon, and I decided I would get fit enough to run it.

So easy to say. So hard to follow through with.

But I was determined, and I started training: road running and running on a treadmill at the gym. It hurt. I hated every second. The gym was full of smug dudes who looked like *Men's Health* magazine models. Running the streets was cold, and friends of mine would honk and laugh as they drove past.

One week into my program, I got home from a run and started wavering. 'This is ridiculous', I thought. 'I am too old for this rubbish', I reasoned. 'I don't need to run a marathon to get fit', I tried to persuade myself. 'I am far too busy. I have travel coming up. There is no time to get fit for this', I tried to convince myself. By the time I got to my warm living room, I had decided to give up the stupid half-marathon idea, and I was on my way to the fridge to grab a beer (which I had given up for nine weeks, too, by the way!).

Suddenly an image flashed across my mind. I was sharply reminded of a conversation I'd had that afternoon with a recruiter in the business I was running. This recruiter was good but young and relatively inexperienced. He was going through a rough couple of months – many offers turned down. He was despondent and told me he was unsure 'if recruiting was right for him'.

During that conversation, I did not hold back. He was a good lad with potential, and I did not want to see him give up because of a few hurdles. I talked about persistence. I spoke of the fact that nothing worth having ever came easy. I spoke of courage and character. I told him stories about bad patches I'd had and how determination had turned things around, and I examined how building a reputation and a genuine business took time. I shared that you often feel as though you are getting no traction, but that all the work he was doing would pay off in time, and when it did, he would feel pride, self-esteem and a sense of achievement.

And every word I told him was accurate. But, as I hesitated at the fridge door, about to grab the beer, I realised what a hypocrite I was. How could I tell this guy to knuckle down and persevere in the face of something he found difficult when I was giving up on my half marathon after only six days of training?

I closed the fridge and hit the road again the next day. Over the next two months, I trained four or five times weekly, and I hated it. I got a calf injury and came close to giving up. I made so little progress for the first month that I felt I was getting *less* fit. I had to travel overseas for work, and the temptation to give up training was overwhelming. But I held firm, training in hotel gyms and jogging along the murky Singapore River in 90% humidity when I could have been in the relaxed bar of the Marriott Hotel.

School holidays came around, and I took the family on holiday to Borneo with only two weeks to go until the race itself. I resisted the hotel in-pool bar and jogged down the main street of Kota Kinabalu instead – to the utter amazement of the locals who were sensibly resting under shady trees or sitting under fans drinking iced tea.

But that conversation with the Sydney recruiter kept coming back to me. *Don't give up. This will pay off. You must put in the hard work before the rewards come.*

One week out from the race, I went to the Royal Botanic Garden Sydney and ran 15 km. I did the distance, but it hurt so much that I wanted to lie down under one of the giant Port Jackson fig trees that line Sydney Harbour. I came so close to giving up on the race there and then.

On race day, I nearly didn't get out of bed. It was cold. I knew that 15 km had almost floored me. How could I run 21 km? At the event itself were 10,000 runners. And trust me, this was no 'fun run'. No one was pushing prams or dressed in Superman outfits. These people were serious! They all looked like East African Olympians: skinny and with all the right gear. I felt well out of place and like I wanted to slink off and go home.

But I did the race. And I was pumped and sped through the first 15 km as though it were a stroll in the park. It got harder after that, but I finished, running every step, and I did it in a better time than I expected.

And it felt great. I was quietly proud. No doubt, it was worth all the hassle and the pain.

And so is it with our jobs. So often, people have early success in their career. A good match, a bit of good fortune, a client or two inherited. It can make you look good, and there is nothing wrong with taking wins when they come around.

But real success? Building a reputation that will last? Developing sophisticated skills? Building a portfolio of loyal clients? Evolving into a trusted advisor? Generating referrals and word-of-mouth talent? Generating repeat business? Securing clients who use you exclusively?

That takes time, perseverance and effort. It takes consistent activity. It takes courage to do difficult things, like cold calling. It takes strength of ego to withstand rejection and poor results. Finally, it takes an open mind to learn new skills and work at the things you are not good at. And, slowly but surely, the rewards will come.

With recruitment or running, the only place success comes before work is in the dictionary.

12 | Recruitment reveals character

Let's build on the theme of the previous chapter: the character required to overcome a challenging situation.

There is no doubt that agency recruitment is an exceptionally tough business, with many disappointments, obstacles and constant learning. However, it's also true that facing these challenges will burnish the resilience and determination you already have.

But, on this issue, I have a marginally controversial view that not everyone agrees with. So many refer to working in recruitment as 'character-building', but succeeding in recruitment does not build character. No, it reveals it!

To succeed in a job like recruitment, you must have resilience, toughness, determination and the drive to achieve built into your DNA over the long term. The rigours of our profession will reveal it (or not!) and no doubt refine it, but it will not build on what was not already there.

This is my opinion after almost 45 years in this profession, including hiring and managing thousands of recruiters.

I have seen supremely talented individuals fail because they do not have the intrinsic attributes to cope with the inevitable disappointments. No amount of 'experience' fixed that issue. In fact, it made it worse.

I have also seen moderately talented people thrive and forge long careers because they have the innate determination and drive to overcome. (I am an excellent example of that myself, especially the 'moderately talented' part.)

This is not an esoteric discussion. On the contrary, this is a crucial understanding as you decide who to hire, invest in and promote. You might also want to consider your career choice with this insight in mind, after some deep personal reflection.

Recruitment does not build character. It reveals it.

13 | The meaning of 'resilience'

Resilience is a core requirement for success in our profession, and maybe in modern life in general. But what does 'resilience' really mean in the context of recruitment?

Old-school recruiters thrived on the cult of toughness. The mantra was, 'Make 100 calls and get 100 rejections, but keep going because the 101st will be successful'. Still today, resilience is often defined as some combination of ego, strength and an almost mythical 'macho' capacity to 'never give up'.

Well, I don't see it that way.

Recruitment is an exceptionally demanding profession, so, to me, it's human to show your frustration. I'm totally fine with the odd tear, swear word or walk around the block to defuse the many disappointments that will come your way. It's not weak to show your emotions when you really care about the outcome of your efforts. It would be weird not to!

Resilience in recruitment means depowering what you can't control and owning your response to the situation. I consider real resilience to be summed up by a word coined by a UK football coach 20 years ago. I am not sure it's a real word, but I know what it means, and so should you: 'bouncebackability'.

The recruiter who has had a shocking day – with three offers turned down, candidates bombing out of interviews and clients being rude – does not allow that negativity to affect their next interaction. When faced with a new conversation with a client, candidate or colleague, they allow no trace of those disappointments to contaminate the fresh engagement. They bounce back and tackle each new situation unhindered by previous disappointments.

That is real resilience – being able to recover fast from disappointment and not allowing any stakeholder to sense that you are dragging your wasted emotion into their life (chapter 125).

So easy to say, so hard to do. (But it's not rocket science. LOL.)

14 | Take a chill pill

So, resilience is a prerequisite for success in recruitment, and so are determination and self-belief. But we are not machines, so we will feel the pressure. It will mount up. It will feel unbearable at times.

Stress at work is dangerous. It can lead to medical issues and harm your relationships and overall quality of life. I have seen it time and again. Felt it, too.

And that is bad for us recruiters because we do one of the most challenging jobs. Unfortunately, it seems that the 'all or nothing' nature of what we do is designed to induce stress.

Over the years, I have seen recruiters reduced to highly destructive and antisocial behaviour because of their stress as they strive to achieve targets, deal with major disappointments and cope with rude clients and ungrateful candidates. Drinking too much. Drug abuse. Anger directed at colleagues. Wild mood swings. Dishonest dealings. Depression. Rapid weight gain or loss. All unfortunate. All harmful.

But what can you do about it? Pressure and stress are part of what we do. They're not going to go away. The reality is that we need to learn to cope. We must all have some releases that ease the pressure and redress the balance.

In a world teeming with life coaches and mindfulness seminars, I feel unqualified to dictate anything on this topic, but here are a few things I recommend when it comes to battling the stress tsunami because they work for me. I have seen them help many others, too.

Look for catharsis

Have a good cry, maybe. Seriously. Or, once the phone is put down, let off some steam. As long as it's not directed at a colleague, as long as it's quick, as long as you bounce back fast, it's okay (chapter 13)! In fact, given our job, it would be weird not to melt down occasionally. I was not much of a crier myself but, when things went seriously wrong, it was not unknown for me to let slip a few choice expletives, punch the desk and bang my head on the wall. It's okay. Let it go. You will feel better afterwards. But then move on!

Get perspective

Breathe. Again, I am serious. Push back from your desk. Suck in the big ones. Deliberately and consciously shift your thinking. Dump the negatives. Tell yourself, 'It will go well', or 'This too will pass', not 'It's all going down the gurgler'. I believe in PMA (positive mental attitude; chapter 20), and I also think that we can control how we react to situations. Jump off the stress treadmill. Take a chill pill. Recalibrate your attitude. Whatever crappy thing just happened, it's not that serious. Emotionally, right now, it is huge; but, intellectually, we know that it will be almost forgotten in a week. Meaningless. Focus on that. The sun will shine on you tomorrow!

Recognise the warning signs

This is simple but big. If stress is building and you feel it getting worse, sometimes discretion is the greater part of valour. Take evasive action. Avoid that annoying client call. Stop making sales calls for an hour if you are getting nowhere with rude clients, and call ten of your best candidates instead. They will be pleased to hear from you, cheering you up right there! Leave work early; you can make it up tomorrow. Call someone who will cheer you up.

Also, recruitment leaders need to be skilled at detecting the signs of stress in others and suggesting a diversion or evasive action, endorsing a break or a change. That is authentic leadership. You should not be banging the desk and asking for more effort when the recruiter is at breaking point.

Set an achievable goal

Set a goal that you can get, and that will make you feel good. This is key. If a massive sea of work is swirling up all around you and you can see no way you can get it done, every call you take seems to pile up more and more on you and the 'to-do' list is getting ever longer, here is the trick: cross out everything on the 'to do' list except the top three to five big, hairy, essential things that must be done. Forget the rest. You were not going to get to them anyway, were you? Scratch them out and get the big three to five things done. Then go home feeling successful. So empowering!

Sweat a little

This is my most personal tip. I reckon exercise reduces stress exponentially. No doubt there is empirical research confirming that. I have a month's gym sessions in my diary ahead of time – three or four a week – and I don't change them for anybody (unless my wife tells me to, obviously). And I used to go in the middle of the day, just around the corner from my office. It suited me because I worked long hours, and it did not really matter when I took the break, as long as I took it. For you, it might be different, but if you feel the stress building, don't hit the grog or buy that burger to give you the comfort you crave. Run, gym, bike or even just take a brisk walk. For me, it's a lifesaver. Someone even told me that, if they need to have a difficult meeting with me, they try to arrange it for after my gym session because, inevitably, I am 'much calmer' – not a great reflection on me but proof of the efficacy of exercise on stress.

*

Being a recruiter means stress. It never entirely goes away, no matter how good you are. You must manage it because, as we already agreed, if you can manage the pressure, being a recruiter rocks!

15 | There are two types of recruiters

Plenty of you reading this are not going to enjoy this chapter. But I don't like the gym even though I know it's good for me. This chapter might be very good for you, so proceed with an open mind, please.

There are only *two* types of recruiters. You are in one group or the other. And the group you are in decides your recruiting future.

First, there are the *honest* recruiters: honest about their ability, their effort, their behaviours, their temperament. They are mostly very aware of their shortcomings, weaknesses and failings, and they are prepared to work on them – to improve, grow and evolve. (They are all over chapter 7.)

Honest recruiters do not blame the market for their poor performance. They don't talk about 'bad luck' (remember chapter 8?). They don't blame the database, colleagues, boss, candidate-short market or anything else. They are *honest*. They know the job is hard, they know that they can control much of what determines success and they focus on managing those factors. They know that consistent, high-quality activity leads to success. When they fail or underperform, they admit their activity, quality or both are too low (chapter 23).

They get stressed, have doubts, feel the pain of offers turned down and counteroffers accepted, and have bad months. But they don't deflect, blame, whinge, accuse or finger-point.

They bounce back. They try to learn and improve and work harder and be more innovative. They might believe they are good, but they also know they are not *great*, and so they work towards constant improvement.

Then, there are the *dishonest* recruiters. They are *not* unethical or shady recruiters; they are just fooling themselves and in a constant bubble of denial. They have no self-awareness and are always mired in wasted emotion (chapter 125), telling themselves all the massive lies I spell out in chapter 16.

They build themselves up. They take the credit. They big-note themselves. They preen.

When things go wrong, and there is nowhere to hide (because recruitment is so beautiful in its clarity and measurability), they blame everyone and everything. They are on a treadmill of mediocrity and denial, and nothing is ever their fault.

When things go well, they take all the credit. Often, that comes with the ugly traits of arrogance and entitlement. But, when challenged on this behaviour, they are shocked and deny everything. Because they are dishonest.

In the end, the house of cards collapses and they fail – or the market shifts and, like the emperor with no clothes, they are exposed as shallow recruiters with limited skills. Which in itself is not a crime. But *not owning it* is.

Then they leave in a flood of tears and recriminations and vindictiveness, blaming 'recruitment' as the door slams behind them.

Be honest. With yourself.

16 | Never lie, including to yourself

This chapter may be another uncomfortable read.

So many recruiters tell themselves huge lies. It ties in very neatly with the behaviour of 'dishonest recruiters' described in the previous chapter, but we are all guilty to varying degrees and at various times. I did it when I was a recruiter, and I did it when I was a manager, too. I do it now when things go off track. But I stop myself fast.

It's a human trait on a broader level as well: it's a well-documented psychological behaviour. We believe what we perceive to be true, and we mould the way we see the world based on those perceptions. We finesse reality to make ourselves feel better.

We tweak the truth to make our failures less painful, and we exaggerate our contribution to meet our egotistical self-construct. And it's dangerous for our career health!

COVID-19 and lockdowns made things worse because they gave us many *real* reasons to feel sorry for ourselves. And an economic downturn will create a whole new set of ways to justify our shortcomings.

But is it possible we are making excuses for some of our failings, wrapping them up in neat packages of self-pity and self-delusion?

I don't want to go all psychobabble on you, but I see it every day. I am guilty of it! We like to feel *good* about ourselves, even if we must distort reality to make it all 'fit'.

And it matters because it stunts growth and learning. It closes doors that otherwise could be pried open, and it reduces our credibility in the eyes of others, who can often see through the lies we tell ourselves and, sometimes, them too.

Told yourself these lies lately?

- **It's the market!** It's not your fault you can't generate any fees! There are no available candidates in your sector! No one is moving. Candidates are ghosting you and accepting counteroffers! No one is hiring. The clients won't see recruiters. There are no jobs. It's not you. It's 'the market'. (Never mind that you live in a city of 5 million people and thousands of people accept jobs daily, and there are 500 competing recruiting companies who all seem to be doing fine, thanks for asking.)
- **That is my client:** That client only works with you. You have every job exclusively. In fact, she loves you. She would never go elsewhere. Moreover, she only uses your recruitment company because of you. (Love that one. So common.)
- **The client put the job on hold:** Yeah right! No way on God's green earth that another agency could have filled it, right? It is on hold, and on hold, and on hold, until... 'Oh, sorry,' says the client, 'we filled it "elsewhere"'.
- **My company has never done anything for me:** Totally! Never trained you. Never paid you. Never generated marketing. Never given you leads. Never provided you with an ATS (applicant tracking system). Never fed you a client. Never run ads on your behalf. Never supported you through that lean patch. Never looked after you during COVID-19, when

the owner was scared about losing her company and house. Never, ever, ever! You did it all yourself.

- **I don't need to attend training sessions; I know about all that stuff:** Of course! You are fine. You have three years' experience, after all! What could you possibly learn from training? What is there for you to learn? It's all good. 'Recruitment isn't rocket science' after all.
- **Technology change won't affect me:** Sure! You have your database in your head. Your memory is infallible. You mention that quite often. You have been a big biller for years. You talk about that a lot, too. You survived every other technological change. Just keep doing it your way. What could go wrong? No risk there at all!
- **It's not me, it's them:** You always pass on leads. You always pick up the phone if the receptionist is away. You always do your admin perfectly. You always wash your lunch plates. You never snap at the admin staff. You are always passing on candidates for other consultants' jobs. You never keep anyone waiting on a Zoom call. It's not you! It's them!
- **She is not that good a recruiter, just lucky:** We spoke about this in chapter 8. It's nothing to do with the fact she works harder, does more business development, does more activity, sources better candidates, delivers better quality and provides better candidate service than you. No, she is just plain lucky.
- **Of course I look after my candidates!** All of them. Especially ones you can't help, and the ones who miss out on the offer or the shortlist. You keep them informed. You return their calls. You treat them with respect. Always.
- **Of course I hit all my KPIs!** And all the stats you provided are 100% accurate, especially when working from home. Promise. No, really, seriously…
- **Of course I have called every candidate on the database:** You've searched every conceivable way. There is nothing there. Guess you'd better run an ad…

That's not the complete list, is it?

Don't fool yourself. Confront the reality. Then you can respond to it.

17 | Think like an immigrant

'Think like an immigrant' might seem like a strange thing to say. Is that advice for a recruiter?

Well, yes, it is. Excellent advice, too. Stay with me.

Modern Australia was built on immigrants. They came in clearly defined waves. The British and Irish. The southern Europeans. The Asians. Many other countries are the same, and most pay homage to those immigrants now.

I am an immigrant myself. I arrived in Australia two weeks before my 21st birthday.

I am the son of an immigrant, too. My dad emigrated to Africa from the UK after a long, brutal war, including three years in Changi POW camp in Singapore.

You think and behave differently when you are an immigrant or an outsider. This I know from personal experience. It's a tiny bit like the first week at a new school: everyone else is chilled, knows the ropes and is very familiar with everything, even complacent. You are alert, watchful, looking to learn and needing to be brave.

Now more than ever before, recruiters need to think like immigrants.

A strange statement? At first, maybe. But consider this in the context of a rapidly changing recruiting landscape. We know a great deal has changed, and more changes are coming. But are we adapting?

We need to have and do what immigrants have and do, right now:

- **Immigrants are massive optimists:** By definition. They have moved somewhere new because they perceive a better life. They want to be here. They need to succeed. It gives them an edge. Are you sharp and edgy? (Chapter 20)
- **Immigrants are brave:** They need to be. Every step, every corner rounded, is a new experience. They need to experiment.

To ask a lot. To be prepared to fail a few times. To bounce back. They act as if they have no safety net because they typically don't. Do you have the courage to try new tactics? Get out of your comfort zone? Reinvent? (Chapter 19)

- **Immigrants learn new skills:** They must. Language, maybe. Driving on the 'other' side of the road. Food. Local traditions. Sports. Are you learning new skills? Smashing your paradigms? Pivoting your approach? (Chapter 7)
- **Immigrants are opportunists:** They typically don't have much, so they are alert to a 'chance'. They see a gap and they take it. They don't have the luxury of waiting for something to 'turn up'. They seek it out. Immigrants do not have the sense of entitlement that locals might. Are you a little complacent? Lacking innovation and creativity? (Chapter 123)
- **Immigrants embrace new ideas:** They still hold on to what is dear to them from the past, but they absorb the new. They search for new ways in most cases. Their paradigms are not set in concrete. They don't limit themselves because they don't assume limits on what is achievable. Are you making assumptions? Closed to change? (Chapter 27)
- **Immigrants are humble:** They will do any job that sets them on their way. (Me? Cleaning toilets at a caravan park in Coolangatta. Barman at the Arkaba Hotel in Adelaide. Storeman/packer at R. M. Williams.) They know that they don't know what they don't know. So, they don't limit what they are prepared to do for success. You? A little 'I have been doing this for ten years' hubris?
- **Immigrants work harder to get ahead:** They must. They are 'on their own' – no 'old boy network'. It's make or break. Persistence is in their DNA. I love the new flexibility, work from home and work-life balance, I do; but, trust me, hard work still pays off. Are you prepared to do the extra work needed to be great at this?

All these immigrant traits are also those of the modern recruiter – or should be.

In a sense, all recruiters are immigrants, because we have just arrived in this 'new world of recruitment' where everything is changing. We must embrace that world, using the skills we learned in the 'old country' – if they still apply – but wide open to change, hard work and fresh thinking.

Twenty-five years ago, I had a client say to me, 'Greg, I only hire people with at least one grandparent who cannot speak English'. That's a baffling remark at first glance, and certainly politically incorrect and probably illegal, too. But what he was alluding to is that he liked to hire sons and daughters of immigrants because he valued the way they thought, the work ethic they displayed and the values they brought. It's hardly scientific or unbiased recruitment methodology, but I have never forgotten that comment, and I daresay it has influenced my hiring decisions since.

Do not discriminate based on what language candidates' family members speak, but hire people who *think like immigrants.*

18 | 5% better, 50% more

You only need to get 5% better to bill 50% more. Roll that around on your tongue and let it sink in. It sounds so illogical.

The real value you bring to recruitment is your influencing skills. Pretty much all the rest can and will get automated (chapter 24). The bit that counts is your ability to connect, engage, question, understand and influence the outcome.

For example, through your credibility, knowledge and communication skills, you encourage a candidate to chat with you, consider your role and then go for the interview. Get 5% better at that and you will get ten more great candidates a year in front of good clients. Half of them will be hired. How much money is that?

The client is taking eons between the first and second interviews and is losing all the good talent, but she just can't see that she is the problem. So, you meet with her, talk her through the realities of a candidate-tight market and tell great anecdotes about how innovative companies are capturing the best talent. Finally, your client sees the light, takes your advice, ups her game and starts to hire!

Get 5% better at that conversation; being brave enough and articulate enough to have that conversation will lead to multiple happy matches that would otherwise have gone begging.

Candidate outreach and client process management are just two of the many 'moments of truth' in recruitment in which your credibility, advice and influencing skills can make all the difference. Taking a job order. Briefing a candidate on a role. Debriefing the client on candidates after an interview. Presenting a shortlist to a client. The job offer itself. There are many (all covered in detail in this book!).

These are the moments that differentiate average recruiters from good ones and good recruiters from great ones. Not searching the database, running an ad or even screening – essential they are, but they are not the leverage point!

You need to keep working incrementally at improving all these moments of truth in recruitment, these critical snapshots of time in which you can influence the outcome for the greater good – shape the process, architect the deal. Moments in which your credibility, consulting, advising, storytelling, persuading and influencing skills can make all the difference. It's in these moments that the magic happens.

A good recruiter knows when their skills create a beneficial outcome. The feeling is indescribable. It is where all the fun in this business is. And, when you are having fun in recruitment, your clients and candidates get what they came to you for, and then the money just follows.

Think about that previous paragraph. It is smarter than it sounds.

Get 5% better. When you have done that, get 5% better again.

19 | Ten seconds of courage

The phrase 'ten seconds of courage' is not my own. I heard my brother say it in a speech, and he later confessed to having lifted it from an elite Australian athlete. No matter: it is the concept that's important here.

It may sound strange to evoke the word 'courage' to describe a white-collar desk job, but you do need to be brave in this job. Often.

One of the characteristics of a great recruiter is that they constantly stretch themselves to better manage the critical 'moments of truth'. That often means saying 'no' to a client, giving bad news to a candidate or confronting challenging interpersonal scenarios. And, indeed, as your career evolves into management, you will face many situations that you need to tackle head-on. Be brave. Say what is challenging to say but what needs to be said.

The tip is this: do your planning, consider your strategy and then, as the nerves and doubt surface, tell yourself that all you need is 'ten seconds of courage' to start.

I started in recruitment in retained executive search when I was 21. Every person I met – client or candidate – was older, more imposing and more experienced than me. I had hardcore imposter syndrome for at least two years.

I used this technique all the time, even though I did not have the phrase 'ten seconds of courage' to label it with.

I remember sitting in my car, white-knuckled, outside a client meeting, with a big-deal CEO – twice my age and infinitely more experienced – waiting to meet me. I told myself the same message: *Be brave, just start.*

You might confront it often. For example, selling exclusivity to a client on a job order might provoke stress and nerves for you. But, once you believe in the benefits for the client, have role-played the pitch and have predicted the objections that might come (chapters 99 to 103), you just need to tell yourself to have 'ten seconds of courage'.

And then you start: 'Ms Client, the way I can fill this job for you is…' And then you're into it; and, before you know it, you are through it!

Ten seconds of courage: you need it just to start. It will make all the difference.

20 | PMA

I mentioned PMA (positive mental attitude) in relation to Graham Whelan, the best recruiter I've ever met, in chapter 2.

I have noticed that, over the long term, the most successful recruiters include what I would describe as 'realistic optimism' in their portfolio of attitudes and behaviours. This isn't as frivolous as it might sound; approaching a job as demanding as ours with a positive mental attitude makes all the difference.

I don't subscribe to some airy-fairy, quasi-spiritual philosophy suggesting that if you simply hope something will happen, it will. But I believe that, if you exude confidence and express belief in positive outcomes, those around you will be influenced and excellent results will become more likely.

Plenty of recruiters get beaten down by the inevitable setbacks of our job, and you hear the negativity in their voices and see it in their demeanour: 'I have a third interview this week, but that'll probably be turned down like the one last Monday'.

If you talk like that, if you think like that, if you behave like that, that is likely the outcome you will create.

Talking to candidates with positivity and encouragement, communicating with clients with enthusiasm and belief and sharing your optimism with colleagues has a domino effect.

Realistic optimism, as embodied in PMA, won't protect you against things going wrong: you will have your share of disappointments. But it will carry you through far more often than not.

21 | Maintain perspective

This is a short chapter, which is ironic because it took me 30 years to learn what I share here. Read carefully, please: this will save you a world of pain.

When things are going well, when the results are good, when it seems you can do no wrong, be sure you don't get taken in by your own bullshit. *We are never as good as we think we are.* And be careful, too, not to surround yourself with yes-men, sycophants and brown-nosing acolytes who feed you what you want to hear and seduce you into complacency and arrogance, for it's just when you do that the biggest fall is imminent. Self-satisfaction stifles growth, innovation, risk and hunger.

Equally, when everything goes wrong, every decision seems to backfire and your dreams are crumbling, do not believe you have no talent just because, at that moment, *others around you are not able to recognise it.* Before you write yourself off as a failure, as wrong, as mediocre, as 'not up to it', just check you have not surrounded yourself with deadbeats, dingbats, drop-kicks and doomsayers who bring you down and stunt your dreams.

That's it. Maintain perspective. On yourself.

22 | What will your tombstone say?

I conclude Part I by waxing a little philosophical. This is not recruitment advice, more life advice.

My life? '1958–2043'. That's what my tombstone will say – if the Shiraz does not get me sooner and I last that long. It could easily say '1958–2023' (although I sincerely hope not!). But that's the point: the dates are not that important – as long as they are a reasonable period apart.

The important thing about that inscription on my tombstone, and yours, is the *dash* between the dates. It's incredible to think but, in the end, that 'dash' represents everything that makes up a life. All of us – you, me, everyone we know – are reduced to a tiny little piece of punctuation. Oh, but what a great deal it can signify!

What's your dash? Dreary repetition? Mediocrity? Excuse-making? Wasted potential? Self-pity? Meanness of spirit? Petty gossip? Missed opportunity? Sunny days spent on a sofa looking at your phone? Empty promises about what you will do 'tomorrow'? Blaming and complaining? Regret and remorse?

But what a life that little dash *could* represent! Not a life that shook the world, necessarily: you don't have to be Nelson Mandela to make a difference. Use every day. Give it your best. Be brave. Stretch yourself. Be kind. Build others up rather than tear them down. Have a real go at reaching your dream. Take a few risks. Absorb failures with fortitude and relish the wins with humility. Be loyal. Laugh off the crap. Learn. Be tolerant. Be generous, in every way. Forgive easily.

Mend fences. Laugh a lot. Love your family and friends, and make sure they know it.

On a tombstone, your dash, my dash, Mandela's dash – they are all the same, give or take a few years.

But what does it stand for? What will your dash represent when the tombstone goes up? What did your life mean?

Maybe it's this: don't worry so much about the length of your life. Just make sure you explore the entire width of it.

PART II

BEHAVIOUR AND ACTIVITY

Once you have your attitude and mindset right, the next competency all great recruiters display is consistently delivering the right activity level and engaging in productive behaviours.

The people who deride KPIs as 'micromanaging' have done our profession a tremendous disservice. Indeed, KPIs implemented poorly by inept leadership can be counterproductive. However, you can't manage what you don't measure and, if there ever was a truism in our profession, it is that consistent, quality behaviour drives success.

The COVID-19 lockdowns brought this into even greater focus. Many recruiters allowed the process to become shallow and superficial, and the relationships with clients and candidates became increasingly remote. This meant that managing the 'moments of truth' became difficult – impossible, even – and outcomes deteriorated.

I believe in clarity around activity goals. Forty-four years in this business have taught me that. But the many factors that ensure long-term recruiter success are changing as the market changes.

The magic cocktail is doing consistently high levels of activity, doing them at an ever-improving level of quality, and doing them with the right people.

It's all about practical, positive activity management. Whether you are leading a team or just managing your own efforts, the industry needs recruiters with high self-esteem, who retain a sense of autonomy and hit their activity numbers because they believe in them and see the link between activity, quality and success.

Most of our energy goes into focusing the recruiter on the outcome. It is more effective to focus the recruiter on the activities that are proven to lead to success.

As you will see in this Part, recruitment is a marriage of art and science. You need to not only do enough of the critical activities but deliver them via highly sophisticated influencing skills to create the best outcomes.

23 | The formula for recruiting success

This is one of the strongest messages in my book. It took me years to learn and it has always held true. I sometimes refer to it as my 'magic formula for recruitment excellence': success in recruitment comes from *lots of activity, done well, with the right people.*

Activity + Quality + Target Market = Success

Activity is key to the ongoing success of any recruitment professional. It's not all about activity, but activity counts. You must do a certain amount of 'stuff' to get the desired results. Those activities might vary a little depending on your sector, your experience and the depth of your customer relationships. Still, they are likely to include all the usual suspects, such as client meetings, submitted résumés, follow-up calls, candidate interviews and client-candidate interviews. These days, there are new activities to add: networking events, content creation, making connections, engagement and candidate outreach activities. I have never seen a successful recruiter who does not consistently churn out the activities that drive the outcomes we seek.

But activity is not enough, is it? Too much activity of the wrong kind or of inferior quality is counterproductive. Hundreds of low-quality, ill-thought-through cold calls, for example, will not enhance your billings or reputation. Nor will desperate, pushy InMails to source people on LinkedIn or indiscriminate résumé-spamming around town.

That's why the second component of the success formula is *quality*. You have to have lots of activity to be successful, but it needs to be activity of the highest quality – and by quality, I mean quality through every step of the process. Your job is made up of hundreds of discrete interactions (chapter 21), and your success is driven by the volume of those interactions (activity) and, crucially, by the quality of those interactions. That is where a real recruiting professional will display their well-honed questioning, influencing, counselling, persuasion and negotiation skills.

So, success is about activity, and the quality of that activity. But there is a third factor to the equation, one most recruiters fail to spot. We must do lots of activity, yes. We must maintain high quality, yes. But we must do that high-quality activity with the right *people* in our target market! If you do ten client meetings a week, and the quality of those visits is superb, you can still fail if you meet with two-bit companies that do not need your services, or people who are not decision-makers.

In five decades of coaching recruiters and running teams of recruiting professionals, whenever I have seen someone go off track or a team start to fail, I have always found the answer by applying this formula:

- Are we doing enough activity?
- Is that activity of the right quality?
- Are we doing it with the right people?

It has never let me down. The reason for the failure will be found in one or more of these areas.

So, there it is, the holy grail of how to be great at this job: activity plus quality plus target market.

24 | Owning the 'moments of truth'

This might be the most crucial chapter in this book (or was that the previous chapter?).

If you hide behind digital technology, you will fail as a recruiter. Of course, you must be excellent at using technology, but the differentiator is building relationships, garnering trust and influencing outcomes. All of this starts with credibility, which allows you to be consultative and not transactional (chapters 4 and 5). You must get 'closer' to your clients and your candidates – close enough to influence their behaviour and decisions. You must master the 'craft' of recruitment.

Recruitment comprises a series of critical interactions between people, the outcome of which can be impacted by an intelligent question, a piece of advice or an injection of encouragement. I call these interactions 'moments of truth'. Of course, great recruiters own the moments of truth.

You call a candidate about a new opportunity. She is hesitant. She has never heard of your client. She is not too keen to proceed. But you know the opportunity is suitable for her. You sell your client's merits and how they meet her goals. She agrees to the interview. She goes. She loves it. They love her. She gets the job! Happy client, happy candidate, happy you (chapter 3).

You made that happen by managing the moment of truth.

The client feels that $100,000 is the ceiling they can offer for a role. First, you tell stories about the changing market. Then, you provide some data on salary movements. Finally, you encourage the client to consider $120,000 for the right person. They are persuaded and agree. You recommend a perfect candidate at $110,000 who would never have considered $100,000. They get the job.

You made that happen.

There are many moments of truth in recruitment. Following are the primary ones. Some of these have four or five 'sub-moments'; you must own them all. And, of course, they are all covered in detail in this book. So, you have no excuses, do you?

- The candidate 'outreach' call (chapter 66)
- The initial candidate interview (chapter 69)
- Selling a job opportunity to a candidate (chapter 84)
- Preparing a candidate for a client interview (chapter 85)
- The post-interview debrief (chapter 86)
- Pre-closing the candidate after the final interview (chapter 87)
- Preparing the candidate for an offer (chapter 88)
- Delivering the offer (chapter 88)
- Managing the resignation (chapter 89)
- Handling the counteroffer (chapter 74)
- The sales meeting (chapters 39 to 41)
- Taking and qualifying a job order (chapter 96)

- Selling 'exclusivity' to clients and candidates (chapters 101 to 103)
- Advising clients on the recruitment process (chapter 93)
- Selling a client on your shortlist (chapters 105 and 106)
- Prepping a client for your candidate interview (chapter 108)
- The client debrief after the interview (chapter 109)
- Negotiating the job offer (chapter 111).

Without a doubt, the future of all agency recruiters depends upon excellence in managing these fundamental interactions. Most of the rest of the job will be automated anyway.

This is where the magic happens!

25 | More remote, more engaged

So, we need to own those moments of truth, but how do we do that in a changing world of work?

The secret is that, work from home or not, as recruiting gets more 'remote', you need to be more 'engaged'.

Many recruiters used COVID-19, working from home and the Zoom meeting process as an excuse for sloppy, superficial interviews in which needs were not fully understood, assumptions were not questioned and pre-closing was not drilled. And then it's tears, moans and 'woe is me' when the candidates ghost them or accept a counteroffer.

As others get more slapdash, you go deeper!

When others prepare candidates for an interview or debrief them afterwards with an email (God help me!), you have a 20-minute phone conversation or, better still, meet them for coffee, where you can look them in the eye. Ask the questions. Study the body language. Listen to the tone.

Finding candidates does *not* provide the significant edge in recruitment anymore, challenging as that is. Engaging with candidates, building trust and credibility and *managing the process* are where it gets spicy, and seeing it through to an offer accepted and a job started is where the value really is. Just because you *can* use technology, that is not a reason to automatically default to it.

Make no assumptions. Constantly check in. Seek regular updates. Conduct continuous, consistent, courteous candidate communication.

The client dynamic is no different. Why would a client take your advice on evolving their hiring strategy when you have never met and hardly speak, and everything is via email? Where is your credibility? How strong and deep is your recruiter equity (chapter 5)?

You interview a candidate on Zoom for ten minutes and seldom return their calls, and then you squeal when they ghost you or accept a counteroffer without telling you. You have no relationship, no engagement and no right to expect anything.

So, any recruiter blaming 'the skills shortage' for their poor results is sadly deluded. The only skills shortage that matters is the lack of *consultative recruiting* skills. My rec tech and AI-frenzied friends will beg to differ, but it's true.

Recruitment is more art than science. Stock your 'skills briefcase' accordingly (chapter 7).

26 | Soft skills are hard

The term 'soft skills' is often thrown in as an afterthought. It is even mentioned with a slight smirk in some cases. As if 'soft' skills are nebulous. Not real. Fluffy, even. Or, at best, less critical.

Time for a rethink.

What's a 'hard' skill in recruitment? Usually, it refers to working the database, constructing a Boolean search string or following a system. Even following a regimented interview process could be described as a 'hard' skill: you are reading the questions off a form, most likely.

These 'hard' skills are typically focused on specific tasks and processes, such as using certain tools, equipment or software. All good. All important.

But what of the so-called 'soft' skills: you know, the lightweight 'fluffy stuff'? Asking great questions. Listening to understand.

Not making assumptions. Influencing outcomes. Resolving conflict. Building trust and credibility. Countering a counteroffer. Calming post-acceptance wobbles. Selling retainers. Coaching clients on the market and an improved process.

Do you think these are easy? 'Soft' does not mean 'easy'.

It's the *soft* skills that are *hard*. Hard to learn. Hard to replicate. Hard to coach. Hard to excel at. And it's the soft skills that determine success, too.

If a person has a moderate level of intellect – enough to learn the hard skills – I always hire based on the soft skills, or at least the potential to master them, because that's where the magic lies.

27 | Making assumptions will hurt you

The most significant cause of recruiting screw-ups is recruiters making assumptions.

It leads to so much angst and wailing over things gone wrong and the unfairness of it all, which is all blamed on 'bad luck', flaky candidates and fickle clients. But it's not bad luck at all; it's terrible recruiting (chapter 8). Specifically, the *craft* of recruitment is lacking.

The status of a candidate's job search or a client's job brief is a fast-evolving, dynamic cocktail of an ever-changing reality. The job you took on Friday in which the client said that $80,000 is the absolute top he can pay? Guess what: it's $100,000 now. The candidate who will not cross the bridge to work on the north side of town? Well, she is interviewing over there now.

I sit in recruitment offices most days, surrounded by recruiters. I hear their conversations, and we are all making many assumptions all the time. You must constantly check in, confirm, question, calibrate, test and reconfirm.

This is the big question I encourage you to ask at the start of every conversation you have with every candidate and every client throughout the process: 'Has anything changed since we last spoke?'

That simple question is loaded: loaded with opportunity and loaded with money.

What's changed? Is the candidate out on other interviews? Has he been offered more money where he is? Has he got cold feet? Has his dad told him that there is a recession coming and not to change jobs? A thousand possible changes might have occurred, none of them known to you – unless you ask!

What about the client? Are they looking at internal candidates? Have they seen someone from another agency who just 'happened to call'? Are they now open to diploma-holders instead of degree graduates? Have they lifted the salary?

Making assumptions will hurt you. A lot.

Drill down and ask; ask differently, ask every time: 'Has anything changed?'

28 | Great recruiters are great listeners

Most recruiters are great talkers. But communicating is listening, too, right? So, surely, 'understanding' is the foundation of it all?

'Active listening', then, is a crucial business skill. It is most definitely something a consultative recruiter excels at.

I am a poor listener. Or, rather, I was, but I have worked hard at this because this weakness was holding me back. I still lapse.

How did I actively improve? I learned to:

- listen to understand, not to formulate an answer
- stop interrupting (I am disgracefully guilty of this)
- be more 'present' – to not allow my mind to wander, and to focus and concentrate on the other person
- stop assuming that I know what the other person is going to say
- listen to the 'whole person'; in other words, to be attuned to body language, tone and other non-verbal signals
- approach every conversation with a more open mind, with more empathy
- be 'slower to understand' – to not jump in with a solution too fast, and think more before I talk

- ask more and more thoughtful questions so I really do understand
- not be defensive when I sense criticism or a different point of view.

Most of us need to worry far less about being right and far more about being right about what the other person thinks and feels.

We must remind ourselves every morning that nothing we *say* today will teach us anything. Only by listening will we learn anything new.

When someone really listens to you, you feel respected. Validated.

29 | The power of pushback

How often has a client said something that you know is wrong or you suspect is not in their interests, but you let it slide because 'they are the client'?

There is a risk that one might interpret 'pushback' as a form of confrontation. This is not how I am using the word at all. I'm talking about a recruiter with self-belief having the courage to offer the client a different point of view that will be in the client's best interest (chapter 4).

I've found that challenging a client on one of their assumptions or their hiring strategy builds respect and trust between the recruiter and the client (chapter 93).

It doesn't have to be something huge. For example, the client might say that they liked the two candidates they met today and suggest a second interview in ten days' time. In that situation, you need to push back and explain to the client the urgency of the situation and the risk of losing quality candidates.

Pushback encourages open dialogue between yourself and the client and establishes the rules of engagement. A recruiter who doesn't push back when they know they should inevitably ends up conceding to the client's whims, regardless of what they might be.

Pushing back on a client's direction when you know you should provides an opportunity to demonstrate your value, prove your worth as a trusted advisor and confirm that you genuinely have recruiter equity (chapter 5).

Of course, tone, language and facial expression are all important, because you are not trying to be aggressive or condescending. You are a professional expert advising your client for the greater good.

Respectful, consultative 'pushback' builds credibility and better relationships.

It is also excellent for your self-esteem, which is no bad thing.

30 | The golden perm recruiter metric

Bring it in tight, everyone. Only one thing ultimately drives success for a perm or search recruiter: the golden metric. *How many of your candidates are sitting opposite your clients?*

That is it: 'client-candidate interviews', or CCIs, as I call them.

Yes, our ultimate goal is placements and the happy clients, happy candidates and happy us that will result from lots of placements. But placements are the outcome. We don't make the job offers, so we can't control the outcome. We need to focus on the activity that *leads* to the outcome.

What is the *one* thing that must happen for a person to be hired? They must be interviewed! Everything you do in this job either leads up to that happy moment or supports the outcome of that event. (Of course, quality counts, too. You must take qualified job specs, find great talent and make a great match. But that's a given, right?)

If you arrange for one candidate to sit opposite one client in one week, you can make, at best, one placement – and only then if all the recruiting gods are smiling on you. But if you get three interviews on different jobs, you could get three placements. Or, three interviews on the same job exponentially increases your chance of one placement. And if you get 15 candidates sitting in interviews…

The point is that you have to secure lots and lots of interviews! So obvious, I know, yet I often hear what a fantastic week a recruiter had and, when I dig a little, find that they've been busy, busy, busy… *but secured no CCIs!*

It's in the CCI that the magic happens!

So, you have had a 'busy' week. Go, go, go. You are so tired, so satisfied you have given it your all. But, ask yourself as you open that first beer at 6 p.m. on Friday, *How many of my candidates are sitting down opposite my clients due to what I did this week?*

31 | Smart KPIs for fun and money

Recruiters *love* to be busy. Or, to be more accurate, they love to *feel* busy.

The same goes for many recruiting managers. If everyone is *busy, busy, busy,* they are happy.

Happy, but dumb. Because, yes, activity is vital in recruitment. But *smart* activity is what we want (following the formula in chapter 23).

The key to working on the *right* activity, and getting recruiter buy-in to that activity, is 'backwards planning'. Don't focus on the outcome; focus on the activities that are proven to lead to success. Goal setting and KPIs are a science, not a whim.

Table 1 shows my 'classic backwards plan': your primary starting point to make sure you are working on the right stuff. It is designed for permanent, contingent recruiters. For a perm recruiter, CCIs are the *only* metric that matters (as discussed in the previous chapter), so let's put some science behind our daily goal.

Table 1: The classic backwards plan

Metric	Method	Figure
Quarterly billings target	Insert the gross profit ($) required to hit quarterly goal	120,000
Average placement value	Insert the average fee ($) per placement	6000
Placements required per quarter	Divide the first figure by the second figure	20

Metric	Method	Figure
Placements required per week	Divide the previous figure by the number of weeks in a quarter (12) and round it to get your weekly goal!	2
Client interviews per placement	Insert the average number of CCIs per placement	5
Interviews per week to meet goal	Multiply the previous two figures to get your crucial KPI!	10
CCI interviews per day to meet goal	Divide the previous figure by 5 to get your easy-to-digest daily goal	2

The table explains itself if you follow it carefully, but you start with your gross profit (GP) goal and divide it by the average placement value. That gives you the goal of 20 placements per quarter. Most recruiters don't even know that figure. Then you can determine that you need two placements a week to hit your goal. Next, work out your average interview-to-placement ratio; your ATS will tell you this (if you enter that data into it, of course). That tells you that you need to set up 10 CCIs per week, or two a day.

Bang! Now you have a *real, achievable, measurable* daily goal proven by science to lead to $120,000 in fees per quarter.

Table 2 shows the second backwards plan for a perm recruiter: the magic 'job-order backwards plan'.

Table 2: The job-order backward plan

Metric	Method	Figure
Quarterly billings target	Insert the GP ($) required to hit quarterly goal	120,000
Average placement value	Insert the average fee ($) per placement	10,000

Metric	Method	Figure
Placements required per quarter	Divide the first figure by the second figure	12
Job orders per placement	Insert the average number of job orders per placement	3
Job orders per quarter to meet goal	Multiply the previous two figures	36
Job orders per week to meet goal	Divide the previous figure by 12 to get your job-order weekly goal!	3

Again, it's simple. Do you want to bill $120,000 in a quarter, and each placement is worth $10,000 on average? Then, you must make 12 placements in a quarter, right? But you only fill 1 job out of 3 that you take. Your ATS will tell you this. (Mind you, it's more likely to be 1 out of 5, but let's not go there.)

That means, if you fill 1 out of 3 job orders, and you need to fill 12, that you must take 36 job orders in a quarter. That's 3 new job orders per week.

And it's science, not opinion.

Now, the other way to increase your billings is to improve your ratios! If you can move from filling 1 job out of 3 to 1 job out of 2, everything improves. That would need some considerable work to achieve, but it makes the point. If you don't measure, you don't know what lever to pull, and you will never improve.

Backwards planning adds science to your daily work effort. Set achievable, digestible, understandable and effective goals to drive results.

32 | Smart KPIs for temp and contract recruiters

Revenues generated by the global recruitment and staffing profession exceed US$550 billion, and the vast majority of that comes from temporary and contract placements.

A strong temporary business is the backbone of a resilient recruitment company. So, table 3 shows the temp/contract backward plan, which, by the way, is very different. You still start with the goal and work backwards, but you target *different* metrics.

Table 3: The temp/contract backward plan

Metric	Method	Figure
Quarterly temp billings target	Insert the temp net margin ($) required to hit quarterly goal	250,000
Average net margin per hour	Insert the average net margin ($) per hour	10
Billed hours required per quarter	Divide the first figure by the second figure	25,000
Average assignment length	Insert the average assignment length (hours)	150
Filled assignments per quarter to meet goal	Divide the billed hours by the assignment length	167
Number of consultants	Insert the number of consultants	3
Quarterly filled orders target per consultant	Divide the filled assignments per quarter by the number of consultants	56
Weekly filled orders target per consultant	Divide the previous figure by 12 (weeks in a quarter)	5
Daily filled orders target per consultant	Divide the previous figure by 5 (days in a week)	1

This plan is for a temp/contract *team* because that is often how they are viewed in a business, and usually how they are paid: as a team. However, it can very simply be adjusted for each individual by making the figure in line six (number of consultants) '1'.

So, let's go! You start with the target for temp GP billings for the team, which in the temp/contract context is net margin. Then you insert the average net margin per hour (after taxes and so on) and divide the total net margin by the margin per hour. This immediately gives you a very cool number you should recite in your sleep, which is the number of temp hours your team needs to invoice to hit the goal: 25,000.

Now, here we drop in a funky little number: the average assignment length (in hours). Get this from your ATS or payroll: total hours billed last year divided by the number of assignments filled in the year. Bingo! That is the number! It's 150 in my example. Why? Because now, when you divide the number of hours you need to bill by the average assignment length, it tells you that you must fill, as a team, 167 assignments per quarter! Now, what a gorgeous, sexy, alluring number that is!

Because it's science – and science cuts through the BS – and because we have three consultants on our temp desk, *each* of them must fill 56 assignments for the goal to be hit. And, if you divide the 56 orders by the 12 weeks in a quarter (one week is always lost due to sickness or holiday), you now know that each recruiter must fill 5 orders per week (or, if you like, the team must fill 15 per week).

That's 1 a day per recruiter, or 3 a day for the team.

Simple, achievable, measurable – and totally undeniable! That, my recruiting friends, is a contract recruiter KPI to love and cherish!

Then, focus on the measurable, manageable, vital activities that lead to broader success.

33 | Reinventing your KPIs

Updating some of your old KPIs and changing what you measure is essential. After all, the whole point of measuring and reporting is to ensure that the recruiter is always focused on the most productive activities in the current market. And so much is changing in recruitment, especially marketing, branding and business-winning.

For this chapter to make sense, you must believe that it's vital for recruiters to build their personal brand (as I do), that social selling is more potent than relentless, untargeted cold calling (as I do) and that digital relationship-building is often the forerunner to opening doors to business relationships in real life (as I do). (For more on building brand and social selling, see chapters 58 and 59.)

Don't rush to consign all your old performance measures to the garbage. Many activities we have always measured need to be measured still. But open your mind to new deliverables, which fall into three broad areas: catchment, conversation and conversion.

1. Catchment

Here we measure building an audience and a community. This is key to modern recruiting because old-school sourcing techniques, such as job boards and LinkedIn, are becoming less effective. So, too, are old-school business development techniques such as unsophisticated, untargeted teleselling. Measure growth in targeted LinkedIn connections, for example. For me, LinkedIn is more about branding than sourcing. Measure growth in blog subscribers on blogs published on the company blog or on LinkedIn, job-alert subscribers, and Twitter followers or social connections. Set KPIs around 'following' goals per week and total connections achieved by a specific date (a growth target).

2. Conversation

Conversation is all about measuring engagement as a KPI: building an audience and a community is step one, but engaging and building relationships with that audience is the next phase. Well-run recruitment businesses have always measured 'keeping in touch with current candidates'. I remember organising candidate phone nights to reconnect with candidates 30 years ago at Recruitment Solutions. Now, though, the measure is engagement with both current and future candidates. It's tapping into the 'talent community' you are building via catchment, and starting the nurturing process on social, via email, over coffee, on Twitter, on LinkedIn and so on. So, you're connected on LinkedIn to the Digital Director of a big-target company? Good, that goes against your KPI for the catchment. But now, the next activity is to engage. Share her material. Comment on her blog. Start a meaningful conversation. I know it might feel forced, but it's smarter than making cold calls to her voicemail, which she never returns and which only serve to irritate and alienate.

There is much you can do to engage and converse, but you need to measure it to manage it. Set KPIs around a number target for engagement activity.

3. Conversion

Conversion is where the magic happens: where all the catchment and conversation are converted into a real live candidate or client.

So, this is the measure of, for example, a person who was not initially looking for a job that you connected with on social via catchment and secured via your digital conversation, who has now been converted into a fully active candidate prepared to listen to live opportunities and be managed through the job-search process. Or, it's a potential client, unknown to you and without any prior relationship, who is reeled in via digital and who accepts a client visit or places an order (you must decide how you define a conversion as far as a hiring manager goes). Set weekly or monthly goals, and measure the GP eventuating from these conversions.

*

The 'catchment, conversation, conversion' method is ideal as an activity platform for building a brand and converting prospects. But the real point is that a great recruiter will always focus on the activities needed for success at a specific time. Many of these are 'timeless', but others are 'market driven'. Measuring activity is not the goal. It is just a tool to ensure we are being effective. The real goal is high-quality activity with the right people.

34 | Post-holiday bounce-back

We all take regular breaks from work: Christmas, New Year, summer holidays, Golden Week, Chinese New Year and others. But at what cost? We don't bill while we are on the beach and, when we get back to the desk, everything is stone cold. No activity, no momentum. What a task to crank up the action again! It could take weeks.

Is your break going to cost you a whole quarter? Maybe your job?

We know that it is a pipeline of critical activities that drives success (chapter 23). Any fall-off in that pipeline and a rapid decline in your placements and revenue is as predictable as night following day.

The activities that need to fill up your pipeline could include a wide variety of things (chapters 31 and 32), but typically you need to meet quality candidates and clients. Those are the metrics that drive the ultimate match.

Think about it most simply for a moment. If you are running a perm desk:

- You only earn money if people get hired.
- And people only get hired if people get interviewed by the client.
- And client-candidate interviews only happen if qualified job orders are secured.
- And qualified job orders typically result from prospect or sales meetings.

In addition:

- People get hired only if they accept job offers.
- And job offers come to quality, qualified talent.
- And, of course, qualified talent is typically uncovered through a thorough interview with the recruiter.

So, if you believe the bullet points above, you must maintain a pipeline of consistent activity, or the desired result – placements, fees and, therefore, fun and money (which I define in chapter 120) – will not eventuate. And taking time off dries up the pipe.

But it does not have to be so.

Here is a simple strategy to keep that pipeline healthy, even if you go away. Ten days before your holiday starting, you set a few simple goals. *Before I leave on holiday, I will have arranged:*

- ten sales visits for the first ten days after I get back
- ten candidate interviews for the first ten days after I get back.

That's it. And you make it happen.

It's a lot easier calling clients and prospects and arranging a meeting for three or four weeks' time. Then, it can be done relatively quickly. Same with candidates.

Be honest. 'I will be away for a couple of weeks. But, as soon as I get back, let's get your situation moving. I will see you in two weeks. How about 10 a.m. on Tuesday 12 January?'

Sure, some meetings will be cancelled. But here is the point: instead of getting back to a dead desk, weeks of grinding the activity wheel and maybe months before the money flows, you hit the ground running. You get back from holiday and have no orders to work on, but you have two client meetings on day one. And another the next day. And two more the day after that. Plus, you are seeing fresh candidates immediately.

You will be in full swing by the end of the week after your break. Feeling busy, being busy.

Yes, you can take a holiday and be a successful recruiter. But make sure a two-week holiday costs you two weeks of downtime – not six weeks.

35 | Do what David does

For about five years, I worked out of brilliant offices in Pitt Street, Sydney, when I was running Aquent and then Firebrand Talent Search.

I am a coffee drinker. It's my biggest vice (and I have a substantial portfolio of those!). So, at least two, maybe three times a day, I would need a hit from Pronto, the coffee shop below the office, which meant nipping downstairs and putting in my order with the friendly crew.

Eventually, I sold Firebrand and moved away from the Pitt Street end of town. So, for five years, I had not been into Pronto – until one day, I was striding past and fancied a caffeine hit, and so in I strolled, with no expectation of recognising anyone who worked there.

How wrong I was.

'Hello Greg', came the cheerful cry. There was David, the owner. (I had forgotten his name, of course, but his face and his persona were instantly recognisable.) 'Flat white, no sugar, isn't it?'

I was gobsmacked! I had not been there for five years, and this place must serve 1000 people daily. And he remembers my name and my order?

We chatted. I had to ask for his name. He was unfazed.

But it gets better.

'How is your son's cricket going?' he asked. Had we even discussed that? All those years and coffees ago? 'Fast bowler, isn't he?' Correct. (Well, not fast enough, but let that slide.) 'Is he enjoying X School?' David continued with a smile, correctly mentioning the school my son attends.

After our chat, I left with a handshake and great coffee. But I also left reflecting on what a great talent David has. I remembered now that he had always greeted his customers by name. But I was a five-year lapsed customer!

It is an incredible human talent to make people feel special, and I admit I left that coffee shop on a high.

Great recruiters do what David does. They take enough interest to remember. In chapter 2, I wrote about Graham Whelan, the most outstanding recruiter I have ever met, as having an incredible memory for people and their lives. He makes people feel special.

The ugly side of technology is that it has dumbed recruitment down. It has weakened the human skills that made great recruiters so special. So many recruiters today hide behind technology and avoid real interaction.

David, I salute you.

Recruiters, including me, take heed: there is nothing sweeter to the human ear than the sound of your own name.

PART III

SELLING IS LISTENING

Recruitment is often described as a selling job. And it is – but not in the way most people think of 'selling'.

Selling in recruitment actually means influencing outcomes, not hardcore pressure-selling. It means introducing jobs to candidates and candidates to jobs. A good recruiter will sell daily, managing each moment of truth. It means influencing, advising, consulting and creating excellent outcomes.

Of course, we also need to learn how to sell our differentiators. What this really means is having the ability to articulate why candidates and clients receive an advantage by working with you. So many recruiters have never really thought this through. You must identify, hone and polish why you offer something different to your competitors. Remember, it doesn't have to be something unique. Often, it's a combination of specialisation, years of experience, track record and network reach. But you need to know what those differentiators are, and you need to know how to communicate them with conviction.

The final area where recruiters need to be super fit in sales is in articulating their value. I often see recruiters flounder when it's time to explain why they are worth their fee. The compelling value to clients is the ability to access candidates they can't access themselves, bring those candidates to the hiring table and manage the process through to acceptance. The value to candidates is advice, insights, job-search coaching and acting as their agent in a crowded marketplace, which means representing them to the best possible employers, according to their goals.

When linked with recruitment, the word 'selling' unfairly became a bit grimy. But, in reality, excellent sales skills are something to be proud of! And you need to excel at them.

36 | In recruitment, everybody sells

In recruitment, everybody sells. It has ever been thus.

During the ten-year recruiting boom that ended in March 2020 when COVID-19 hit, recruitment companies got away with squadrons of non-billing managers and platoons of people with sexy job titles and no discernible responsibilities. Productivity declined before COVID-19 but, in a downturn, the last thing you want is 'administration managers' poring over spreadsheets, number-crunching, tweaking budgets, checking KPIs, planning, strategising, reviewing, assessing and (God help us!) calling (Zoom) meetings.

Of course, most of those things have some value. However, they're not a full-time job, except perhaps in the largest of organisations (and even then, I doubt it). Why else is it that these roles get cut the moment the market dips? They provide the most negligible value, and everyone knows it. (These administration managers were the first people, along with rookies, fired by the big players in recruitment when COVID-19 hit, too. At the time of writing, it looks like a full-on economic downturn may be on the way, so by the time you read this it may be happening again.)

In recruitment, everybody sells! The actual 'selling' will vary, but everybody sells – CEO included. And when I say 'sell', do not automatically think cold calling or relentless 'hard selling'. It's likely to be sophisticated, consultative, ambassadorial, relationship-based and sometimes digital, but the point is that everybody *bills* or directly engages in activity that leads to billing.

A recruiter sells all day. A resourcer or candidate manager sells to candidates and supports the recruiter in selling to clients. The 'team leader', supervising one or two people, must hold a full personal fee generation budget. The 'manager', running a team of up to eight consultants, will still bill, but they will increasingly farm work out to consultants in support; however, that 'billing manager' still sells, even if they handle just a few jobs. The placements dwindle, but they still rain-make, account-manage, see clients and front networking events. So, as the team grows, billing drops, but *selling* does not.

If you are in marketing in a recruitment agency, that's all good, as long as your work results in selling opportunities for people on the sales front line. During the 2008 Global Financial Crisis and other recessions prior, this took care of itself, because recruitment companies cut out middle management and everyone went back on the desk. And it happened again during COVID-19, just much faster.

My advice to you is to *not* allow non-billing managers to emerge as things improve, and to be careful about a role in recruitment in which your link to sales is unclear.

Your CFO, if you have one, should see clients. So should your HR manager. Why not? Undoubtedly, they must be as connected as possible to the ultimate customer. Likewise, admin staff should be brought into sales meetings and rewarded for sales growth. Your senior management should have sales responsibilities, which might include a goal for client meetings or running key accounts.

In my last 'corporate' role, I was the CEO of Firebrand, a company with ten offices in eight countries, and I did my share of selling. I did 100 client visits in my final year before selling the business (chapter 40). I also sold via my 'ambassadorial' role, speaking at conferences and events where clients and candidates were among the audience and creating PR and branding opportunities. (For the full story of Firebrand and the other business I founded and ran, read my first book, *The Savage Truth.*)

Whether the market declines or the market improves, don't lose focus. Everybody sells!

37 | When the client is talking, you are selling!

Most recruiters are good talkers. We do it all day, right? And most recruiters think that 'selling' means 'pitching', 'persuading' or 'spinning'. 'Good chat' is highly prized.

But there is a problem with that, and it raises its head at the most critical time, often undermining recruiter success. I was guilty of this mistake for many years. I must still fight the urge every day.

What urge? The urge to 'tell'. The instinct to jump in and 'preach'. The innate belief that 'selling' means 'talking'.

Most recruiters at a client meeting (remember those?) or in any version of a 'pitch' can't wait to tell the client what they can do.

How good they are. How they are different. Some even start the meeting with that. In minutes, you can see the client's eyes glaze over. And that's when they are in right front of you! Imagine what they are doing on the phone.

It is natural to want to talk. You want to impress. Get your credentials across. Show the client you have the answers. You are passionate. You believe you can help.

But that is not selling. Selling starts with *questions* and *listening*.

Think about it. The client says they are frustrated. Other agencies are providing 'second tier' candidates. Quickly, you leap into a rant about how you have the best database and understand the market intimately, and start to quote your job-fill ratios! No matter how articulate you are, this is likely to sound pushy, even cocky. And, anyway, you do not *know* what the client is saying yet.

It's so much better to explore:

'In what areas are the candidates you are seeing most deficient?'

'What categories of candidates do you see this happening with most often?'

'Why do you think they are doing this?'

'What specifically are you looking for that you are not getting?'

'What is the profile of a "tier one" candidate as far as you are concerned?'

The client explains. You probe. The client elaborates. The real issue is uncovered – by the *client* doing the talking!

It's precisely the same with candidates. And it's never more critical than in a skills-tight market (as it was when I wrote this book).

Be 'slow to understand'. The candidate says they are looking for 'career progression' as a reason for a job change. Of course, plenty of recruiters will write that down and move on. But that is only the beginning!

'What does "career" mean to you?'

'Have you discussed your career aspirations with your current employer?'

'What else is important to you in your next role?'

And that is just the tip of the iceberg. You are burrowing in deep! Peel the onion and find the real motivators, and then help that candidate rank those motivators to move! (Much more detail on these skills is given in chapters 70 and 71.)

You are not showing yourself in a good light by leaping in at every opportunity. People like to feel they have come to a decision themselves. They want to be heard. Also, intelligent questions build trust and credibility, and people take advice from people who they trust and find credible.

I have said it for years and it shocks recruiters every time: at a client meeting, the client does 70% of the talking. Not only that but, for the first 30 minutes, you do even less than 30%.

Selling is *not* talking. Certainly, when you do talk, it needs to be spot on – that's for sure. But what you say will depend on what you *hear*. And what you hear will depend on the questions you ask.

So, never forget: when the client is talking, you are selling.

38 | Look for clients in pain!

A client in pain is an excellent thing.

Stay calm. Not *physical* pain.

But it *is* true that when a client is under pressure, when a client is facing issues, when a client has deadlines, they are more committed to getting an outcome and, therefore, more likely to be committed to our process and us. And that is why getting the client *talking* is so critical. We need to understand their situation, their pain points, the real need. We do this by asking questions and listening.

So, what does this mean? Well, as you make your judgement on which clients to work with and where to spend your time, ask the questions that allow you to assess where one or more of these situations exist:

- The client has just had a key person resign.
- They suffer from high turnover in their team.
- They have just won a massive piece of work from a client.
- They are under pressure to perform or deliver results.

- A direct competitor has just launched a new product or service, and you know your client is under pressure to compete.
- Their high season is about to start and the pressure is on.
- It's salary review time, and you know their staff are underpaid and will be asking for raises.
- They have a massive personal workload with many deadlines just when they're starting to hire.
- They have no HR or admin support, yet are no expert in interviewing, recruiting, hiring or onboarding.

There are many more examples, but I think you get the picture. Look for a client under pressure, with deadlines and workload issues, and you will find a client in pain. Excellent! When we are in pain, we seek help and don't care how much we must pay to fix the problem. So it is with your clients. They need a solution. And *you* are there to ease that pain.

We are not looking to take advantage of their situation. Not at all. But a client in pain, properly managed, is a *committed* client. And that is where you will do your best work and solve their problem.

39 | Reasons sales meetings fail

For most of my recruiting life, client meetings have been vital. They are where you win business, earn trust, uncover needs and build rapport.

COVID-19 disrupted this dynamic, but it remains true that it is in a face-to-face meeting that the magic happens. This is where your credibility is established and the business is won or lost. Here, a recruiter can win exclusivity, secure multiple temp orders and resolve pricing and service dilemmas.

At the time of writing, intelligent recruiters are starting to engage with clients face to face again. They will thrive. How all this plays out remains to be seen but, be it face to face or via video-conference, winning business will most definitely be a perennial recruiter requirement.

Yet, too often, the visit or meeting is a wasted opportunity at best and an unmitigated disaster at worst.

There are many reasons why a client meeting can go belly-up, and some may not even be the recruiter's fault. But, too often, one or all of the following reasons makes a client meeting (face to face or digital) a wasted opportunity.

Wrong target market

Firstly, make sure the meeting is worth having at all! Yes, that's right. Is the potential client in your target market? Do they use recruiters? Are they a long-term prospect with ongoing hiring needs? Are you seeing the decision-maker? A visit for its own sake is a sad waste of time. Think before you meet. Remember, the formula for recruiting success in chapter 23 included the right 'target market' as a fundamental requirement.

Lack of preparation

You have a *huge* opportunity to see a significant client's CEO or marketing director. It's your one big shot. So much hinges on it. It has taken months to secure the meeting. And what do you do to prepare? *Nothing!* This is so common and so avoidable – it almost brings me to tears.

You must do everything possible to give yourself an edge in that meeting. Yes, do the standard research on the company and its products. But also, google the person you are meeting. Find out their history. If they have given an online presentation, read it. Press releases are to be studied. Check out their LinkedIn profile.

But you need to do more, too. Who are this company's clients? Who are their competitors? How are their trading results?

I once saw a prominent communications group CEO for a cold sales meeting. I googled him and found a YouTube video of him being interviewed in the week he started in the role. He explained his vision and his plans. How much do you think that helped me in framing my questions and my comments during the meeting? After that, we got on like a house on fire.

Your planning needs to be micro, too. How long will it take you to get to the client site? Trivial, you think? Not at all. A client meeting is stressful enough without arriving 20 minutes late. Why put the client offside before you have even met them? Check your database, too. Has your company worked with the client before? Was the client contact a candidate of yours once?

Knowledge is power. Get the knowledge!

Attitude

That's right, give yourself a sharp uppercut before the meeting starts. Don't be subservient. Don't be apologetic. Yes, your client is a senior executive expert in his field – but you are a professional recruiter who is an expert in yours! Act like an expert: not arrogant but confident. The client relationship is peer-to-peer. It is a partnership, not a slave-and-master relationship (chapters 5 and 6)!

Structure

Many recruiters conduct a visit like a pinball in a pinball machine. I have seen it 1000 times: they're all over the place with questions and anecdotes, trying to sell, then asking questions. It's a disaster!

You must have a plan. You are controlling the meeting – subtly, yes, but still, you know where it's going. You make sure it starts with the client talking about their company and their responsibility, and then you lead the conversation to their team and their staffing mix. Then you guide it to hiring challenges and their recruiter likes and dislikes, then on to specific opportunities. Finally, after all this has been done, you talk about your service and how you can solve the client's issues. Structure. Plan. Agenda.

Poor questioning skills

Oh yes! In this industry we are great talkers. I am no slouch myself. But the secret to a great client meeting is asking great questions. Unfortunately, most client meetings fail because the recruiter does not ask questions at all. Or asks the wrong ones. Or wimps out on the important ones.

Talking ratios

Guess what? In a good client visit, the client speaks 70% of the time (chapter 37). You talk 30%. Job done.

Missing the needs

Often, we are so anxious to 'sell' – so quick to leap on a client comment and tell them how we would handle the situation, so desperate to include all our differentiators – that we miss the client's 'hot button': the pain points, the critical need they want met.

Poor closing skills

Not long ago, one of my new recruiters told me they thought asking for the business at the end of a client visit was 'too pushy'. Lord, help me. Why do you think you are there? For the cup of tea? A well-structured client visit, in which all questions have been asked, needs unearthed, objections resolved and your offering clearly sold, must end with you asking for the job order. If you don't do that, or can't do that, guess what? You just wasted the whole exercise.

40 | You must achieve credibility at a sales meeting

Meeting a recruiting client for the first time, either face to face or digitally, is a nuanced and sophisticated skill.

Many recruiters don't seek out this critical opportunity. Some avoid it. In the post-COVID-19 boom, many recruiters delivered good results without running a single sales meeting. I fear for their longevity as the market turns.

Those who do run sales meetings often make fatal mistakes that harm their chances of building strong business relationships.

Of course, there are many things we want to achieve in that hour we spend with the prospective client, much we wish to communicate and plenty we must learn. However, there is *one* outcome we *must* achieve at *every* meeting with a client or prospect (and this is true with candidate meetings, too, by the way). It's non-negotiable, and your ability to win business and start a professional partnership hinges on this crucial outcome. I would go as far as to say that, without achieving this, the meeting fails, and so do you.

Credibility. At every meeting, you must earn credibility with your client.

It's like any other meeting with a professional service provider: your lawyer, accountant, architect, doctor, even hairdresser! You will not move forward with those people, commit to them or give them your business unless you believe they are 'credible'.

Credibility is made up of a complex cocktail of your personal presentation, your interpersonal style, your questioning skills, your market knowledge, the insights you offer, your track record of success, your ability to articulate your offer, your differentiators and the confidence you instil in the prospect that you can deliver what you promise.

So, from today, your goal in every client visit is to earn credibility. Ask yourself as you leave each meeting, *Was I credible?* That might be subjective, but my experience is that, if you are honest with yourself, you *know*. Remember, good recruiters are honest (chapter 15)!

You want empirical evidence that you were 'credible'? These are signs:

- You secured a job order.
- You were able to qualify the job order fully.
- You got it exclusively.
- You sold a retainer.
- There was no job order, but you got the client's commitment to using you next time.
- You got a follow-up meeting or action.
- The client did most of the talking.
- You got referrals to other decision-makers in the business.

Essentially, you must get the meeting to the point where you can *ask for the business* and be given the affirmative. For that to happen, the client has to believe you are a credible option.

If clients will not meet you, it means they don't believe you have a chance of being credible enough to warrant their time. Don't waste yours on them.

Credibility is the platform on which a consultative recruiter builds a real career.

41 | A great sales meeting

I cannot imagine a genuinely skilled recruiter who can't run great sales meetings. Developing business, opening doors, prospecting, understanding a prospect's needs and delivering a compelling pitch are fundamental requirements.

It was the part of the job I loved most. The prospect was sceptical, even cold. But, by the end of the meeting, we were chatting freely, the trust had begun and the opportunity to work together was agreed upon. Best feeling ever.

Many recruiters lost this skill during COVID-19 and the post-COVID-19 period. Many more never developed the ability: starting their careers in a tight candidate market, with work from home prevalent, they have never even done client meetings to sell their service and capability. The wheel will turn on that one, maybe even by the time you read this.

Sales meetings often go wrong. Many recruiters dread them, and some of the reasons they go wrong are outlined in chapter 39, but let's drill down on the risk factors so you can avoid them! Figure 2 outlines the anatomy of a great sales meeting.

Figure 2: The anatomy of a great sales meeting

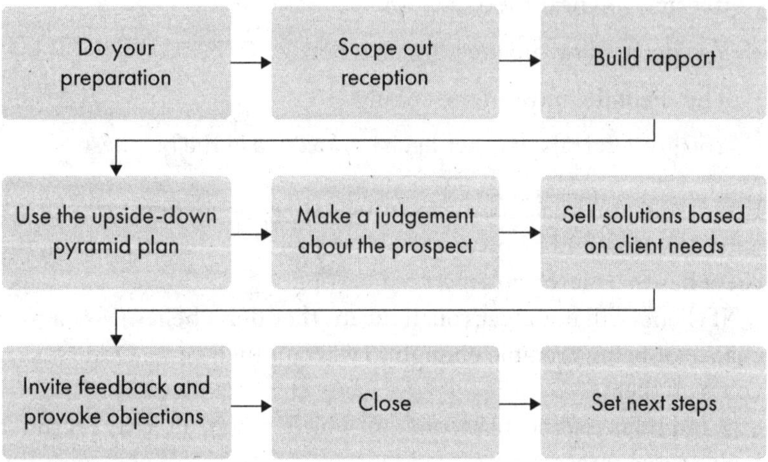

Do your preparation

A lack of preparation is one of the primary reasons meetings go wrong or could go better. There is so much you can do and so much you simply must do. You are only likely to get one opportunity in front of a prospect in real life or on a video call, so stacking the odds in your favour is innovative business.

Before leaping into a sales meeting with a potential client, here are some steps that professional recruiters take to prepare:

- Check if your business has dealt with the contact before. Are they in the database? Maybe they have even been a candidate in a previous life. Does anyone in the team know them?
- Check if your business has dealt with the prospect company at any time or place. What about another division of the business? A different branch? Years ago?
- Check if you are currently representing any candidates who work at the business you are about to meet with. That could be awkward later. Knowledge is power.
- Research the social profile of the client contact: through LinkedIn, obviously, but also Google.
- Research the company, of course. Their website is a good start but go deeper: press releases, interviews, reviews, Glassdoor.
- Research their hiring structure. What can you learn about their talent acquisition team, for example?
- Research current vacancies. Look at their careers site. Review job boards. Are they hiring now? What types of positions?
- Assess distance and travel logistics. Don't arrive at your prospect meeting late because you did not plan ahead. Why make a challenging meeting infinitely harder by annoying the prospect before you even meet them?
- Prepare your marketing collateral: salary survey, brochure, whatever else you might have.
- Search LinkedIn for the types of employees that report to the prospective client.

- Based on the point above, consider bringing profiles of potentially matched candidates to the meeting. (Get the candidates' permission first, of course.) If the meeting goes well and the prospect admits they are desperate for UX designers, for example, imagine how fantastic would it be to reach into your briefcase and say, 'My research told me that might be the case, and I have here the very best UX designer I have seen for a long time, and she is very interested in your company'.

Scope out reception

So, you have done your preparation and you arrived on time. What can you learn while you are waiting in reception? What can you do during this period to gain information and extract an advantage?

Many recruiters sink into a chair and get lost in their phones or daydream. You can give yourself an edge!

- Engage with the receptionist if there is one. This is a brilliant opportunity to learn critical snippets of information and make a potential ally for the future.
- Read the wall: the plaques, the awards, the company slogans.
- They are rare now but, if there is a visitors' book, plunder it! Don't steal the book, obviously, but see who has been visiting lately. Your competitors?
- Assess the culture. What's the buzz? How do people interact? How do they look? How do they behave?
- Pick up the brochures and pamphlets on the table. You will glean great information, which could be helpful in the next hour but also when briefing candidates.
- Focus. Get your thoughts clear. Have an opening line ready for when you meet the prospect. Review your meeting structure plan.

Build rapport

I was always standing up when the prospect arrived. I wanted to be ready, alert and in a position to greet the client eye to eye, not scrambling to get out of a chair while dropping my phone.

It is critical to build some rapport as soon as possible. There is always tension when two people meet for the first time, especially if one of them is nervous that they are about to be 'sold to'.

Defuse it. Get chatting with the prospect. Avoid the banal, like the weather, but as you walk to the meeting room, how about an ice-breaker? 'Great offices, Ms Prospect. How many people do you have onsite here?' Silence will raise anxiety and get both of you on edge.

Remember that your primary goal in a first-off sales meeting is to earn credibility.

Use the upside-down pyramid plan

Now that you are in the prospect's meeting room and the small talk is flowing, how do you begin? It's not just a friendly chat. It may include that, but you need a plan, a structure, to make sure you glean the pertinent information and earn the right to ask the crucial questions. You need the upside-down pyramid plan (see figure 3).

Figure 3: The upside-down pyramid plan – start general, drill down, get more specific

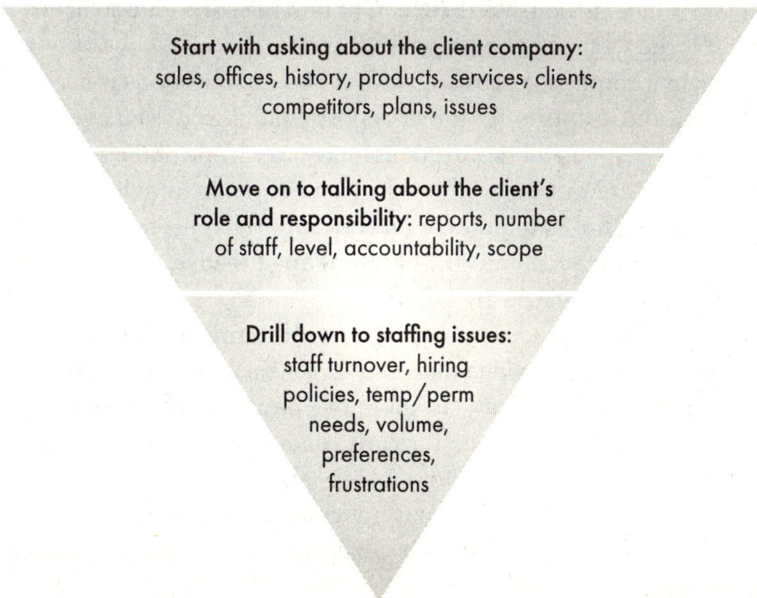

You can't approach a meeting with a random set of goals and no plan. Nor can you kick off the meeting with a sensitive yet essential question without having built trust and paved the way.

For example, imagine asking this as your first question: 'So, Ms Prospect, how much did you spend on temp agency fees last year?' That would be inappropriate and probably impertinent, and unlikely to provoke a constructive response.

But you *will* ask that question *later* in the meeting, when you have earned it – when you have been on the journey with the prospect.

Start with broad, open-ended questions about the company – non-threatening questions that make perfect business sense. For example, 'Ms Prospect, of course, I have done my research on XYZ PL, but would you tell me a little more about your organisation?'

Some prospects are verbose, others more taciturn. You drill down with a few prompting questions, including about ownership structure, company history, sales, offices, staff numbers, products and services, significant clients, competitors, expansion plans and and critical business issues. This might take five to ten minutes.

When you feel you have enough information, move down the pyramid. Now you focus on the prospect's area of personal responsibility: 'Where do you, Ms Prospect, fit into the corporate structure? What is the scope of your responsibility?'

Again, prompt the prospect with follow-up questions if needed, covering title, reports to, direct reports, number of staff, level of staff, staff responsibilities, accountability and scope of the role.

Now we are moving to the pointy end of the pyramid! You have been chatting for 20 minutes or more. Rapport has been established. The client has been doing 80% of the talking because, after all, when the client is talking, you are selling!

It is time now to address staffing and recruitment issues.

I would use this bridge question to get there, but you can do it any way you wish, as long as you move down to the sharp end of the pyramid: 'Thank you. I clearly understand your marketing department, Ms Prospect. Do you have much staff turnover?'

The answer to this question is not essential in itself. It's a vehicle to allow you to say, 'So, when you have hiring needs, Ms Prospect, how do you solve those?'

And, again, you drill deep: How do you recruit? Why do you use those strategies? Do you use agencies? Which ones? What do you like about the service you get? What do you not like? Do you use temp/contract staff? In what situations? Is it seasonal? What types of staff? How many? Where from? What is your annual budget for temp staff?

When the client is talking, you are selling. The meeting has been going on for 30 minutes. You have done about 15% of the talking.

You have not tried to sell your company or your service. This is critical. Do not be tempted to jump in and tell the prospect how you can solve their issues and how great your agency is. Not yet.

Make a judgement about the prospect

Now, you are ready to judge the prospect against the following questions:

- Are they the decision-maker?
- Are they a real prospect in terms of roles and volume?
- What is their hiring history? How have they recruited to date?
- Do they have current agency relationships?
- What are their likes and dislikes when using agencies?
- What are their 'hot buttons' when using agencies?
- What frustrates them or makes them happy?
- Where is their 'pain' (chapter 38), and how severe is it?
- What other hiring issues have you identified?

Remember, a client in pain is a good thing (chapter 38).

Sell solutions based on client needs

Now it's your turn! Sell your specific solutions based on the prospect's identified needs:

- Focus on their pain points.
- Speak to a problem they need to solve.
- Focus on your differentiators and how they will work for the prospect (chapter 42).

Do not regurgitate every feature and benefit your company has. Instead, tailor your pitch to what you know your prospect *wants* to hear. Do not oversell. Don't cloud the clarity and power of your solution with anything irrelevant. It's not one size fits all. Each pitch is tailored to how you have heard the client answer your 'pyramid questions'.

Don't focus on what your company is or has. Instead, focus on what you have learned about your prospective client's wants and needs.

Invite feedback and provoke objections

After you have delivered your pitch, the client may ask some questions, which is an excellent sign. If not, ask for feedback. Indeed, provoke objections:

- Do you have any questions?
- Can you see how my processes might help you?

Objections and questions are good because they mean the client is interested.

Then, make a judgement about the client's readiness to commit to using you and your company.

Close

It is logical and appropriate to ask whether the client has any current temporary or permanent recruitment needs. Hilariously, they will often be forthcoming with roles they are trying to fill, despite having said at the beginning of the meeting, 'I am happy to chat, but I have no needs right now'. That's all good. It just means you have earned credibility and they are now ready to engage. Well done!

Asking for current roles is a 'close'. If they offer you an opportunity, you start taking the brief, and that is 'job done'. The position is not filled, but you got what you came for: the prospect is now your client!

However, quite likely, the client has no current vacancies right now. You must get their verbal commitment to using you next time.

This proves that you have satisfied their criteria and is also a subtle 'promise', which I have found prospects often keep. Say something to the effect of the following:

> *'Ms Prospect, I have appreciated your time today. I feel I have a good understanding of what you expect when hiring temporary and permanent staff. I hope I have explained how I can meet your needs. When you next have a hiring need, may I have that opportunity to work with you?'*

You will get a 'yes' if you have done an excellent job. And it's crazy not to ask for the business. Everyone knows why you are there, and you have earned the right!

However, it's not time to leave just yet. Make sure you wrap up a few essential extras:

- Ask the client for the names of other hiring managers and ask permission to contact them 'with your introduction'.
- Ask for permission to send a LinkedIn connection request (and do it!).
- If appropriate, introduce names of other recruiters in your company who recruit in different disciplines. Get an introduction for them.
- Introduce and offer your marketing collateral, brochure and salary survey.
- Discuss and agree on terms of business, if appropriate.

Set next steps

Finally, do not dare leave that room without your next contact steps nailed:

- A follow-up meeting date
- An invitation to a client event
- A brief to float in or reverse market key skills (chapter 48).

You have done all the hard work. But, unfortunately, a 'sale' may take several contact points.

Set yourself up for the next one.

42 | Selling your differentiators

The previous chapter mentioned 'selling your differentiators' at the vital moment in the sales meeting. Of course, you need to be very skilled at that, but you also need to be prepared to sell why you are different and why clients and candidates should work with you at any time during the process.

Clients and candidates often view recruitment companies as being 'all the same'. I have heard it often. That's a problem if you wish to stand out.

Start by explaining why you and your company have skills, processes or advantages that should incline clients and candidates to work with you. What sets you apart? What can you claim as yours?

When I joined Aquent in 2001, I was shocked that the organisation offered a blanket 110% money-back guarantee on any permanent or temporary placement that went wrong, no matter the reason. Initially, I was against the idea, but that was both naïve and arrogant, because it was a magnificent credibility, marketing and differentiation strategy. Very few placements went wrong and, when they did, most clients simply said, 'Hey, don't send the money back. Just refill the job'. Which we routinely did. In the infrequent circumstance that we did refund the placement fee, 'plus 10% for their troubles' (which was our mantra), it was deeply appreciated by the client, who would inevitably offer us more work in due course. (Learn about the incredible story of my time at Aquent in *The Savage Truth*, my first book.)

For our recruiters it was a real 'wow' factor to be able to say in client meetings, 'We are so confident in our ability to do a good job that, if it does not work out, we will refund the fee plus 10% for any stress we caused'. It looked huge in the eyes of the client, when in reality the cost to us was minimal and the rewards fantastic.

I always encourage recruiters and companies to identify their differentiators and then learn how to articulate them.

Firstly, think about this in the context of what matters to the client. This is not as obvious as it should be. I often hear recruiters say – and read on websites and marketing blurbs – statements like, 'We have been operating for 15 years'. This does not tell the customer anything other than that you have been able to survive. Not a compelling argument. Even this is better: 'We have been operating for 15 years in the life sciences sector, have over 150,000 candidates in our database and work with all of the top 15 life sciences companies in the UK'. That is a strong claim. It's meaningful and tells them that what you offer is proven and works!

Your differentiators need to speak to the client about how you will solve their problems, make their life easier and deliver faster and better outcomes. Remember, your differentiation doesn't have to be some unique technology or bespoke process: you simply need a set of competencies and advantages you can claim as your own. Proven access to exceptional candidates is most potent. Evidence of benefits in cost, process or consistency always resonates. Quality and productivity will catch the client's attention.

You also must have differentiators to outline to candidates. These should mainly centre around how you treat them as human beings, your regular communication processes, your understanding of their niche, your ability to access the best roles, your leverage with clients and your access to the decision-makers.

When identifying and articulating your differentiators, you must consider the *value* you bring to your customers. Your differentiators must be tangible, with measurable business outcomes that you deliver, and they must speak to critical issues that customers in your market are facing.

If you can quote specifics, metrics or statistics, that's very powerful. For example, 'We have 150,000 candidates with funds management experience in our database', or, 'In the last 24 months, we have filled 90% of our roles within 18 working days'. You need to be accurate, but this is what your market is looking for: proof of quality and swift outcomes.

It is sadly true that very few recruiters can articulate their differentiators with confidence and pride. Few recruitment companies work on identifying them, and fewer still consistently train their teams on what their differentiators are and how to sell them.

As a result, it turns out that knowing and being able to sell your differentiators *is* a differentiator.

43 | Lessons from 2000 client meetings

Have I done 2000 client visits? At least that many. All over the world.

I did not count them, obviously, but one a week over my recruiting career takes me well over that number – and it was way more than one a week.

So, did I learn anything? I like to think so. Do the following lessons resonate with you?

1. Just doing a visit is not enough. You must craft a great meeting with structure, agenda and key outcomes.
2. A great meeting is not a 'friendly chat'. Of course, it could be that as well, but it must be an exchange of meaningful information that ends with a road map for the future relationship and communication plan.
3. The more (quality) visits you do, the more business you win and the better relationships you build.
4. The visit is the start of the relationship getting real.
5. The fundamental goal of a prospect meeting, the one thing you must achieve, is 'credibility'. Do that and the rest flows.
6. You can learn a considerable amount that will help you in the meeting while in reception.
7. Meetings fail because of a lack of structure, no planning, poor questioning skills or the consultant talking too much and missing the actual needs.
8. A client 'in pain' is a good thing. Meetings help you identify clients in pain.
9. You can qualify a job order immeasurably better at a visit, and qualified job orders get filled more often.
10. After you visit a client, your commitment to helping them get the best staff increases – or decreases. Either outcome is excellent because you know your level of commitment.
11. When you meet clients, you make better matches.
12. Your preparation and research make all the difference to the quality of the visit outcome.

13. Allow enough time to get there on time. Why make a stressful situation worse by annoying the client by pitching up late?
14. Intelligent questions are the backbone of a successful meeting.
15. Clients become candidates, especially after they have met you.
16. Clients often lie.
17. An effective client meeting will have the client talking 70% of the time and you 30%.
18. Client meetings are like a first date: the more you talk about the client, the more they like you and the smarter they think you are.
19. Don't give the client any collateral, brochures, salary surveys or anything other than your card until the end. If you do, they will read that and stop listening to you.
20. A prospect who is cold, sceptical, brusque and disinterested in the first meeting can be friendly and chatting by the end of the meeting and your lifelong client after six months. That is the power of a great client meeting and some of the best fun this industry can offer.
21. Suppose the client keeps you waiting too long in reception, takes calls during your meeting, haggles your fee and is generally disrespectful. In that case, this client will inevitably jerk you around forever after.
22. Start client meetings with non-threatening questions like, 'Could you tell me about your company?' or 'What is your market like?'
23. However, by the end of the meeting, you should have addressed all the hard questions, like 'Who do you use?', 'How much do you spend on third-party recruiters?' and 'What do you like and dislike about the agency service you get?' But you must earn the right to ask these questions!
24. You must close. That means taking an order or getting a commitment to work on their next order. And you must ask for the business before you leave.

25. If the prospect is seeing you, there is a reason. They did not agree to meet you because they had nothing else to do that day. An opportunity exists there. Even if the client says it doesn't, it does – maybe not right now but in the future.
26. When the client talks about fees and discounts, you know that you have not sold your service well enough. You need to go back to talking about your value, not your price (chapters 51 and 52).
27. No two pitches to prospects are the same. You don't have a 'one size fits all' presentation that you wheel out on every occasion. Instead, you tell the client what they want and need to hear, and you know what they want and need to hear because you have asked the right questions and unearthed their needs and 'hot buttons'.
28. A demeanour of confidence and self-belief, and an attitude that says, 'I am an expert in my field', overcomes just about everything. Without that self-belief, you will never earn 'recruiter equity' (chapter 5).
29. Selling exclusivity and retainers is immeasurably easier in an in-person meeting than over the phone (chapters 101 to 103).
30. Never say to a client, 'I know you are busy. I won't keep you long'. You are busy too. Your time is valuable too. The meeting will take as long as it needs to take. Be always respectful to the client, but don't belittle your value.
31. Always agree on the 'next steps' before the meeting closes. That might be another meeting, a call back at a specific time or an open brief on skills needed that allows you to be back in touch with particular candidate profiles.
32. Ask for referrals. Who else in the group hires?
33. Don't put your phone, keys or folder on the client's desk.
34. Don't take a phone call in the client's office. (Obvious, but some clowns do it.) Don't be on the phone when the client greets you in reception. Don't even have your phone visible during the meeting. And do not allow it to ring, beep, ping or play 'Highway to Hell', either.

35. Dress for your client, not for your party that night.
36. The best fun in the recruitment business stems from meeting clients. That is when the adrenalin pumps. Most of the rest of this job is glorified administration – or unglorified administration, for that matter. It's in the client meeting that the magic happens!

By the way, if you think I was exaggerating about doing client visits 'all over the world', I was a bit, but not much. I have conducted recruitment client meetings in all of these locations (which was a privilege and taught me so much): Australia, New Zealand, South Africa, Singapore, Malaysia, India, Hong Kong, China, Japan, Korea, the United Kingdom, the United States, Canada, Poland, Czech Republic, Germany, the Netherlands, Spain, France and Ireland.

44 | Credibility is built on insights

One of my recruitment-agency-owner clients told me a fascinating story. It's elementary – obvious, even – but instructive about one of the critical dynamics in the agency recruitment market.

One of his recruiters had a candidate down to the wire with his client. In fact, after three interviews, the client had made an offer to the candidate, and both the recruiter and the client were convinced that the candidate would accept.

However, as so often happens, there were other things afoot with this candidate and she took another job. The recruiter was disappointed but professional, and called his client to convey the bad news: 'I'm sorry, Mr Client, our candidate has not accepted your job, and indeed she's taken a role by another means'.

The recruiter thought he had done his job, but that is when things turned: the client asked the recruiter, 'Do you have any feedback for me?'

The recruiter was somewhat taken aback. 'Feedback? Specifically, regarding what?' asked the recruiter, which wasn't a great response, but that's the story's point.

The client was very articulate in explaining what he meant:

'Why did she turn our job down?'

'What specific aspects of the other role trumped ours?'

'What was the deal-breaker regarding her not accepting our job?'

'What salary did she accept in contrast to our offered salary?'

'Did she have any comments or feedback about our recruitment process?'

'Did she have any comments about our culture or any other aspect of our business?'

'Was it anything to do with me personally?'

This goes to the heart of differentiating through consultation and credibility. Even in a bad-case scenario, you can improve trust with a client. In fact, it's the best time. Clients are looking for *value* from the recruitment consultant. They are seeking an ally and a credible, trusted advisor. So, even though this placement didn't go through, it was an opportunity for the recruiter to *strengthen the trust* and the equity with this client by providing helpful market feedback.

The client felt he had lost a good candidate and didn't know why. To him, the recruiter was vague and maybe even dishonest (which wasn't true, by the way). I can't express how important it is not to lose sight of the fact that we need to *build relationships, prove credibility* and *strengthen client trust.*

This situation exemplifies that there are many opportunities to go the extra mile to show that we are more than just 'résumé hacks' – that we are *partners* with our clients.

That list of questions the client asked should be your template when a candidate rejects your client's offer. Go back with the bad news – that's your job. But also bring *insights* and *value.*

As I write this, it's a candidate-driven market. So, that recruiter could write this episode off and pick up another client if this one is unhappy. However, the wheel will turn in the recruitment market and, if you don't have a strong bond with clients that is built on a track record and credibility, you will sink like a stone when the downturn comes.

45 | Develop your chat

The title of this Part is 'Selling is listening' and, indeed, the foundation of any sale is to ask, listen and understand. But when you *do* talk – and, obviously, you need to – you must have something compelling to say!

The sad truth is that many recruiters flounder at this stage. They stumble over their pitch, unable to define their differentiators, spouting worn-out clichés and offering little in the way of insights or valuable information.

Creating a powerful *narrative* is an essential recruiter skill and a platform for being able to impress, build credibility and ultimately influence outcomes. A recruiter should have one narrative for clients and one for candidates, each constantly evolving depending on the market and new trends.

We must flip the selling and business development dynamic in the recruitment industry. Instead of asking clients for something from them – 'Do you have any jobs for me to fill, Ms Client?' – you should be *offering* something to the client or prospect, which is usually a clear, robust and informative point of view. You need to develop something valuable to say, providing insights and ideas.

This narrative, or 'chat', could cover a wide range of topics but will typically revolve around issues important to the client or the candidate.

With clients, you might talk about salaries, working conditions, talent availability, benefits and compensation, candidate confidence, improved hiring processes and specific issues emerging in your market at that particular time.

With candidates, of course, you will elaborate on job demand, high-demand skills, salary developments, work-from-home arrangements and a wide range of other topics that are of interest to people considering a career move.

This narrative or point of view is not something the recruiter should simply 'wing'. Most of us are not good enough to do that. Instead, you need to work on building and refining your narrative. You need a point of view that points the way. It's not a rehearsed script; it's a thought-through set of opinions and insights.

A sophisticated recruiter has developed the skill to spark positive conversations with clients and candidates, which makes them memorable and valuable, and separates them from the average recruiter. Even if you can run a solid recruitment process, that is not enough. You must offer ideas, insights, information, market intelligence and informed opinion.

Develop your chat. Then, you will be remembered for it.

46 | Two great selling questions

Selling does not have to be 'hardcore'. You should be subtly selling to clients and candidates throughout the process.

If you did not know it yet, you are in a selling job: 'selling' in the most positive sense of that word.

So, in this chapter are two simple questions you can ask every client, whether you deal with them often or sporadically. These questions will spark conversation, uncover opportunities and open doors; and, if you go a little deeper and 'peel the onion', they will offer a path to stronger relationships, new business and information you have been missing.

Here they are:

1. 'What else?'
2. 'Who else?'

As in:

1. 'What else can I do for you? What else are you grappling with? What else needs solving? What other vacancies do you have? What else do I need to know?'
2. 'Who else can I talk to? Who else recruits in your business? Who else can you recommend? Who else can I introduce you to from my business?'

There they are. Just build them in. Use your own words, if you prefer.

What else? Who else?

The questions are just the beginning. It is a journey. But, if you don't ask them, the journey never begins.

47 | Do cold calls – but don't!

For most of the history of agency recruitment, cold calling and hard-core business development (BD) were front and centre as recruiter skills and responsibilities. In the post-COVID-19 boom, they waned as job briefs became plentiful and candidate availability dried up.

By the time you read this, they may be back on the front burner – in which case many recruiters will have been found out, as they will have no idea what to do or say.

BD skills are imperative but, mostly, telling recruiters to mindlessly 'cold call' is poor advice.

All recruiters indeed need to develop clients, identify prospects and find ways to build sustainable relationships. Often, that means connecting with people you have never dealt with. So, yes, we are business developers, and that becomes even more critical in a tight job market. But, if possible, *don't cold call.*

Random, untargeted, unprepared cold calls are most likely to fail and even do brand damage. In addition, they will undoubtedly provide the recruiter with self-esteem damage.

However, don't misunderstand me on this one: *you do have to make those calls and initiate that contact.* The key is that you should do everything possible to ensure that the call is not stone freezing cold.

Move your *cold* call to a *warm* call. Instead of making hundreds of random calls to people who don't want to hear from you and in which your pitch is little more than 'Got any job orders I can fill?', do the research to find a point of common ground that turns the call from 'cold' to 'warm'.

There are many ways to do this, but here are ten good ones:

1. Approach ex-candidates, even if you did not place them, who are now in roles that mean they may become clients. (I hope you looked after them well!)
2. Get a referral from another division or office in your company. For example, 'Mr Prospect, I am calling because our Singapore office has done a lot of work with your colleague, Michael Chew, over there, and he suggested I give you a call'.

3. Get a referral from another current client: 'Ms Prospect, I work extensively with Michael Chew at Apex Industries. He mentioned you had worked with him there and suggested I call you to see how we could assist'.
4. Connect first in a neutral environment and follow up later: 'Ms Prospect, it was a pleasure to chat with you at the Marketing Institute Conference last week, and I would enjoy a chance to talk more about your comments on SEO trends'.
5. Follow up on previous placements, no matter how long ago: 'Mr Prospect, you probably would not realise this but I placed Roberta Clarke with your predecessor quite a while ago. I would love to come down and see how she is doing and introduce myself to you'.
6. Engage on social media first: 'Ms Prospect, I have enjoyed our banter on LinkedIn, and thanks for the connection, by the way. I am in your part of town next Tuesday and would love to drop in and learn more about the new training system you were posting about'. (A rec to rec did precisely this to me while I was in London recently. I met her.)
7. Follow up on a talk given by a prospect, a blog written or a piece of PR they have received: 'Ms Prospect, I loved your blog on the impact of ChatGPT…'
8. Do your research and call a candidate who has the skills this prospect may be interested in. The good old 'reverse market' is timeless in its efficacy (chapter 48).
9. Call with insights: a salary survey, information on hiring trends, the latest strategies around managing remote work… whatever is likely to interest the prospect.
10. Approach senior contractors of yours who have finished up with you and are now working at companies that are not your clients. That's an opening right there.

Be creative about this. Brainstorm it with your team. You don't want to be manipulative or trite, but you want to start your BD call from a warm position, get some connection and then move on.

Of course, the more you have built your online brand, the easier this becomes (chapters 58 and 59).

48 | Reverse marketing candidates

The reverse marketing tactic is as old as the recruitment hills, but it is still a highly effective way to achieve outstanding outcomes. We are talking about identifying a highly skilled candidate in a niche and then contacting a targeted prospective client to represent that candidate to that potential employer. In this situation, you don't have an actual brief to fill, but your market knowledge suggests that the client or prospect will likely be interested in your candidate's skill set.

Let's consider the broader benefits.

Firstly, reverse marketing quality candidates has a substantial impact on growing your *personal brand* and your *company's brand.* This is because you are seen to be an expert. You are seen to have access to top candidates, and you are seen to be making an intelligent match.

Reverse marketing sends a strong message to *current* clients when you contact them with prospective hires, particularly if you've already briefed those hires on your client and can say with authenticity that the candidate is interested in working with them.

This tactic demonstrates to both candidates and clients that your company is a specialist in a particular niche, has contacts and can make things happen.

And, of course, this is an outstanding warm business development activity. As outlined throughout this Part, we must go to clients with something of value to them. What better offer can you make than a highly skilled candidate with a difficult-to-recruit skill set?

So, it's a great idea to reverse market candidates, but *how do you do it?*

Start by asking clients on an ongoing basis what types of skills they are routinely on the lookout for. Most companies can nominate a profile or two. In addition, you can sometimes set up 'standing briefs', whereby a client acknowledges that you will contact them if you see an exceptional candidate with the right competencies.

To reverse market candidates, you need to understand the skills of your candidates deeply. You only select outstanding candidates to reverse market. You represent candidates that have hard-to-find skills that are in high demand.

Importantly, you get the candidate's permission to represent them to the specific companies you plan to approach.

Make sure you are transparent with the candidate that there are no guarantees and that you don't have an open order with this client right now. You are 'acting as their agent and representing them to the best employers'. (Feel free to steal that phrase. I probably did. It is very effective.)

You can approach current clients, which is obviously a warmer call. You can also call prospects. When you do, the language you use might be something like this:

> *'Mr Prospect, we haven't spoken, but my name is Greg from GregSearch and I represent the best creative and design talent in Australia. This week I interviewed one of the most outstanding and talented UX designers I've met in some time. He particularly mentioned that he would like to work at your company. Would you like to have some details?'*

Remember, great recruiters tell no lies, and the above statement will be true because you would have said to your candidate, 'Bob, I think you might fit in with ABC Ltd. Here are some details about them. Would you like me to represent you to them?' Once your candidate has answered in the affirmative, he has specifically said that he'd like to work at that company.

If the client were to suggest that they're not looking for UX talent now, you would acknowledge that and then prompt a conversation about their *current* hiring needs.

Reverse marketing is a *door-opener*. It's still a massive success if you come away from that call having secured a different brief, or maybe agreed to have a coffee with the prospect, or possibly set a time for a follow-up call in three months.

It's outbound, proactive business development, compelling and, done well, is appreciated by both prospect and candidate.

49 | Flex your BD muscle

No matter what the market, business development (BD), sales and client penetration are part of a recruiter's role. Danger emerged post-COVID-19, when jobs were plentiful, and many recruiters lost any sales skills they had – or, in the case of new recruiters, never acquired them.

Individual recruiters must take control of their futures by asking these questions and being confident in the answers they come up with:

- What will happen when the market turns?
- How will I react when there are more candidates than jobs?
- Do I know how to start a search for job orders to fill?
- When last did I flex my 'BD muscle'?
- How would I cope if permanent fees dropped 50% and temporary margin by 30% in one month, and they did not recover for two years? (This is typically what happens in a full-on recession.)
- What skills do I have to cope (or not!) in that market?
- What relationships have I built that will soften the blow?
- What should I do now to mitigate the risk of a market downturn and a sharp slowdown in job orders?
- In the last month, have I spoken with every client I have placed with in the last five years?
- In the last 60 days, have I reached out to every client who lodged an order I did not fill to re-engage and update?
- Have I spoken to every candidate I placed in the last five years?
- Have I contacted every 'good' candidate I did not place in the last five years?
- Have I visited face to face (or, as a fallback, via videoconference) my top 25 customers?

- When last did I do a BD outreach call to a prospective client? Do I have that skill?
- Can I run an effective business development prospect meeting (chapter 41)?
- Can I sell my differentiators in the face of multiple recruiters selling theirs to my clients and prospects simultaneously (chapter 42)?

And these questions are just the tip of the iceberg.

You don't want to go into 'sales mode' when the market declines: that's too late. It is better if you are always in sales mode, because this insulates you against a market decline. Take the actions in this list ASAP, then set the cadence for regular follow-up. Set your own schedule as you see fit, but make sure you follow through.

This will make much more sense to you when we have a severe downturn.

Till then, please take my word for it.

50 | Client nurturing

In chapter 41, I outlined how to conduct a prospective client visit, which sets the platform for an ongoing relationship. In chapters 96 and 105, there is a detailed explanation of how you build that relationship through the job-order qualification process, setting up interviews and advising clients through the process. However, with most clients, working on a job-order will be a sporadic activity, and it's critical to set up a system of ongoing communication, nurturing and relationship-building.

Some great tactics for this are outlined in chapter 113 – which asks the provocative question, 'Are you client fit or client flabby?' – but also consider the ideas in this chapter.

Whether you're initiating a relationship or trying to keep an existing one healthy, it's important not to approach your client with the banal. For example, 'I am just calling to see if you have any jobs' or 'How was your vacation?' are likely to annoy.

You must think, *What's in it for them?* not *What's in it for me?* So, go to your client with something useful or interesting *for* them, not always to ask for something *from* them.

Many recruiters feel unsure at this point, but conversations, insights and information are the foundation for nurturing a client relationship. Indeed, a great way to do this is with targeted, appropriate-candidate reverse marketing (detailed in chapter 48). However, any opportunity to deliver pertinent news will be appreciated, as will updates on the market or events of interest.

You might tag or reference a client on social media, particularly LinkedIn. As long as you are not breaching any confidentiality, this can be very powerful, especially if you bring their attention to an interesting, relevant issue, or perhaps even showcase something they are doing that others can learn from.

Another digital idea to keep front of mind with your client is to share their social posts when appropriate. Don't overdo this because it can look needy. Still, suppose one of their LinkedIn posts is particularly relevant to your community; in that case, sharing will help your connections and remind your client of your existence, because they will notice.

It can be a door-opener to reference-check a candidate you have met who used to work for your client. Of course, you may not even need that reference check right now, but it's a wonderful opportunity to engage and initiate conversations about the market or hiring prospects.

You could invite your client to an event that is relevant to them and even go with them to that event.

If you meet another client or supplier, or an industry professional who you think would be a good contact for your client, drop them a note to offer an introduction. This can be extremely powerful and appreciated.

You do have to approach all of this with caution, as you don't want to appear to be a stalker, nor do you want this to appear inauthentic. Be very considered in your approach.

On the other hand, keeping client relationships oiled – particularly when they are framed around what's valuable to your client – will ensure you get the call when the next order is available.

51 | The fee negotiation mindset

I wrote at some length in my first book, *The Savage Truth*, about negotiating fees and proving your value, but it's worth enlarging on that here.

It's a fact of recruiting life that clients will push you to negotiate your fees. With so many recruiters quick to drop fee percentages to secure briefs, this can be a challenging discussion.

The starting point for successful fee negotiations is, strangely enough, to get the conversation *off the fee percentage* and onto the question of what your fee is actually for. Bundled up in that conversation is your ability to sell your differentiator (chapter 42). That is the secret sauce. What have you *got* and what do you *do* that gives your client *unique value*?

Now, please understand that this strategy only works if you do, in fact, have meaningful differentiators. So, here is the bad news: if you do not have parts of your process or abilities that offer unique (or at least advantageous) value, you won't be able to hold your fees when things hot up at the negotiating table.

However, if you have worked hard to create differentiators – and you must – that is where you want to focus.

At Aquent and Firebrand Talent Search, for example, we emphasised our deep sector focus; our unmatched access to creative, marketing and digital talent; our multiple branches in the Asia-Pacific, the USA and Europe; our specialist knowledge and understanding of client needs; and our proprietary testing software, which meant we knew candidates had the design skills they claimed to have. This was all wrapped up in a 110% money-back guarantee.

That was (and still is) a compelling argument. (I am sold just reading the previous paragraph!)

It's also vital that the differentiators you nominate have relevance for the client and are centred on the advantage you bring regarding access to talent.

52 | Don't talk fees, talk value

So, when a client does ask you to drop your fee, *don't talk about your fee!*

Go through your entire recruitment process, explaining *everything* you do to secure the right person. Take your time. Start at the beginning and don't leave anything out. Talk about your screening, interviews, and candidate generation strategies such as social media, events, referrals and networking. Don't assume your client knows about these!

Focus mainly on your ability to find candidates that *other recruiters and the client cannot.* That's the sweet spot! Talk about your database and the fact that you have several offices (if you do) tapping into talent. Explain how you act as an *advocate for the client* and how you will qualify each candidate concerning cultural fit, salary and skills.

When you drill down, you find that we recruiters do a lot! That's the point – so, tell your client.

The biggest reason clients want to push down fees is that they don't perceive the value in what we do. Usually, they don't recognise it because *they don't know what we do* to earn our fee. They don't know what we do because *we don't tell them*!

So, tell the client everything you will do to solve their staffing problem, chapter and verse! Then, and only then, ask the client why they feel a reduced fee is appropriate. This is important. *Put the ball firmly into the client's court.*

The client is asking for a discount. *They* should be squirming, not you! When it comes to fee discounts, you don't have to justify *why not* – they must explain *why*! This shift in the dynamic is very compelling indeed.

Sometimes the client pushes hard for a reduced fee. Don't feel pressured. Don't get emotional. It's a purely commercial decision, and it's your decision to make. Are this client and this order so attractive that they are worth a lower fee?

Remember this before you discount next time. Don't think of the fee only as dollars gained or lost: think of the fee as what your service is worth.

A discounted fee means a discounted you. Never forget that.

53 | Feel you must compromise on fee?

Sometimes you will feel it is worth compromising on your fee to secure a special opportunity. In these cases, remember one golden rule: never reduce your initially quoted fee without *extracting a concession* from the client.

In other words, if you say, 'My fee is 20%', the client asks for a discount and you reply, 'Okay, 15%', you have just signalled to the client that you never believed in your value proposition and your service in the first place. You will struggle to get that client's respect again, and you will never get your fees back up.

So, if you reduce your fee, always ask for something in return: a retainer, maybe exclusivity, or for the client to give you multiple orders or advantageous payment terms. Or, perhaps you may waive the guarantee.

Make sure the negotiation involves *both* sides giving. This way, an equal partnership stays intact.

So too does your self-esteem – and, in our business, that is crucial.

54 | Don't fear the 'C' word

It can be intimidating when a client is determined to negotiate the fee. I understand completely. And, remember, the client has almost certainly done it before with other recruiters, and they likely got their way quite quickly.

But, you will not be an 'average' recruiter, will you? You have pride and believe in your value. So, you will address each tactic the client rolls out – and they can vary!

Sometimes in a fee negotiation, the client will utter the dreaded 'C' word. This word often scares recruiters, leading them to concede too early and by too much.

The 'C' word? 'Competitors'!

'But your competitors charge less!' says your client triumphantly.

I love it when clients use that word.

Suppose they do start to talk about competitors' low fees. In that case, your response is to ask, 'Can you tell me about a situation,

Ms Client, in which you were charged less than the fee I am suggesting today and got the level of service and the calibre of talent you want?'

True, this is a gamble. However, the fact that you are there in the client's office (or even on the phone) taking the order means that it is most unlikely the client is happy with their current supplier. After all, why are they even briefing you if they are getting great candidates and excellent service at a lower fee?

It amazes me when a client spends 20 minutes bagging another recruiter, telling me how hopeless they are, and then when I quote my fee they say, 'Hey, but the other recruiter only charges 15%!'

Of course, they do: they are no good! *You just told me that.*

By the way, *you* never say that the other recruiter is no good. The client states that if they wish. You simply ask, 'Are they delivering at that low fee?' Which they are not, obviously.

That is the time to remind the client that a low fee, quoted by a supplier who does not deliver, is not a benchmark against which you will measure your fees – and nor should the client.

Be prepared to stand your ground on this with your client. Quoting a fee is easy and meaningless. *Delivery at a fair price* is what counts.

You need to say, 'I can deliver at this price'.

Then, make very sure that you do.

55 | Negotiating temp margins

It is time now to dive into the wonderful world of negotiating temp rates and margins – a recruiting minefield if ever there was one. Even experienced temp recruiters struggle with this, and I often find that recruitment business owners are pretty vague on how to tackle this, too!

When negotiating with clients about temp bill rates, the 'big secret' is to shift the client's focus from the rate to the total cost!

If you allow all the focus to remain only on the dollar value of the hourly rate, then you have very little negotiating leverage. If the client quotes another agency that will charge less for the same job and you argue about the hourly rate only, you have nowhere to go. The client will say, '$45 is less than $50, so what's to debate?'

However, you have plenty to discuss if you focus on the *other* part of what the client said. I am referring, of course, to where the client said another agency will charge less 'for the same job'. That's the weak spot to tackle in a client's argument.

Will the client indeed get 'the same job' done by the cheaper option? 'No!' is your response. In fact, it could cost the client plenty.

So, for example, let's say you advise a client that a mid-weight freelance web designer will cost $50 per hour. The client says, 'That's expensive – I can get a designer from your competitor for $45'. So, you see, the client focuses on the rate only (and tosses in the 'C' word to shake you up!).

Most temp consultants cave at this point and reduce the bill rate to win the assignment. But, unfortunately, that teaches the client that your rate is negotiable and immediately reduces your margin.

That is bad.

A more appropriate strategy is to direct the client's focus to the comparative cost of the entire project. Get the focus off the hourly rate. How? Well, this usually works:

> *'Ms Client, all our designers have been interviewed, screened and tested for their skills and attitudinal fit to do freelance work. The person I propose to provide you with for this role has worked for us many times before, and I have many glowing testimonials of her work, initiative and accuracy. Ms Client, the person I will provide you with will come in and start being productive in the first hour. She will make minimal mistakes and need no supervision, and the quality of the outcome will make you very happy indeed. Moreover, she will do this project within the two-week time frame you need. We need to pay $50 per hour to get someone of this calibre; $50 times 8 hours times 10 days is a total cost of $4000.*
>
> *'If you take the cheaper option, Ms Client, you may pay $45 per hour, but it is most unlikely that you will get the calibre of individual and the quality of work I can promise you today. Your $45-an-hour person is likely to take longer to do the job, absorb more of your time and quite possibly make more mistakes.*

In this case, $45 times 8 hours times 15 days is a total cost to you of $5400.

'The so-called cheaper option, Ms Client, will ultimately cost you far more! It's quality work done at the best cost that I am offering you, and that's why I am suggesting my talent at $50 is in your best interests. What day can she start?'

That's the way to sell quality temps! Think about it: BMW does not compete on price with Hyundai. They are both cars with engines, seats, GPS and reverse parking cameras. However, people will pay far more for a BMW because the quality and value are there.

It's the same with your temps. If your client wants an excellent freelance, temp or contractor experience and their problems solved quickly and accurately, the price may be a little higher but the value will be measurably better!

There is a temptation for many temp recruiters to concede in this situation: *It is just one assignment, and I am still getting a $10-an-hour margin.* This is flawed and dangerous thinking. Denuding your margin like this adds up to a fortune over time (chapter 92). It also teaches your client all your quoted margins can be whittled down, and that is a disaster.

56 | The madness of temp-to-perm discounts

This is one thing our industry has all wrong: we give away our temps at discount rates. I know the market is competitive. I appreciate a dollar is still a dollar. But I also know that clients are screwing us with all their might, and most recruiters are pushing back with all the vigour of wet lettuce.

A temp on your payroll is always a precious asset. So, in talent-short times, I cannot fathom why anyone in our industry would give a substantial discount on the fee when a temporary employee turns permanent. (This is called a 'conversion fee' in some markets and a 'buyout' in others.)

It's just so illogical. A temp-to-perm or conversion fee is a once-off hit, which is nice when it happens, but we seem to forget that, in the process, we have lost a tried, tested and hard-to-replace revenue-earning asset: our temp worker.

I have heard all the arguments from clients; they simply don't wash.

Let's start with the classic, 'But you really should discount the permanent conversion fee because you have already earned so much margin on the temp'. What hogwash. The temp margin is for the temporary service rendered: finding, managing and insuring the temp. We are also paying them, sometimes up to a month before the client pays us. The perm fee is for the acquisition of a permanent staff member.

There is no leveraging one against the other.

We must be clear with the client that it's far from a celebration for us when a temp converts to a permanent position. A temp-to-perm fee is scant compensation for the lost revenue that the temp could have earned on future assignments.

We are happy for our candidate if that is the role they want. We are delighted for our client that we have found them a permanent solution. But it's no commercial windfall for us! You need to make that clear; clients routinely *do not* get it.

Some clients will even try to use the 'hire purchase' argument. 'But, can't you see,' they say, 'It's like me renting a car and then buying it: it's always cheaper to buy a previously rented car'. This sounds neat but it is fallacious. A car is a depreciating asset: the more it gets used, the less it is worth. A human being is an appreciating asset in a contract assignment where they are getting trained, absorbing the company culture and learning the systems. The perm fee should be *more*, not less.

Now, I know that in many markets discounting temp-to-perm fees is embedded in the industry ethos, and some recruiters almost give their temps away. That is no reason for you to cave in. You need to be part of the change and part of the solution, not perpetuating the dysfunctional dynamic.

Make sure you have your commercial terms of business carefully worded, train all your consultants and stick to your guns. Temps and contractors are not 'slaves' to be bought and sold, but an 'introduction for a fee' is a legally enforceable agreement. It's a fee for the service, not the human being.

You have done the work, you have solved the client's problem and you have been successful. This is proven by the fact the client wants to hire your contractor. So, by definition, you got it right!

Charge a full fee. You earned it.

57 | Don't pro-rata perm fees for long-term contract assignments

Say your client wants a person for six months. That's a temp job. However, they want to pay a one-off payment and put the person on their payroll. That's okay. However, the client wants their one-off perm fee *discounted* because the job is not for an entire year. Don't agree to that. That's dumb. You lose.

Keep the distinction between temporary/contract and permanent crisp and clear. (I know that in some countries your hands are legally tied on this, but in many countries it's about negotiation.)

If it is a fixed-term assignment, it's a contract role, and therefore it's a timesheet hourly rate with your margins on top or it's a fixed weekly or monthly rate. Don't for a minute think, 'Well, it's a six-month role, so we will take our perm fee and divide it by two because it's half a year'.

Firstly, was the candidate easier to find just because it's a six-month gig?

Secondly, do the arithmetic! A permanent placement fee of 20% for a $75,000 placement is $15,000. If a client wants to pay half the perm fee because it's a six-month gig, then you get $7500. However, the margin you will earn on a temp valued at $75,000 over six months, at a margin of 22%, is $12,500 (based on industry norms).

That's $7500 versus $12,500 – you can see why the client likes the idea!

Sure, if the client wants to pay a perm fee instead of a margin for a six-month gig, that's cool. However, it's the *full* perm fee they will need to pay. That's fair and proper.

If you are not convinced, think about this: if you owned an investment property and rented it for five years to a lovely young couple, and then they wanted to buy it from you, would you give them a 25% discount off the sale price because of the rent they had previously paid? I don't think so. So, why would you give your temps away cheaply?

Believe me on this. We have nothing else to sell besides our service and talent skills. Don't give away the farm.

58 | Social selling

A billion words have been written on the subject of social selling, and at least a few are helpful. I will restrict myself to just a handful of observations that I trust will help you evolve into a fully rounded recruiter who gets both digital and human, in-real-life influencing. After all, recruitment is a marriage between art and science.

In an era of rapid digitalisation, transactional keyword-matching and 'dumbing down' of the recruitment process, there has never been a greater need for differentiation through brand, reputation, thought leadership and partnership.

There is a tendency for clients and candidates to view all recruiters as 'the same'. You may have heard that line.

You may be tempted to dismiss much of this book as 'old school', and it's true: some of the concepts I preach are as old as recruitment itself. But you will still teach your children to look both ways before they cross the road, won't you? As your parents taught you and their parents taught them. You won't dismiss that advice as 'old school', because it is timeless – just like this book's advice.

However, it is also true that I have a much larger digital footprint than 99% of recruiters. So, I'm not entirely old school after all. I have built my recruitment businesses on digital branding, and I started doing that before social media was even a serious 'thing'.

So, please take my advice when I say that you must own the real-life moments of truth, as I expound on many times throughout this book, but you must also *build your online brand* and *excel at social selling*.

Social selling is using social media to create online conversations that will eventually convert into real conversations and, quite possibly, real-life business relationships. It's a slow burn. It's an investment in the future. It acts as a door-opener. There is no 'hard sell' in social selling; instead, it hinges on providing value through outstanding content and engagement that resonates with your target community.

Many people who buy this book will do so because of what they have read from me online. *That is social selling.*

Great social selling through content provokes engagement and ultimately creates inbound inquiries.

When I founded Firebrand Talent Search in 2010 (via a management buyout), we found ourselves with a ten-office company spread across eight countries. Yet, we were a start-up with little money, so we had to build a brand using the fledgling opportunity offered by social media at the time. We focused on building awareness through content and engagement and were soon perceived to be much more prominent and influential than we were.

We found that it warmed up the sales process early (chapter 47) and created credibility, familiarity, authenticity and believability for our consultants.

My social selling framework spells it out for you (see figure 4).

Figure 4: Your social selling framework

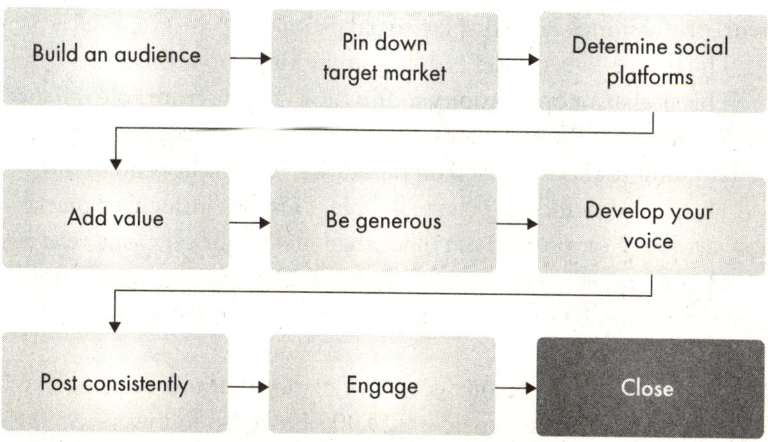

You first need to build an audience. That audience needs to be very much focused on your target market, which means potential candidates and clients in your niche.

Then, determine which social platforms will reach that audience: LinkedIn, most likely, but also other channels as they emerge and are favoured by various groups. The primary premise upon which you will base your content is adding value, informing, sharing, providing advice and being generous.

It's essential to develop your voice, which means speaking with authenticity and sincerity, which people value more and more. Posting consistently is crucial as well.

Finally, your social selling strategy will include engagement, which is the most challenging part for most people because it requires investing time and effort to respond, thank, refer, congratulate, encourage and advise. But engagement is the secret sauce because it illustrates that you care and are real, which will likely lead to authentic conversations and enquiries.

For most recruiters, branding on LinkedIn will deliver the best return.

59 | Branding and LinkedIn

Everyone is looking for credibility and authenticity in the service providers they engage. Therefore, they are attracted to engaging with professionals who display social proof.

The future-fit recruiter is doing something about this!

This is also an opportunity to flip the dynamic from sole reliance on hardcore, outbound, sales-driven business development to consistent, inbound leads based on reputation, credibility and brand.

This is not marketing cliché babble. I am no 'influencer marketing' acolyte. For a start, I am older than just about everyone reading this book and started in recruitment in 1980, so if anyone should have 'old-school' views, it's me. And I do on many things.

But not this.

I base what I tell you on decades of personal brand-building. And it has worked – if you consider 321,000 LinkedIn followers, 55,000

Twitter followers, a million blog readers a year, over 10,000 copies of *The Savage Truth* book sold (and hopefully *even more* of this book) and 2000 subscribers to the Savage Recruitment Academy evidence of brand-building success.

My business as an advisor over the past ten years has come from inbound enquiries based on my online brand. I am currently on the boards of 16 recruitment companies and turn away several such appointments each month, and I have conducted hundreds of recruitment masterclasses worldwide, which routinely sell out. None of this is because I am so clever – I am most definitely not. Most of it is because of content marketing and brand.

It is hard work, but it pays off – and it will pay off for recruiters, too.

Here's how to build a digital brand:

- **Take a long-term view.** It takes persistence and perseverance. It's a question of months and years to build awareness and a following. There is no 'quick fix'.
- **You must be consistent.** Daily posts. LinkedIn and the rest are 'streams', so people will not see everything you post. You must be consistently visible.
- **Content is an opportunity to differentiate.** You need to differ from the vast mass of recruiters who clients perceive as bland and beige. You are interesting, with a point of view – a thought leader, even! To show that, most of your content must be unique to you.
- **You must have targeted connections and followers.** The volume of connections is essential, but so is relevance. Remember, no matter how great your content is or how witty your updates are, they are all wasted unless you have followers and connections! Posting to a handful of followers is like putting on a musical in an empty theatre: it might be great, but who knows? Proven ways to build your following include posting quality material consistently, sharing and engaging with potential 'customers' and influential people in your sector, and targeting and connecting with the key people in your audience.

- **Speak 'to' your audience.** I need to emphasise this. You are posting to entertain, inform, help and share – for the community you want to engage with. It's for *them* you post, not for you.
- **Generosity.** This is a key to social media that so few seem to understand. Think *What can I give?* – not always *What can I get?* Share ideas and insights. Give away research, tips and tactics. Answer questions. Introduce people to each other. Open doors. Be kind.
- **Authenticity.** Be real. I don't mean be blunt or rude. However, be yourself. Be 'you'. People can tell if you're not being authentic or are finessing your posts to impress or show off, and they will switch off.
- **Engagement.** Some people only use social media to 'broadcast', just pumping out links and content. Engagement and interaction are what build trust and connection. On LinkedIn, for example, the more you engage with others, the more reach your posts get!

Understand me, please: branding and social selling do not replace traditional business development. You still sell. You still open doors. You still make calls. You still meet prospects. Most of the chapters in this Part have been about precisely that.

The cold call used to be the conversation starter. Social selling is now the conversation starter, but it can be leveraged into a telephone or face-to-face conversation – only this time the initial IRL contact is 'warm' (chapter 47)!

Let's focus on LinkedIn, an incredible resource that most recruiters do not make the best of. LinkedIn is less of a *sourcing* platform and more of a *branding* platform. This is deeply ironic because the better you use LinkedIn for branding, the more effective it will be for sourcing! This is true for both candidates and clients.

Here is your LinkedIn branding and social selling action plan.

Complete your LinkedIn profile

LinkedIn acknowledges that the more complete your profile is, the more likely you will surface at the top of a search. So, make your profile as rich as possible. Have a professional photo of your face.

Avoid using group photos, personal photos or photos with a busy background. Make sure your headline says what you actually do and offer. Your summary (or 'about') section must be detailed, using sector keywords, selling your expertise and track record. Fill out the 'experience' section in detail using industry-recognised titles, and elaborate on what you have done and achieved, using keywords again.

Craft a killer headline

Your headline is one of the most visible parts of your LinkedIn profile. It is a massive factor in a person's decision to reach out to you. So, make it count. Try to grab attention in as few words as possible. Help the reader understand *what they'll get from you* and put the benefits to them upfront.

Nail your LinkedIn banner design

Your LinkedIn banner image (the horizontal rectangle behind your profile picture) helps tell your brand story to your contacts and provides an immediate first impression. Your banner can really help you stand out from the crowd. Look for imagery that represents who you are and what you do, or use a simple infographic of your services.

Choose your skills strategically

Every LinkedIn profile can list up to 50 'skills'. You should choose relevant skills to fill all 50 slots, so think strategically about what skills to include. The 50 skills you choose should align with the skills that potential candidates or clients will be looking for.

Post regularly

You should post content every workday for maximum impact, but three times a week is a solid start. You can post links to your own content, such as a blog or relevant content your company publishes. Links to general industry-relevant information are okay occasionally but if it is not bespoke to you and drives readers to a third-party website, that is not ideal. Sharing relevant content taken from what your clients publish is an intelligent move. However, the most significant impact you will have is with your own opinions, your insights.

Research suggests photos do well. So, do polls (two answer options is best), but don't overdo them and don't make them frivolous, please. If you include links in your post, you get significantly less reach. Don't do it.

If you use video, make it native to LinkedIn – that is, upload it directly to LinkedIn.

So many recruiters shake their heads and recoil at this: 'I have nothing interesting to say'. So wrong. You are in the market 365 days a year. You are an expert. You know hiring trends, candidate behaviours, salary movements and changing market dynamics. All this and so much more can be shared in a concise paragraph. Remember, what is obvious to you is news to clients and help to candidates; sharing these insights positions you as a recruiter with a voice, a recruiter who has ideas. It is so powerful and it will open so many doors.

Engage!

Don't just broadcast content. Engage. Start conversations. Show a human face. Here are a few ways:

- Reply to comments and questions. Research suggests that getting comments drives extra engagement and replying to those comments gives your post an extra boost in reach.
- Thank others for feedback and input on your posts.
- Answer questions.
- Ask questions.
- Connect your community to relevant information and interesting people.
- Share and like others' content.

Join LinkedIn groups

LinkedIn groups are a missed opportunity for many people. You can join 50 groups. Many will include your target audience. Joining groups gives you a considerable increase in search reach. You are visible to, and contactable by, all group members. You should check groups daily for new jobs and pertinent discussions that you can contribute to. You can start your own discussions and share your content with your target market. You can connect to group buddies, get free 'in-group' messaging and view group members without being connected. It is astounding how underutilised this free resource is by so many recruiters.

Deliver daily nourishment

You can set your LinkedIn notifications to inform you when your connections get promoted, start a new role, have a work anniversary and more. Set aside 20 minutes a day to nurture your LinkedIn community. Share, connect, congratulate, like and engage based on these updates. Refresh dormant relationships and start new ones. This is quick, easy and very powerful.

Constantly connect

Build your audience. Every relevant connection is now in your community and will see your updates. Start by connecting with all current clients and candidates, many of whom *you will not be connected to* (I bet you). This is such a missed opportunity. Then commit to connecting with:

- every client you meet
- every prospect you talk to
- every relevant conference attendee you meet
- every (worthwhile) candidate
- every referee you speak to
- your service providers.

Ask for permission in your initial conversation or early in the relationship. Then, follow up fast with the connection request and make sure it is personalised.

Check your social selling score

Guess what? LinkedIn tells you how you are doing with your branding and selling by giving you a social selling score. Check yours here (you must be logged in to LinkedIn): linkedin.com/sales/ssi.

60 | Build the talent acquisition and agency recruiter relationship

Everyone wants things to be different between agency recruiters (AR) and in-house talent acquisition (TA). Typically, the debate ends up being adversarial, even quite acrimonious. Yet, we all want to improve cooperation, communication and outcomes.

The reality is this: TA and AR need each other! And it all starts with your attitude and mindset, no matter which side of the recruiting fence you are. But, then, you need to make it happen.

I am an 'agency guy'. That is true. But I am not taking sides here – quite the reverse. I want to help all parties see their role in making this work better. In the very end, we have the same core goal: client companies hiring more great talent.

So, we must be self-aware and acknowledge that it starts with what you *think*, which impacts what you then *say* and, ultimately, what you *do*.

AR should dump this type of thinking:

- TA are failed agency recruiters.
- TA are jumped-up admin assistants.
- TA are control freaks and power junkies.
- TA love to jerk AR around.
- TA do not understand how we work.
- TA are only about saving money.
- TA block access to line managers and information.
- TA only care about the volume of candidates.
- TA will never consider a better fee or an exclusive order.

TA should cease this type of outlook:

- I was an AR but I am better than that now (the 'reformed smoker' approach).
- AR are 'used-car salespeople'.
- AR are KPI-driven recruiting hacks.

- AR only care about commissions.
- My job is to screw AR on the price.
- AR do not deserve communication and respectful interaction.
- AR do not understand my business.

Also, lose the 'master-servant' tone.

AR, your job is not to screen, match and fling candidates at TA. Sure, you need to screen and match effectively, but your real job is to find candidates TA cannot find and bring them to the hiring table, and then help manage the process to acceptance. You are an advocate for the TA brand, an ambassador.

TA, never mind what your board, or your boss, told you. Your job is not to 'save money on recruitment agencies'. Your job is to *make* money by ensuring the best hires!

When a TA director starts boasting about how much money they saved by cutting out recruiters or screwing them on fees – and I have seen them do it online and at conferences countless times – it's time to fire them. It makes me cringe. For them. Because they are not doing their job. They are doing the *reverse* of their job.

Their actual job is to grow the business, serve the customers, support the leadership and execute the company vision *by hiring the best possible talent in the market*, no matter where it comes from.

That is the competitive advantage. That is what TA exists for – not to save a few dollars by hiring second-choice candidates, and then stand up and brag about it.

At the time of writing, AR and TA working closely is a commercial imperative for both parties. AR have no 'fat' built in to allow wasted time on uncommitted clients. Global, prolonged talent shortages mean that good AR will work with hiring organisations that work collaboratively (chapter 95). TA will need to access the best talent or their business may lose or even fail.

It's a survival issue. The stakes are that high.

So, now is the time for AR to:

- value themselves and their service (chapters 3, 4 and 5)
- disrupt their entire approach to TA by redefining the expectations of both parties

- stop behaving as if TA is 'the enemy'
- stop searching for ways 'around TA'
- establish credibility and ground-rules upfront
- walk away from bad business (chapter 115)
- refuse to act like a little doggie on the beach chasing the multi-listed, contingent order bone (chapters 99 to 103).

AR must walk away from bad TA business and learn to read the warning signs, which include the following:

- TA won't meet them.
- All communications are via email: video or phone calls to enhance understanding are not forthcoming.
- TA send group emails, including to multiple agencies on the same email. (It's hard to imagine anything less respectful.)
- There's no access to line management.
- Communication on everything is slow.
- TA provides no feedback on résumés, candidate interviews or job status.
- 'Fee' negotiation comes up early before value and process are explored.
- Procurement drives the process. (Run!)
- There's no exclusivity or commitment.

TA must walk away from lousy AR, even if – or especially if – they are the cheapest. A lousy AR:

- doesn't ask to meet
- asks no intelligent questions
- doesn't ask to meet line managers
- sells their service on the price
- overpromises and clearly cannot deliver
- cannot articulate their differentiators (chapter 42)
- has no clearly articulated candidate acquisition strategy
- sends spam résumés that only tangentially fit the brief

- has constant staff turnover
- offers no insights, advice or guidance.

For decades some TA functions have played agencies off each other. They have leveraged them on fees in the name of 'being competitive'. This is so laughably unproductive that I am pleased innovative TA groups are seeing things differently now. The dangers for TA if they create an agency race to the bottom include:

- unique talent being missed
- fishing in the diminishing pool of 'easy to find' job-board candidates
- the best candidates being actively directed elsewhere
- employer brand hurt
- massive time wastage.

Now that so much recruitment is remote and real-life interaction is rare, both parties must work much harder to avoid communication lapses and get the best out of the dynamic:

- Briefs should be given by videoconference, not by attaching a job description to an email.
- Résumé feedback should be sent within 24 hours with a clear explanation.
- Candidate feedback should be given by videoconference, with precise details on success or failure factors.
- An office walk-through should be given via video.
- Access to line managers should be made available when needed (and it is needed).
- AR should possibly provide short candidate videos.
- There should be total transparency on the process.
- There should be constant mutual updates on timelines.

Most AR get this, but it is equally essential for TA to understand.

Multi-listing job orders with multiple agencies is dysfunctional and leads to shockingly bad outcomes for all parties, especially for the TA and their company (chapters 99 to 103).

TA should select AR based on their:

- ability to access candidates TA cannot
- understanding of TA's needs
- urgency and efficiency
- specialisation as it impacts the previous three points
- transparency and communications
- management of the process
- insights and data
- timesaving
- value.

(Did you see 'price' on that list?)

Current barriers to effective AR–TA relationships include:

- transactional mindsets by both parties
- short-term thinking ('Save money on this hire!')
- ego and hubris (from both sides, sadly)
- control fetishes (by TA, usually)
- petty vindictiveness
- lack of respect
- skewed priorities
- lack of empathy.

I am not blaming either TA or AR: all of the above characteristics are found on both sides. Both sides have equal responsibility to address this. TA and AR can build real commercial relationships through:

- fixing their attitudes, as described earlier
- asking questions to understand what the other side needs to be effective
- active listening, not talking down
- constant two-way communication
- empathy for each other's differing perspectives and challenges
- respect, both human and professional

- honesty and transparency
- constant feedback loops
- mutual trust
- developing a hiring plan together
- TA using the right AR at the right time
- agreeing on accountability and responsibility upfront
- sharing data and insights
- sharing the bad news early
- occasional forgiveness
- understanding that it's a journey.

The big secret for AR when attempting to change the perception TA have for you is this: you have *insights*! Flip the dynamic. Go to your TA team with something of value for them!

- Train and practice having 'different' conversations.
- Use phone and email to set up Zoom or IRL meetings.
- Think *What does my TA client need and value?* and not *What do I need and value?*
- Understand their priorities.
- Shift your tone – add value, guidance and advice.
- Engage in intelligent digital marketing (such as webinars).
- Stay very visible.
- Help TA clients visualise the future.
- Offer to pipeline talent for the future.
- Provide data, feedback and advice.
- Be TA clients' 'market eye' *(insights)*.

I have created a road map each for TA and AR. I would love it if these were used internally on both sides of the recruiting divide to guide our behaviours and process. It takes two to tango. Someone needs to start by asking the other to dance.

Figure 5 shows the road map for TA to improve the outcomes they get from working with AR. Figure 6 shows the road map for AR to completely reinvent how they work with TA.

Figure 5: The road map for TA

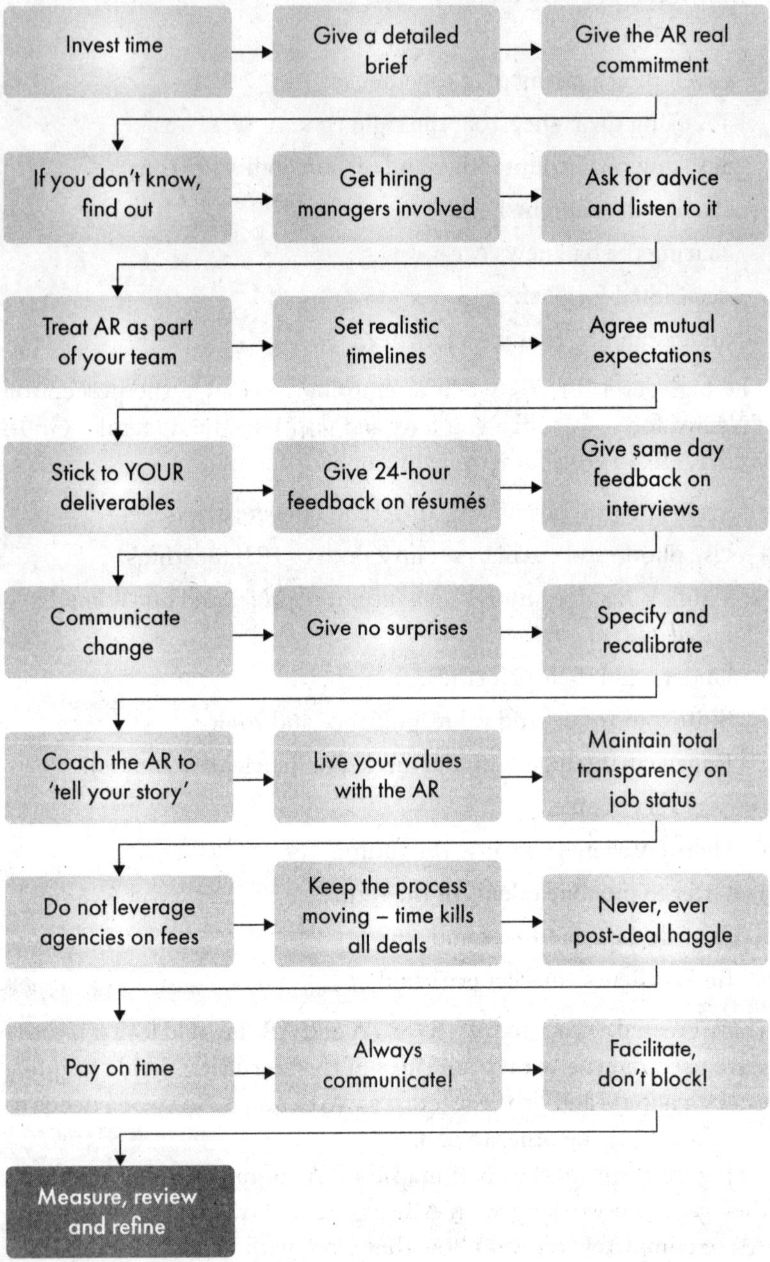

Figure 6: The road map for AR

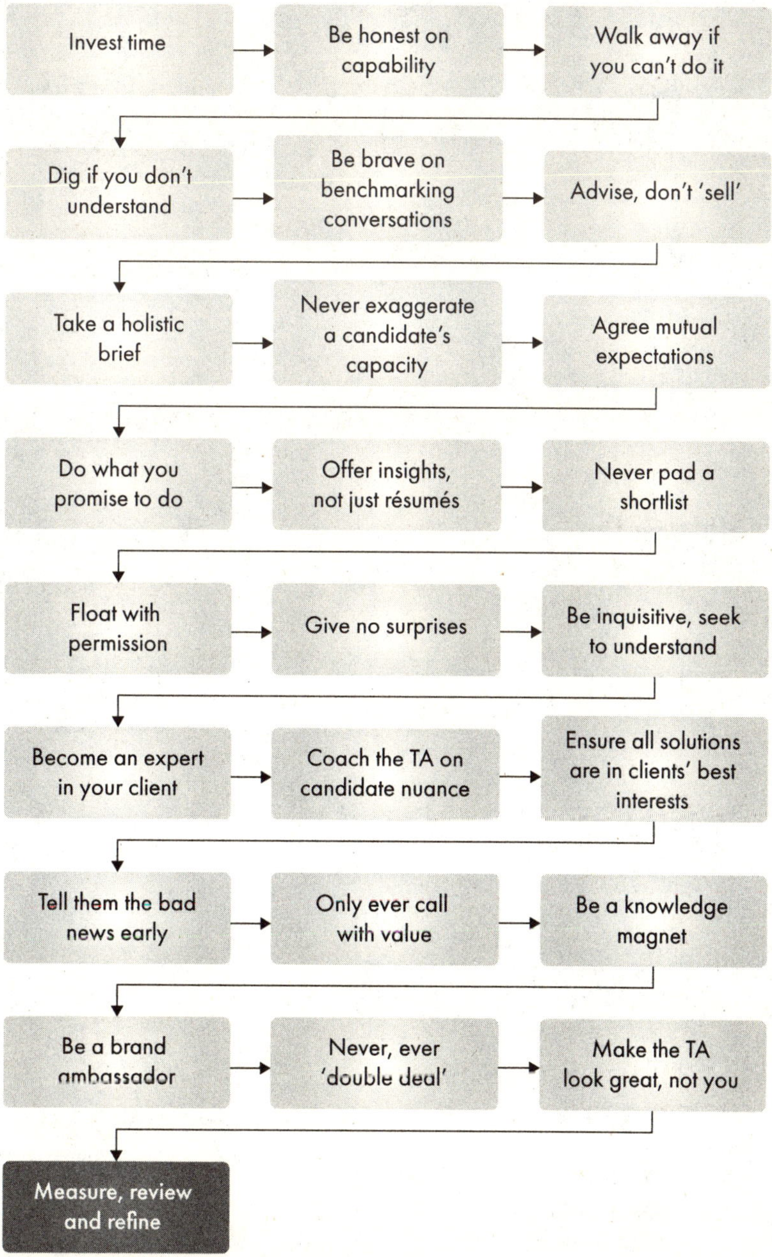

PART IV

CANDIDATE SKILLS

Recruiters compete on their ability to access candidates that their clients and competitors can't find, bring those candidates to the hiring table and manage the entire process through to acceptance. That's where the actual value of a recruiter is.

As COVID-19 drove a more remote recruitment style, some recruiters became less engaged. This is your huge opportunity to differentiate, because truly great recruiters will move from being referrers of résumés to acting as the candidates' agent during their job search.

That takes next-level credibility and influencing skills. You need to become an expert at identifying prospective candidates, which is actually not that difficult, but becoming a world champion in connecting, engaging and bringing quality candidates into the job-search process is exponentially more complex.

All outstanding recruiters understand that assessing the candidate's suitability for a job is the easy part, while managing their expectations, building rapport and controlling the moments of truth are what separate the mediocre recruiters from the great.

61 | Candidate shortages are a good thing!

Let's get real.

I write this chapter in the middle of a massive skills shortage. Created in the post-COVID-19 hiring frenzy, a lack of appropriately qualified people is a challenge. I am not minimising that.

But some recruiters are wallowing in unwarranted self-pity, as though a shortage of candidates is a bad thing! As I heard a recruiter say recently, 'All that's happened is we have swapped the disaster of no jobs in COVID-19 to the disaster of no candidates as we recover'.

Trust me on this, and never forget it, please: when it comes to 'recruiter headaches', candidate shortages are not in the same *universe* as job shortages.

You will grab 'candidate short' over 'no jobs' any day of the week, in any year, in any century. Candidate shortages are nirvana for our profession! If candidates were easy to find, *why would clients come to us?* It's the whole reason for our existence!

Your mantra needs to be, 'Candidate shortages are excellent because my differentiator is that I know how to find them, and I know how to bring them to the hiring table, and I know how to manage the process through to offer and acceptance'.

That previous paragraph is worth re-reading and thinking about. It is the very essence of our value. That's what our fee is for. That's why clients will use us. It's simple.

If there are massive talent shortages, and that is where the pain in hiring is, your job is to become a world champion at finding candidates and managing them through the process.

Don't whine about it. Celebrate it! And master it.

It's not easy, I know. But, if it were easy, all the lazy and incompetent people would be rich, right?

So, hone your talent acquisition skills, candidate engagement tactics, influencing, advising and creating outcomes toolkit.

As you will learn in this Part, candidate care, building relationships, taking a long-term view and managing the candidate process are crucial for recruiter success.

62 | The recruiting dysfunction you must fix

There are twin dynamics at play in agency recruitment that lead to angst, time-wasting and disappointment for all stakeholders. They are so embedded in how the profession works that many within the process can't see it.

Firstly, we have the catastrophe of multi-listed, contingent job orders, which benefit no one. Clients, naïvely thinking they get a better service because they get agencies to compete, get far *worse* service because they actively encourage recruiters to work on speed instead of quality. (This is discussed at length in Part V.)

Recruiters suffer because we can't really 'partner', 'consult' or 'value-add' even if we want to. So, in the end, we only fill one out of five jobs (if we are lucky), destroying profit in many cases and the careers of recruiters who simply burn out, chasing rainbows.

Then, we have the often-ignored fact that *candidates* suffer the most because they do not get service or due care from third-party recruiters, who cannot focus on the candidates' needs because they are chasing mythical job orders in competition with five other recruiters.

If recruiters worked like accountants, lawyers, doctors or even real estate agents – that is, not working on each case in competition – they would work on 20% of the orders they currently do but fill 300% more! And who would benefit the most? *Candidates!* Yes, candidates would no longer be treated as a commodity but rather as crucial partners, as they should be.

However, a parallel dynamic exacerbates the multi-listed job-order farce and leads recruiters to fill only a fraction of the jobs they take, which results in disappointed clients and frustrated job-seekers – and unhappy recruiters, too.

Have a look at my whizz-bang chart in figure 7.

Look at the *left* circle. It represents all the candidates available for recruiters to place in jobs.

Look at the little segment on the right of that circle. That shows the tiny proportion of suitable candidates that recruiters *actually* access. Most recruiters focus on so-called 'active' candidates, those that come from job boards or who are already on the database.

There is nothing wrong with these candidates per se, except that they represent only a tiny percentage of the available people.

Moreover, because they are actively job-searching, they will likely be working with other recruiters already or possibly well down another recruitment process. Which means that you are *not likely* to place them.

Look on my chart at the massive pool of candidates most recruiters *do not* access. *There* is your opportunity!

Now, look at the *right* circle. This represents the majority of clients' commitment to filling the job. We all know that most clients do not give their agency recruiter total commitment. That is what the shaded segment represents: a tiny commitment. Many use third-party recruiters as an afterthought or in competition. Clients' commitment to filling roles goes elsewhere, such as to the internal recruitment team, LinkedIn or their own recruitment strategies.

Figure 7: Agencies access the same tiny candidate pool

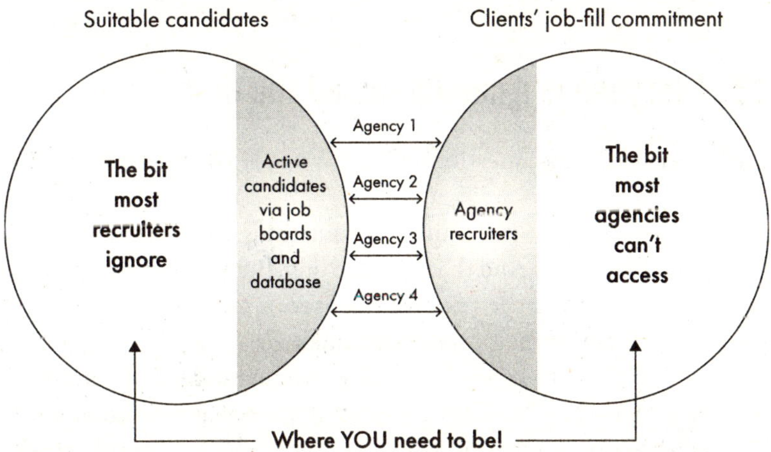

So, right there, you have an incredibly dysfunctional situation.

Most recruiters access only a tiny percentage of suitable candidates and, what's more, secure only a fraction of the clients' commitment to filling the job. This often leads to a vicious cycle of discontent. Clients get increasingly irritated because they deal with low-level recruiters who don't do a thorough job. Ironically, the fault lies with the *client*, who asks recruiters to compete on the *same* position, thereby dumbing down the process. As a result, recruiters get disillusioned, desperate and burned out, and take shortcuts, which continues the cycle.

And, of course, worst of all, candidates suffer.

But it's not all doom and gloom. This chart shows *tremendous opportunity* if you look for it. The prize goes to the recruiter who can develop strategies to access those candidates in the segment of the circle that are not active. This is the skill of bringing top hidden talent that clients can't find themselves to the hiring table.

Those recruiters who can blend technology with the craft of recruitment can secure a more significant percentage of the client's commitment and a greater share of candidates not freely available to everyone else: unique, exclusive candidates (chapters 75 to 77).

So, the winners will be those recruiters who recognise that our work is flawed and who act to access the parts of my circles that most recruiters do not.

63 | Everyone is a candidate, all the time

I ask recruiters this question often: 'What is your definition of a candidate?'

The answer, 90% of the time, is something like, 'Someone who has applied for a job'. And that is not wrong. But it does not go nearly far enough. It shows the reactive mindset of many recruiters – the short-term focus of their candidate thinking.

My definition of a candidate is very different indeed. A candidate is a person who has the skills and presentation that your clients will hire. Whether or not that person is looking for a job is simply a matter of timing! They will be – someday.

Not everyone is *actively* looking for a job, and recruiters know that. But we often do not behave as though we know that. Research (and common sense) tells us that less than 10% of relevant candidates are actively looking for a role at any given time. That means

90% of candidates suitable for your roles are not engaged in job searches. They have not registered with recruiters, are not perusing job boards and are not applying for positions. They are not even particularly unhappy where they are.

But they *are* willing to move! And, even if they are not available to move right now, that day will surely come.

The fact is that most recruitment agencies are failing to be creative in attracting *unique* talent to their databases. We are fishing in an ever-shrinking pond. Our talent pool is becoming a talent puddle.

So, the key to success in the future of recruitment is to change our definition of a candidate.

Most recruiters only consider a person a 'candidate' when that person has 'opted in' to be assessed for a job or seeks help on a job search. In other words, they have applied for a job and sent in their résumé. But, in the brave new world of recruiting, as talent shortages bite and set in for the long term, is it not time to have a fresh look?

When exactly should a talented person become a 'candidate' in your eyes? When they see your advert? When they accept your head-hunt call? When they apply to your ad on the phone? When you get their résumé? When you interview them? When you submit their details to a client? When they follow you on Twitter? When they subscribe to your blog?

Think about it: if they are not a candidate until they 'opt in' (that is, 'apply'), what are they before that?

Someone connects with you on LinkedIn. They have not actively 'applied' for anything. Are they a 'candidate'?

The reality of recruitment is that *everyone* is a candidate, *all the time*, and it is up to us to convert them into *active* candidates – not wait for them to come to us.

And so, that means we must leave 'just in time' recruitment behind: running ads on job boards, relying on the database and even relying on referrals, as crucial as they are. Don't get me wrong; we must still do these things. And, depending on your market, they will still work… to a degree. But increasingly, *they will not work*. Because you will have nothing to offer clients that they can't get themselves. Clients have LinkedIn and in-house recruiters, and they can build talent databases.

That means we must build relationships with talent and communities of people, who we may only place *months* or *years* into the future.

That is a crucial facet of successful agency recruiting: first, identifying, connecting and building relationships with the vast, passive pool of potential placements, then converting them into active job-seekers when the time is right.

64 | Unique candidates

Exclusive job orders are good (and chapters 101 and 102 detail why). However, the significant advantage in recruitment now is exclusive candidates (chapters 75 to 77)!

The candidates you get from job boards are not exclusive, by definition. They approach clients directly, talk to other agencies and comb through search engines and social media. The hard truth is that you have very little chance of placing those candidates, even if they have all the skills. It's a fact. We place a tiny percentage of the people we screen from job boards. (I enlarge on the fundamental industry dysfunction that exacerbates this issue in chapter 62.)

If you have access to the same candidates that everyone else has, then your competitive advantage is driven by speed and price; and, in that case, you are on a slippery slope to recruiting hell.

The modern recruiter is a genius at accessing 'unique candidates': candidates working only with you, who are not available to competitors and, more importantly, unable to be found by your clients, either.

What is more, these unique candidates are at the beginning of their job search. They are not 'out there'. You can act as their agent. This is key.

Take heed – don't follow the herd into oblivion. Unique candidates are the differentiator in modern recruiting. Find unique candidates with in-demand skills, and your clients will not only come to you but will also pay you higher fees for the privilege.

65 | 'Skills hunter' and 'talent magnet'

A core reality of success in agency recruitment now is that you must be able to access candidates your competitors – and, more importantly, your clients – cannot. For that to happen, you cannot rely on talent acquisition strategies that no longer work.

Any recruiter who relies on candidates making proactive applications for jobs is *destined to fail.*

So, what to do?

Firstly, you must reinvent yourself as a 'skills hunter' (see figure 8). This is about being proactive, aggressive and intelligent about identifying, approaching and sourcing candidates. It involves digital, phone and active social sourcing, using social sites as a database of candidates you target and hunt down.

Figure 8: The 'skills hunter'

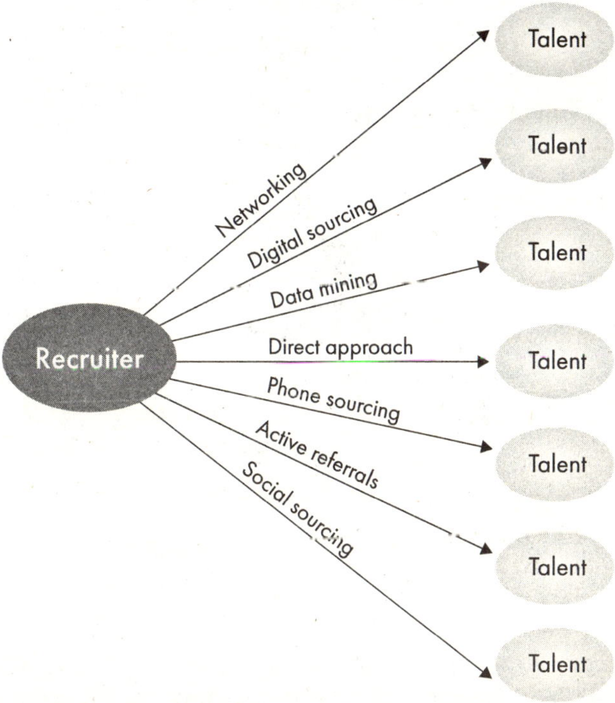

However, the modern recruiter does not rely on *finding* candidates, even though that skill is vital. The future recruiter makes sure the *best* candidates find *them*! That means building a brand that is a magnet for the best candidates.

So, recruitment winners see LinkedIn, for example, as a branding platform more than as a database (chapter 59). They are strong on social media, putting out great content and engaging as they go. But they also build a brand in the real world through empathy, service and mindfulness of the candidate experience (chapter 80). The most successful recruiters will likely work for a company that 'gets it', a firm that understands recruitment has *merged with marketing* and uses sophisticated CRM, automated marketing, SEO and candidate engagement tactics (see figure 9).

Figure 9: The 'talent magnet'

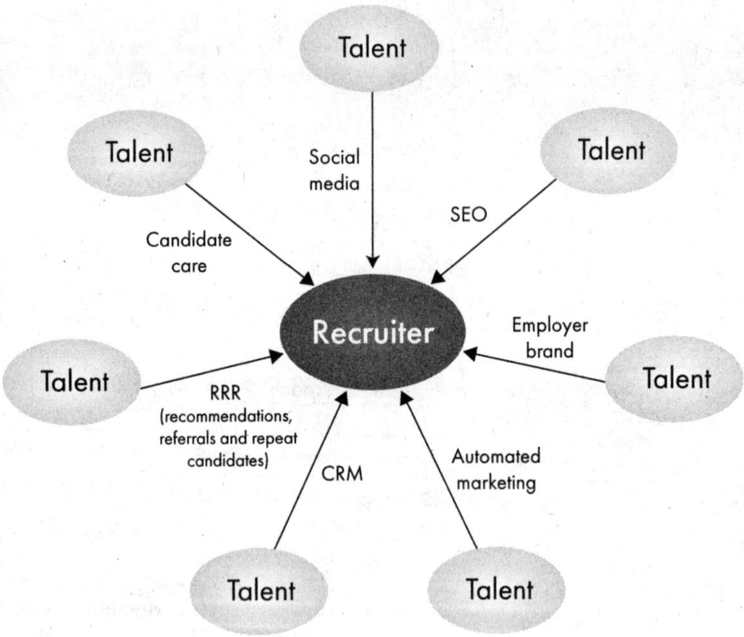

Recruiters who adapt and become highly evolved skills hunters and powerful talent magnets will have the recruiting world at their feet.

66 | The candidate outreach secret

So, we must learn how to 'create candidates' by approaching likely prospects. However, candidates are being bombarded with recruiter approaches, primarily via InMail and email, but occasionally over the phone. So constant has this flood of unsolicited contact become that most candidates *do not read* the messages. Some have even hidden their LinkedIn accounts.

Yes, recruiters *do* need to initiate contact with prospective candidates, but how does a good recruiter differentiate themselves?

There are two simple yet crucial steps to take:

1. Understand the candidate psychology when receiving a cold recruiter approach.
2. Do not approach prospect candidates with a job, as every other recruiter does.

Huh? Well, let's dive in.

We said earlier that a person might not be looking for a job but might be open to hearing about a career change if approached. That is 100% true. However, you are not dealing with a desperate job-seeker here. The approach needs to be subtle. Your InMail was not asked for, and your phone call was neither expected nor canvassed. The approached potential candidate will likely feel cautious, even suspicious. They don't know you. You have no credibility. And they never said they were looking for a job, anyway.

So, all that needs to be considered, as does the language and tone used in the approach. You need to build trust and prove your credentials, and go slow.

Now, the big secret to candidate outreach or 'headhunting': do not approach a candidate with the infamous line 'I have a great job for you', or, 'I have your dream role'.

The candidate isn't looking for a job. Or, at least, they never asked you to pitch them one, did they? It's arrogant to assume you know what they want. How can you possibly know anything? This approach is *riddled* with assumptions. And, even if they are considering a move, how do *you* know what is important to them?

Go back to my first point. If you immediately start selling a job – unasked and unbriefed, with no credibility or rapport building – are you showing you understand the psychology and the concerns of the approached person? I think not.

When you approach a potential candidate for the first time, you don't pitch a job like a sidewalk street hustler. You pitch your *credibility*.

So, start with some commentary on the market. Some insights. Something you know someone in their field would likely be interested in: salaries, market movement, fresh trends.

Then – and this is the big, shiny move – you pitch a career discussion.

Most people in a job are not actively looking for a job. So, pitching a job is like walking up to a stranger in the street and pitching the purchase of a specific brand of car. How do you know he wants a car? Did he buy a new car last night? What car would he want? What does he use his car for? What size family does he have? Does he do sports that need a particular type of car? Can he even drive?! It's ludicrous to start spouting what you sell without first finding out what he *needs*.

Selling is listening, after all (Part III).

It's the same with a job. So, don't pitch a job. Pitch a career discussion.

Short version – make yours better than this:

> *'We haven't spoken, Mary, but I specialise in the careers of digital marketing experts like yourself. Your career has been super impressive, but there is so much new happening in the market that might interest you. Opportunities in your space have boomed, flexible work offerings have changed, job roles have evolved and there are some fascinating new marketing tech developments many of my clients are experimenting with. So, I thought it might be valuable for you if we set a time to chat about the market, your options and how your career could evolve.'*

Just an example. But you get it, right?

Most people are not looking for a job change right now. But most (all?) people are interested in their *careers*. Pitch a career chat, not a job.

And a final tip: specifics are powerful!

> *'In the last six months, I have placed eight people with profiles very similar to yours.'*
>
> *'Three of my clients have recently hired candidates with your profile into management-level roles.'*

It needs to be *true*. Don't build your outreach on untruths. Remember what prospects want from you.

The conversation about specific jobs will naturally evolve from the broader discussion and, by then, guess what? You would have earned the right to discuss a specific role and would be on your way to earning a 'unique candidate' (chapter 64).

67 | The secret sourcing tool

Here is the transcript of a conversation between a bright, experienced (three years) recruiter and me. It occurred five years ago, but the mindset it illustrates has worsened:

> **Bright Recruiter:** *Greg, I am so frustrated. I found this perfect candidate on LinkedIn and she won't respond.*
>
> **Greg Savage:** *What have you done so far to contact her?*
>
> **BR:** *I have sent her three InMails.*
>
> **GS:** *And…?*
>
> **BR:** *And she won't reply. Such a bummer. I must find someone else…*
>
> **GS:** (Exercising considerable restraint) *Have you tried calling her?*
>
> **BR:** (A little condescendingly) *Ah, Greg, but don't you realise most candidates don't list their phone numbers on their LinkedIn profile?* (Triumphant smile)

> **GS:** (Borderline losing it) *Seriously, how hard is it to find someone's phone number if you know where they work?*
>
> **BR:** (Not missing a beat) *I suppose I could find it. But calling someone at work? That's rude, isn't it?*

Right, and spamming them via LinkedIn is polite?

It's an epidemic of missed opportunities. Some LinkedIn candidates get up to 20 emails and InMails a day! And many of those InMails are spammy, untargeted and do not even get read.

Most recruiters do not use the phone to contact quality candidates they identify on LinkedIn or through other sources. Yet, research consistently shows that candidate response rates are *at least* twice as high using the phone compared to different approaches.

Of course, it is 'horses for courses' and, in some situations, email and InMail are better. And, of course, it's not easy to reach people on the phone. But whoever promised you recruitment was going to be 'easy' led you up the garden path.

Many recruiters hide behind technology. They say 'people don't answer their phones' because they lack the confidence and skills to craft an engaging approach on the phone, which is a shame. After all, the dividends are enormous.

Getting candidates that others cannot is your competitive advantage. Typically, the technology identifies, but *human beings* recruit.

As chapter 66 outlined, you are not 'selling a job' when you phone-source a passive candidate. You *will* have a job in mind, but that's *not* where you start. It's a subtle sell at most.

Think about the call this way:

- **Be clear on your desired outcome:** You will have researched the candidate, know their background and have made some informed assumptions about the sort of role that may suit them. You will have identified an actual position and know how its benefits will likely suit them. Your goal is to have a career discussion – now or at a set later date. If it leads to talking about a specific job, then 'happy days'.
- **Ask if it is suitable to talk:** They may be at work. At a party. At the doctor. With kids. Be polite. Check it's appropriate. But

be ready to suggest a better time and make an 'appointment to speak'.

- **Introduce yourself:** Be clear and confident, and keep the candidate's hot buttons in mind. Give your name, your company and your credentials; for example, 'I specialise in helping UX designers grow their careers'.
- **Don't oversell:** Don't push. Get the candidate talking. You are not selling 'a job'; not right now, anyway. This is the key. Don't leap into a conversation about a 'job'. They are not looking for a job, remember? You mention 'job' and she says, 'Not looking', and where do you go from there?
- **Sell the discussion:** Instead of, 'I have got a great job for you', try something like, 'I wish to set up a time to discuss your career'. It's a career discussion. Insights, data, updates, assistance, information, benchmarking: that is what you are offering.
- **Thank the candidate:** End the conversation with clear next steps: a follow-up conversation, a coffee meeting, a date in the future to follow up.

The phone approach is challenging. It's a nuanced human skill. It requires the ability to build trust and credibility quickly. It will often not pan out as you would like – but it often will!

68 | Placeable candidates

Recruiters don't get paid for getting their candidates job offers. The client is happy, the candidate is happy and the recruiter is happy when an offer is made *and accepted*.

It sounds banal, but recruiters often make the most basic blunders working with candidates who are not placeable or less likely to be placeable. And my definition of a placeable candidate is a candidate with the skills, experience and presentation to likely get them a reasonable offer from a client – yes, we get that – but who *also* has the motivation, commitment and incentive to accept it.

This has implications for who you interview and what you look for during the interview. Once the interview is done, you must be confident you know enough about the candidate to be sure that, put in front of the right client, they will likely get an offer. But you also need to know – by asking the right questions and uncovering the *true motivators* – that, if given a fair offer, the candidate will likely accept it.

If you do not do that, you can expect offers to be turned down, which means a lot of work for no money and a wide variety of other intensely stressful outcomes.

69 | The candidate interview is a 'moment of truth'

In the final wash-up, a recruiter is only as good as the number of orders they can close.

In most cases, we get paid for successfully filled jobs. That is it. So, finding someone a job and getting them an offer is only half the battle. Getting them to accept it is the other half.

A good recruiter must learn to control the process to minimise fallout and disappointment for all parties. To do that, we need to understand that assessing a candidate for qualifications, skills and experience is the *easy* part of the interview process. It is critical, of course. It takes skill and expertise to do that well. But it can be learned, and most experienced recruiters can do it competently.

The hard part of the interview process, the part that will make all the difference when getting the acceptance, is assessing the candidate's *true motivators* for a move and identifying lurking barriers to an acceptance. They will not be as obvious as they seem, nor are they likely to be volunteered by a candidate who may not even have thought them through themselves.

Your job is to identify the potential barriers, articulate them and nullify them. That's the 'moment of truth'.

The first interview sets the tone for the relationship with the candidate, which will affect how they communicate with you throughout the process, how transparent they are and whether they will take your advice.

Getting this wrong could waste immense time and lead to ultimate disappointment. The offer is turned down, or the candidate disappears.

So, during that first interview, you will dig deep into why the candidate is changing jobs, what they want from their new role and the 'push and pull' factors. By the end of the interview, you will have tested their assertions and be able to rank their motivators. You will learn and assess how committed they are to a move, agree on their ideal new job and define the position they would accept if the perfect job is not forthcoming (which may be different!). You will manage their salary expectations and counter their counteroffer. And, finally, you will have agreed (if appropriate) that they will work with you exclusively.

The previous paragraph sums up the work to be done in the interview 'moment of truth', and I explain more about each component in the following chapters.

Closing a placement starts here, in the first interview. You must learn to prioritise candidates and put 80% of your time into the 20% of candidates who will get offers and accept them.

Think about that for a while before you read on, please.

70 | Uncovering the real motivators

Wasting time on uncommitted candidates will cause you much pain. Of course, few candidates will tell blatant lies, but most know an interview is a 'performance', and they will try to give answers that they think will position them in a 'good light'.

Take nothing at face value. Instead, probe. 'Peel the onion.' Pose scenarios. Ask questions and leave silences. You are never being combative or aggressive, always very collaborative and supportive. But you want the real reasons, the true motivators.

Pose scenarios that may happen: 'What if your current employer…'?

Make no assumptions. This was my interviewing weakness: I was too quick to jump to conclusions and move on to trying to solve the problem. We need to understand what we are dealing with first.

Question each reason given for a move. For example, 'You mention you are looking for career growth, but your current employer has 50,000 staff. Have you explored opportunities there fully, do you feel?'

Offer alternatives: 'Do you think a frank conversation with your current boss about your career options might be the better first step?'

Work with the candidate to rank the motivators. For example, a candidate might volunteer three reasons for changing jobs: career advancement, more money and more flexible work arrangements. All reasonable. All probably true. But, which is most important? If you do not rank them, you might find this candidate accepts a job via a competitor for the same salary! Because flexible work was the *actual* driver.

Work with the candidate to list their 'deal-breakers'. What are the one (or maybe two) components the new job simply *must* have? Sometimes the candidate can't articulate that, but often they can – you must help them identify it, and then you dig into that and manage it through the process.

When interviewing candidates, you clearly must assess their skills, qualifications, experience, interpersonal profile and much more that will allow you to match them to a job description. But below the surface are the reasons they will accept a job, and on what terms. You need to know those motivators and to have discussed them – maybe influenced them – and ranked them.

It's a classic agency recruiter moment of truth!

71 | Understanding candidate MTA and CTM

Unless you enjoy having offers turned down and counteroffers accepted, you must get close enough to candidates to understand their motivation to accept (MTA) and their commitment to move (CTM). Work to understand these from your first conversation through the interview, and at every point after that.

Just because a candidate says they are ready to accept a new job, that is no reason to believe they *are* ready. Your job is to find out and decipher precisely what it is that will encourage them to accept. That will be a heady cocktail of salary, employer brand, flexibility, work-style, responsibilities, opportunity and much more. Recruitment is more art than science, as you know (chapter 24).

The skill set of today's recruiter involves the subtle art of real discovery. It goes beyond the résumé and includes probing, questioning, checking, confirming and scenario-pitching.

It used to be that recruitment was about finding candidates. That's our job still, of course. But managing the process through offer and acceptance is now the critical skill that separates a good recruiter from an average one.

Plenty of recruiters spend a lot of time complaining about candidate behaviour: 'erratic', 'mind-changing', 'counteroffers', 'ghosting'. That is futile and lacking self-awareness. You don't wait for candidate behaviour to change. Instead, you change your behaviour towards candidates!

Avoiding assumptions and asking, 'What has changed?' is just entering into the field of play. It's no guarantee you are going to achieve anything. You need to assess, calibrate, test and measure their commitment! 'Commitment to move' is now the significant candidate metric. And, to add complexity, it is dynamic and constantly evolving as the candidate moves through the job search.

This is rough and ready, but it's a start. And it is essential. Candidate shortages are a good thing – if you are a world champion at managing the candidates you *do* have.

The candidate will be at one of the following levels at any one time, but they can and will move through the levels – in either direction. The point is firmly this: do you know, at all times, what level your candidates are at?

Flirting

The candidate is toying with the idea of moving. They may even say, 'I am looking to move'. But, are they? Or are they just dipping a toe in? Typically, a move is conceptual at this stage. Hypothetical. An idea. Real goals and consequences are not understood.

Considering

The candidate is seriously planning a move. They are upgrading their résumé and LinkedIn profile. They are doing research. They have made a list of 'must-haves' and 'must-not-haves'. They can articulate the 'ideal job'.

Engaged

The candidate is 'actively looking': applying, going for interviews, researching recruiters and employers and getting salary data.

Committed

There is a massive difference between 'committed' and 'engaged'; this is key. The committed candidate has worked through the pros and cons of leaving. They have addressed the counteroffer possibility and rejected it. They know precisely what salary is suitable for the move. They are taking recruiter advice, returning calls and giving feedback. They have partially 'checked out' from their current role. And you can hear the excitement in their voice.

72 | The ideal job versus the acceptable job

The number of times I've heard frustrated recruiters utter words like these could not be counted: 'I don't understand it. My candidate explicitly told me they must have X, Y and Z to accept a new job, and now she tells me she accepted a job that only had X and Y!'

Understandably, all candidates aspire to find the perfect opportunity when they change jobs. Sometimes, we can help them do that. But the reality is that we all go into a job search with the 'ideal' job in mind and a reasonably clear picture of what an 'acceptable' job would be, especially if the 'push factors' in our current role are compelling (in other words, we really want out). So, the skills a recruiter needs around commitment and motivation to accept (outlined in the previous two chapters) require even more subtlety than previously explained.

You must work out with the candidate their ideal job parameters and work very hard to help them find that perfect role. But, you also must have agreed with them the answer to a question that goes something like this: 'If what you are ideally looking for is not possible to find, what does an acceptable job look like?'

And then explore.

This ties in with the need to rank their motivators (chapters 70 and 71), but it needs to be taken further, fleshed out and agreed upon.

Remember, too, that both the 'ideal' job and the 'acceptable' job will evolve during the job search, and that is why you are always asking 'what's changed' (chapter 27) and assessing the candidate's current MTA.

73 | Managing salary expectations

Successful recruiting is about lots of small interactions handled well – the moments of truth (chapter 24). However, the real job of a recruiter is to manage outcomes in the interests of both the client and the candidate. That is never more evident than in the vital skill of managing the candidate's expectations around salary.

It's not that you want to find a candidate the lowest possible salary you can – not at all. But, it is crucial to know the absolute minimum salary for a candidate to move for the *right* job. That is the key.

Too many recruiters take a stated salary expectation at face value. Often that number is inflated and largely the result of wishful thinking. If taken as an accurate guide, the candidate could miss out on the perfect job because you, the recruiter, did not understand their true motivators.

It can also result in that most uncomfortable of scenarios in which the candidate you interviewed accepts a job you are handling – *through another recruiter!* All because you did not understand their actual salary parameters and were 'out-recruited' by a better recruiter. (Harsh, but true.)

The process of managing expectations on salary starts in the first interview, and it involves coupling the perfect job sought by the candidate and the lowest salary they would accept. Sure, it's a technique and a test, but it clarifies the salary tipping point.

So, firstly, drill down on the job that the candidate seeks. Probe all those nooks and crannies identified in chapter 71. Then ask, 'What salary are you looking for to move?' Do not accept the answer at face value; instead, ask how the candidate came up with that figure. Question a significant gap between current salary and desired salary: ask the candidate to explain, even justify.

Once again, never be argumentative or condescending. You are just working with the candidate to understand 'why'. This is crucial. Obviously, you will act in the candidate's best salary interests, but explain that you would hate for them to miss the perfect job for the sake of a few grand when other factors are so much more important.

And now, the killer question. Work down the salary by offering the perfect hypothetical job. Say the candidate has nominated $95,000 as the minimum salary they will accept: 'If I found the perfect job that met all your wishlist criteria that we have identified today, and it was paying $85,000, would you be interested in hearing about it?'

This will open a very revealing conversation. Sometimes the candidate will hold firm: 'I don't mind how perfect it is. If it's not paying $95,000, I am not moving'. But, more often, it's along the lines of, 'Well, if it is that good an opportunity, I need to consider it'. In this case, you wrap it up by agreeing that, if the job is perfect, the candidate's floor is $85,000, not $95,000.

A key final tip: make sure you end by assuring the candidate that you will look for the *highest possible* salary: $95,000, or even more, is your goal. However, for the right job, they agree that they will look at $85,000.

You must drill down on what the candidate would accept for the *right* job. Each candidate is different in their attitude towards salary. You just need to know that information.

Without that, how can you effectively manage the candidate's job search?

74 | Countering the counteroffer

There is little more frustrating in agency recruitment than doing all the work, securing a great offer and tying up an acceptance, and then seeing it all crumble as your candidate accepts a counteroffer to stay where they are.

There is nothing we can do to *guarantee* that a counteroffer will not emerge or that it will not be accepted. However, there is plenty we can and must do to *mitigate the risk.*

Remember, the candidate accepting a counteroffer is not in the client's interests (the client will blame you, by the way) or, clearly, the recruiter's, but it is also unlikely to be in the candidate's interest either, especially if you identified that the fundamental factors driving their desired change are not really about money.

Here are two of the great truths about handling a potential counteroffer:

1. Countering a counteroffer starts at the very first interview.
2. A counteroffer must never be 'unexpected' for the candidate.

Attempting to defuse a counteroffer after the offer has been made is futile – too little, too late, too bad. You have no credibility and you sound desperate, so it is not going to happen.

It is a big ego stroke for the candidate when a counteroffer comes *unexpectedly*. It's usually a juicy extra money offer with other delectable goodies thrown in, like a job-title change or additional responsibility, and there may be a little employer-induced guilt on top.

And the key word in the preceding paragraph is 'unexpectedly'. It's your job to make sure it *is* expected, and not only expected but considered, analysed… and dismissed! Before they even get the counteroffer!

Making an offer that will be accepted and not counteroffered successfully is not an event – it doesn't happen in a single conversation. It's a progression, a step-by-step process – managed by you (see figure 10)!

Figure 10: Countering the counteroffer is a *process*, not a *conversation*

The process

The process starts the same way as everything in quality recruitment: don't make assumptions. Work through each step. Explore each option.

I said the counteroffer starts at the first interview, and it does. You have agreed on what role the candidate is looking for, and you have identified and ranked their MTA.

Here is the critical skill that most recruiters lack: you do not tell the candidate that accepting a counteroffer is a bad idea. You don't lecture at all.

You take the candidate, in their mind's eye, to the resignation day. You transport them to that moment and *ask the candidate* what's likely to happen. This requires subtlety, patience and the ability to shut up at critical moments.

This is just conceptual – an illustration, not a script – but you could do a lot worse than something like this:

> *'Ms Candidate, I think I clearly understand the sort of role you are looking for. However, if I were to secure that position and you accepted it, what would your current employer say when you go to resign?'*

There are several possible responses to this question. The first is worrying: 'Oh, they would be glad to see me leave'.

Unlikely, but I have heard it. Dig into that! Usually, it unearths previously undiscussed conflicts or issues.

The second is what you are hoping to hear: 'I have thought this through. They will do everything they can to entice me to stay, including offering more money. However, I know staying there is wrong, and I am determined to move on'.

This is promising, but you dig into that too:

> *'What might they say?'*
>
> *'What might they offer?'*
>
> *'Is there any amount of money, within reason, that would make you think again?'*

You are testing their determination to resign (DTR). But, often, this is an evolving conversation. You take your candidate on a journey of self-discovery as they work through the likely response to their resignation:

> **Candidate:** *They would probably offer me more money to stay.*
>
> **You:** *How do you think you would respond to that?*
>
> **Candidate:** *Either 'No way' or 'Depends on how much'.*

Explore the answer in detail. Look at body language. Test how much they would stay for. Offer up scenarios as to what their employer might say.

If the candidate articulates that, for the right money, they would in fact entertain an offer to stay, you go right back to the MTA:

> *'But, Ms Candidate, you told me a few moments ago that your current company has no future. It's too small to offer you a career. They offer no work flexibility. Also, you are bored there and don't believe in their values. How would more money solve these issues?'*

Keep asking questions. Resist the temptation to lecture or persuade.

The goal is for the candidate to conclude that they will get a counteroffer and are determined not to accept it. But *they* must come to that conclusion and articulate it. Lead them there through questioning and 'sanity checking', but don't tell them what to do. It is much more potent for a candidate to tell *you* they will not accept a counteroffer than for you tell them that they should not!

But, maybe the candidate holds firm: 'Greg, I know I said all that, but I probably would if I got offered an extra $25,000 to stay. It's a lot of money'.

If that happens – and I mean this – encourage them to go to their employer and ask for a raise, then coach them on how to do that. You have nothing to lose and everything to gain.

The candidate just told you they would accept a counteroffer, so there is every likelihood you will do all the work to get them an offer and have them use it as leverage for a raise and stay, as they just told you they would. So, if they ask for raise, they will either get it and stay – and you never really had a real candidate at all! – or they will be rebuffed and come back to you very motivated indeed!

However, even if you did all this expertly during the first interview, and the candidate raises the potential counteroffer and emphatically rejects it, your work is nowhere near done.

You raise it again when they are sent out on a client interview (chapter 85). You raise it again during the post-interview debrief (chapter 86). You raise it again before the second interview (chapter 87), and you most definitely raise it again during the job offer pre-close (chapter 88).

Every time, you get them talking. Reaffirming. Don't tell; listen.

Countering a counteroffer is a journey – not a single conversation, and never a lecture.

The final resort

I will be transparent: I think persuading a candidate to reject a counteroffer after the event is 'second-division recruiting'. You must do all the subtle management of that moment of truth at the first interview and throughout the process. However, if you do all that and, at the last minute, the candidate wavers and threatens to accept the counteroffer, here are a few last-gasp tactics that may save you (which is very unlikely, but you have nothing to lose at this late stage – except your credibility, so… think hard):

- 'How does extra money solve all the issues you were initially looking to address by moving?'
- 'Did you know that 80% of counteroffered people leave within a year?' (Make sure you have credible research on hand to back this up – there is plenty available online.)
- 'How do you feel now that you know your boss thinks you are worth more only when you threaten to leave?'
- 'How has your relationship with your boss been affected? Do they trust you now? How will they perceive your loyalty for the future?'
- 'Who will be the first to go when the business goes bad?'

75 | Exclusive candidates – the 'why'

Chapter 64 discusses how 'unique candidates' are key to successful recruiting. Indeed, recruiters often discuss securing exclusive job orders (although few recruiters know how!). But, at the same time, we should really put equal focus on negotiating exclusivity with highly specialised, in-demand candidates.

The rewards for doing so are juicy-sweet. This is particularly relevant in times of significant skill shortages (which is the case as I write this book) – less so in a downturn, when candidates are plentiful and jobs scarce.

Don't misunderstand me: I am not suggesting a legal 'contract' with the candidate or any other restrictive covenant. I am talking about having the credibility, the process and the influencing skills to show an A+ candidate why it's in *their* interests to work with you exclusively, why they should allow you to act as their 'agent'.

In candidate-short markets, it becomes vital to work with our candidates exclusively. But it's critical even in job-tight markets because it increases the chances of a happy outcome for all stakeholders. So, let's think about why it is so good for recruiters:

- Clients come to us for the talent they can't find themselves. That's our reason for being in business. So, the starting point is doing what we get paid for well.
- Any recruiter worth their salt will back themselves to place a highly skilled candidate if they have the time to 'cover the market' for the candidate. If the candidate is not applying directly to employers or meeting other recruiters, the chances of us placing them increase exponentially. So, we will get paid for our effort more often if we work with exclusive candidates.
- Transactional résumé-racing is not a model worth pursuing. Instead, we must become professional and consultative, providing a quality service. A consistent criticism of our profession is of the lack of candidate care and communication. So, let's work with fewer, better candidates, give them far better service and place a higher percentage of them.
- You have a massive competitive advantage if a great candidate works with you and does not go to other recruiters or approach employers directly. It gives you time to do great work, leading to better outcomes for clients, candidates and yourself.
- Suppose clients learn over time that you can access talent others (including them) can't. In that case, you become strongly differentiated, credible and, eventually, their first and maybe only port of call.
- Remember, even if you don't place the 'exclusive' candidate this time, they will come back to you or may become your most prominent advocate because of the quality service, insights, advice and personalised help you can offer.

76 | Exclusivity is fantastic for candidates

This is the key to the whole process: you need to be confident, skilled and articulate in explaining to the candidate why it is in *their* interests to allow you to take control of their job search (if only for an agreed period). You are offering to act as their 'agent', just as a footballer or a movie star has an agent to manage their best interests and secure them the best roles and contracts. That's what you are offering. It's an entirely new dynamic built on a fresh premise.

However, the candidate's first reaction, naturally, might be to feel this is 'restrictive' and in your interests at the expense of theirs.

You must believe it's in their interests; otherwise, do not even try to sell it. Here is why it is great for the right candidates (see figure 11):

Figure 11: Why exclusivity is cool for candidates

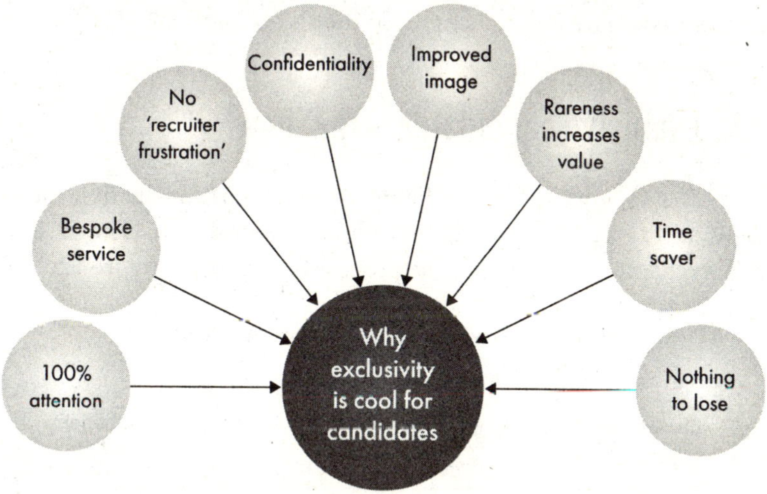

- The candidate gets 100% of your attention. If you agree to work in partnership with them, you commit to finding them appropriate interviews within an agreed time frame. (You can offer this if the candidate is great and the market is tight, right?)

- They get bespoke personalised service, regular contact, access to exclusive jobs, real-time updates and your after-hours number.
- The candidate does not have to 'do the rounds' of recruiters. Trust me, they do not love visiting recruiters, taking time off work or being kept waiting. 'Recruiter frustration' is real from a candidate's point of view, and you will wipe that all away.
- The candidate won't have their résumé sprayed around town. Exclusivity preserves their confidentiality and credibility.
- It improves their image with clients. The client has not seen them elsewhere; they are a 'rare bird'. And rarity increases value.
- It saves the candidate time, as opposed to talking to many recruiters over an extended period – an outcome they will thank you for.
- What do they have to lose? You will only ask for a maximum of a few days, or maybe a week or two. That's all they risk. And you will make sure it does not fail, so the risk is minimal.

77 | Exclusive candidates – the 'how'

The offer to work as the candidate's 'agent' starts at the first interview, after you agree to the candidate's job-search criteria and MTA (chapters 70 and 71). The process is outlined in figure 12.

Figure 12: How to secure candidate exclusivity

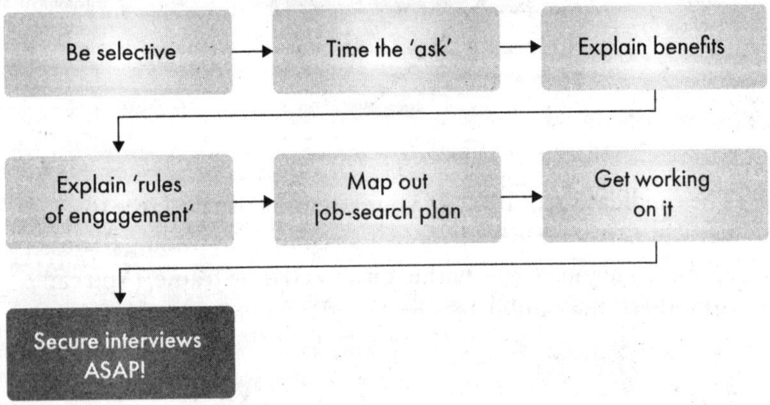

- Be selective in choosing the candidates that you wish to work with exclusively. They must be outstanding and highly placeable (chapter 68). In addition, they must be at the beginning of their job search. (This is why unique candidates are so essential; see chapter 64.) The rule is that you only ask for exclusivity if you know you can secure that person interviews in the agreed time frame. Only do it if you have outstanding matching orders and are confident they will get offers if you get them interviews.
- Ask your candidate for a period of exclusivity. Do this once you have built up rapport and trust through the interview process and shown that you have a range of appropriate job orders. Ask for a reasonable, manageable period: a few days for a junior candidate; a few hours for a 'hot temp' candidate; a week or two for a more senior candidate. But be flexible. It's not about stopping the candidate from job-searching; it's about securing enough time for you to wrap the search up for them!
- Explain the benefits to the candidate. Ask where else the candidate would like to work. Agree on a list of jobs that you will represent the candidate to. Then, agree to approach those companies on their behalf, too. The primary premise is that you have what they are looking for, and 'I will give you 100% of my commitment if you can give me 100% of yours'.
- Explain the 'rules of engagement': you will approach the agreed three or four companies, and the candidate will not go to any other recruiters or approach clients directly for the period of the exclusive window.
- Map out a job-search plan, bespoke for the candidate, in front of them. This outlines the steps you will take, the clients you will approach and the referees you will contact. This is the communications schedule you and the candidate agree on.
- Get actively working on the plan fast, constantly stay in touch and show the candidate you care about them. Give them regular updates.
- Get them one or more interviews with clients ASAP. Show you can deliver. If you can agree on exclusivity and then come

back with an interview within 12 hours, the candidate will be impressed and relieved, and will leave their job search with you.

There is one *critical* caveat to all of this: if you have agreed exclusivity with a candidate and in good faith believed you could get them interviews, but it is not going to plan, you must act. If you are not getting interviews for the candidate as you thought you would, 'release' them from the exclusive agreement early and with a smile. Asking for commitment and then not delivering will harm the relationship forever.

You still try and place them as hard as you ever would. You just never want to be in a situation where you ask for a week as their 'agent' and then, after that week, leave them high and dry with nothing to show for it. It smashes your credibility and their trust.

What I have shared with you in this chapter has the potential to reduce frustration, increase your billings and enhance customer satisfaction on all fronts – not to mention your self-esteem and job satisfaction.

But you must try it (see chapter 19 on ten seconds of courage)! Act today!

78 | The rules of engagement

It is not unusual to hear recruiters bemoaning candidate behaviours, such as sharing details of a role with another agency or not calling them back to debrief on an interview. However, when asked, 'Did you coach the candidate on your expectations?' they go blank.

You cannot assume anything (chapter 27). A good recruiter will also manage this mini 'moment of truth'. It happens in the first interview, and it's probably best not to call it the 'rules of engagement' in front of the candidate – it sounds somewhat aggressive – but rather something along the lines of a 'How we are going to work together?' chat before you agree to work with them.

Even if you have not agreed to exclusivity with a candidate, the basic guidelines shown in figure 13 should be discussed. Depending on your sector and company process, you may add extra components of your own. The point is to pre-empt problems by making the expectations transparent at the start.

Figure 13: Selling the rules of engagement

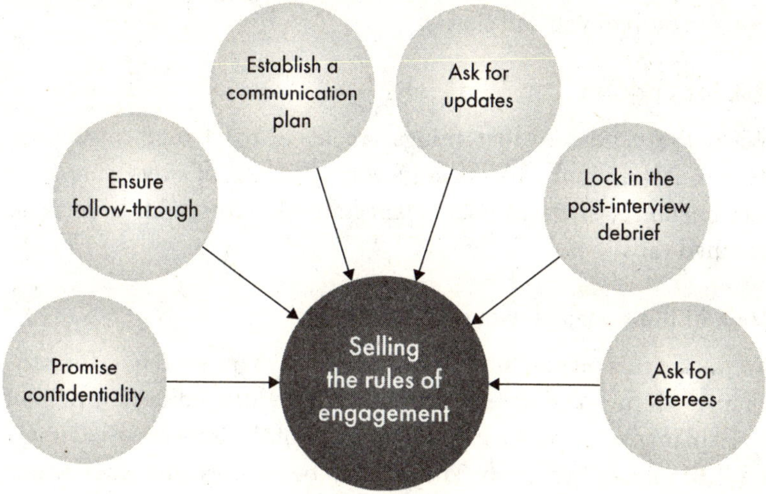

Promise confidentiality

Explain to the candidate that you will never refer their résumé or disclose their name to any client without their permission. Equally, you must ask that they not discuss any role you divulge to them with anyone else, especially other recruiters.

Ensure follow-through

Explain to the candidate that you will call them with an opportunity because you believe it fits their job-search criteria. At that stage, the candidate has every right to reject being considered for that role. They can decide it's not for them and ask you not to refer them to your client – all good. However, if the candidate agrees for you to represent them to your client, they must follow through on any forthcoming interview. This is important. It's professional etiquette to do so, and it's bad for both the candidate's brand and yours not to.

Establish a communication plan

Agree on how often you will be in touch. Confirm the communication method the candidate prefers. Find out the best time to talk. Let the candidate know when you will be in touch and how often. With a temp candidate, you may need to speak daily. Just agree on what's best for both of you and clarify.

Ask for updates

Warn the candidate that things are likely to change during the search. Ask them to please keep you informed of every change in circumstance, such as salary expectations, job-search criteria or planned vacations.

Lock in the post-interview debrief

We tackle this pivotal 'moment of truth' in chapter 86 but, for now, share with the candidate how important the post-interview debrief is. Explain that it must happen on the day of the interview and it will take 20 minutes or more. They should be in a private space where they can talk freely. Explain that it is in their interests because it means you can give the clients quick, positive feedback, which may secure the candidate the job of their dreams.

Ask for referees

Ask for referees even if you don't intend to contact them yet. A candidate's response to being asked for referees can be wonderfully instructive, particularly if they are evasive. (I know this is not appropriate in some countries.)

★

Use the first interview to establish the tone of your relationship with the candidate. It's a two-way street, a partnership. Setting the ground rules will cement that in place and reduce frustration and misunderstanding for both parties.

79 | The candidate is assessing you, too

Recruiters, in-house and agency, sometimes lapse into hubris and complacency.

Don't take offence. It's a fact. I have been guilty of it myself.

The candidate experience has been a disaster for decades, ironically made exponentially worse by all the whizz-bang technology tools added to 'enhance the process'. But now, it's potentially much worse.

As I write this, we are in a talent shortage. So, candidates get marginally better treatment because recruiters and employers 'need them'.

The problem is, we always need them! So, don't be short-sighted when the market turns and candidates are plentiful.

Looking after your candidates through simple behaviours like responding, informing, providing feedback and coaching is the right thing to do as a professional, empathetic human (chapter 80). Especially now.

But, it's also the commercially intelligent thing to do. Candidates will remember the companies and agencies who treated them like cattle, and the names of individual recruiters who demeaned and disappointed them will be burned on their brains.

And they will hurt you – a lot. And you will deserve it.

Remember, please: the candidate is assessing you, too.

80 | Your candidate-care ethos

I discussed the candidate-care ethos in *The Savage Truth* and, if anything, it's more important now than when I wrote that book five years ago. Candidate care in recruitment is like inviting 100 people to a party at your house and then leaving 95 of them outside in the rain.

Don't be like that, please.

'Candidate care' in our profession typically means one of two things: either it's a series of platitudes and clichés on recruiter websites, or it is part of a grand 'program' including newsletters, birthday cards and other marketing-generated activities that, while good, are not personal or engaging in any meaningful way.

The fact is that our profession is predisposed to disappoint candidates. That's right, our model is set up to let people down. Think about it: what percentage of candidates that approach you, or that you interview, do you place? Lower than 10%, I bet. So, that means many people won't get what they want from you.

Understanding and believing that candidate care is a recruiter's responsibility, not a corporate one, is critical. You don't need a candidate-care department. You need a candidate-care ethos.

So, here is your seven-point candidate-care action plan for you, on the desk, to do today – and every day (and, just for fun, give yourself a score out of 10 for each measure; did you get more than 35 out of 70?):

1. **Respond!** The most significant criticism of our profession is that we don't respond: to résumés, to applications on our website, to phone calls, to LinkedIn messages. First goal: get back to everyone. Fast.
2. **Don't keep them waiting:** For an agreed videoconference call. In reception. For news. For your call. For feedback. You know what I mean.
3. **Manage expectations:** Much of the dissatisfaction we cause with candidates is our fault. We fail to manage expectations. Don't say, 'When I get the right job in for you, I will give you a call'. The candidate just hears, 'I will give you a call', and you have set up the scene for disappointment. Instead, tell the candidate you will call if you have a great job and that, given the current market, that's unlikely – but that they should call you once a week for an update if that's what they want.
4. **Return phone calls:** I know you don't. As the guy from the shoe company said, 'Just do it'.
5. **Tell them the bad news:** Don't be weak. Don't be selfish. A candidate wants to know if they have been unsuccessful if that is the case. So, don't leave them hanging. Not only after an interview, but also after you have told the candidate you will be

representing her to a particular employer. Oh and, in case you didn't know, telling a candidate there is no news is news to the candidate (chapter 82).

6. **Shut up and listen a little:** Yes, be slow to understand what the candidate wants and thinks (chapter 28). You already know what you want and think.
7. **Give a little:** Thanks, advice, encouragement, respect and empathy.

When it comes to candidate care, you invited them to your party! You are the host. They are the honoured guest. Treat them that way.

81 | You are not in 'recruitment', you are in 'rejection'

We think of ourselves as 'recruiters', but what is the ratio of candidates we recruit into roles compared to the number we screen, interview or submit?

Our profession is obsessed with the number of placements we make. (Of course. I have run a recruitment business all my life – I am most guilty.) Surely, we need to apply equal attention to the number of people we do *not* place and, more crucially, the treatment they get during that process?

What is your 'rejection' process? I have trained 1000 recruiters on managing the recruitment process, influencing the critical moments of truth, making an offer and bedding that offer down. I don't recall ever running a training session on empathetic candidate 'rejection': the let-down, the follow-up, the next steps. What an indictment that is on me and our industry. I would do things differently now.

Also, what documented automation process do we have to ensure no one falls through the cracks? The successful candidate is sometimes showered with love and attention, including flowers and a bottle of wine. What about the also-ran shortlisted ones? What about the ones who did not make the shortlist but still believe they might (because, you know, we are still keeping them warm on the bench, so to speak, in case our real shortlist falls through)? What about the ones you dismissed at first résumé-read but who are still at home waiting for your call because you never got around to communicating that to them? (It's a terrible job explaining to a keen candidate why they are not going forward, isn't it?)

Even if you ignore the basic manners and human kindness aspect of this, the commercial reality is that annoying a high percentage of customers is a disaster.

Remember, even no news is news to a candidate who is waiting (chapter 82). In tight talent times, this is key.

You need to be a great recruiter, but you also need to be an empathetic, consistent and morale-building 'rejecter'. Truth be told, we are in the *rejection* business. And classy rejection is a skill worth refining.

82 | No news is news

The life of a recruiter can be hectic: so many jobs, so many candidates, so much administration, so many interruptions. Amid all that, it's easy to let things slip. After all, you've been frantically busy. How could you remember every little call you probably should make?

But see it from the candidate's point of view.

You told them they were on a shortlist sent to your client this morning, and you confirmed that you would call them back by 4 p.m. with confirmation that they have been selected for an interview, which you fully expect to happen. The candidate is upbeat and excited. But, at 11 a.m., your client calls you to say he is heading off for two days of golf and will only get back to you on Thursday with feedback on your shortlist. You are relaxed because all your candidates are still in play. It's just a short-term delay. Nothing has changed. As far as you are concerned, there is no news.

But the candidate is waiting for your call. As a result, they become anxious and edgy. In this situation, you can differentiate yourself from most recruiters. Make that call to that candidate, tell them the status, check that nothing has changed, reinforce that you still feel they are a strong prospect for this role, and leave them feeling uplifted and respected.

To the candidate, no news is news. You have taken the stress away and left them feeling valued.

It's certainly true to say that, in time, candidates will forget what you say to them, and they will probably forget what you did for them, but they will never forget how you made them feel.

Proactive, outbound calls to candidates, keeping them informed, checking in, feeding updates and encouraging them: that is the recruiter you want to be.

83 | The CCCCF secret sauce

Candidates are ghosting you, letting you down, reneging on meetings, accepting counteroffers and engaging in a wide range of other behaviours that you 'don't understand'.

The reasons are easy to decipher, and many of the solutions have been spelled out in the earlier chapters in this Part. Let's talk about what to do about it!

Firstly, do *not* make any assumptions. Ask in every conversation, 'Has anything changed?' Over Zoom or not, get closer to candidates than ever before.

Secondly – and this is the 'secret sauce' – CCCCF.

What? Yes! CCCCF: constant, continuous, courteous candidate feedback.

The truth is that most recruiters only contact a candidate if it is in the *recruiter's* interest at that moment in time. You need constant outbound engagement, building rapport and trust.

Remember, no news *is* news to the candidate (chapter 82), and if the candidate calls *you* for an update, you left it *too long*.

Deliver that level of engagement consistently and those behaviours you 'don't understand' will wane.

84 | Presenting a job opportunity

Consider how much work you have done to prepare the candidate for the job-search relationship. You have managed the moments of truth and maximised your control over what you *can* control.

Now it's a couple of days after the candidate interview and the perfect role has come in for that candidate. Your challenge is to present the role in a way that encourages the candidate to allow you to represent them to your client company.

Remember that is the goal of this conversation, and it is another crucial recruitment moment of truth.

Let's think about this very simply. We make a fee when we make a placement. We make a placement when someone accepts a job. People get job offers after an interview. An interview can only happen if the candidate agrees to attend that interview.

I know I'm labouring this point, but your job now is to *sell the job to your candidate* (assuming you are sure that the role in question meets the candidate's job-search criteria). Your goal is to get the candidate to agree to allow you to represent them. Remember, the golden metric in permanent recruitment is client-candidate interviews (chapter 30).

Before you make that call to the candidate, make sure you spend 30 seconds putting yourself in their position. What do they want to hear from you? What will excite them? What will incline them to permit you to represent them to your client for this job? Review your interview notes. What are their hot buttons? What is their MTA (chapter 71)?

Here's how to present the job opportunity to the candidate:

- Never lie. Do not embellish the role to the point where you are not being truthful.
- On the other hand, this is a selling dynamic in the best sense of the word 'sell'. You know the candidate's hot buttons because you isolated their MTA during the interview, right? So, you know precisely what they are looking for. That's the focus. Shine a light on the aspects of the role that meet their needs. Feed the fundamental motivations to move.
- Make sure the candidate can speak freely and is in private.
- Ask, 'Has anything changed since we last spoke?' But you do that every time anyway, right (chapter 27)?
- Start by positioning the company, not the job. This is important. Paint the picture. Build a compelling narrative: the company's

products and services; its resources, location and facilities; its values, ethos and employer brand. Ask for feedback and questions. Deal with those.

- Move on to talking about the role: the responsibilities, the scope of duties. Ask for feedback and questions. Deal with those.
- Talk about the direct reporting lines. Who will their new boss be? Make sure you emphasise positive details. Ask for feedback and questions. Deal with those.
- Build on this by moving on to career opportunities: training, mentors and promotion prospects. Ask for feedback and questions. Deal with those.
- Ask the candidate to reaffirm their salary expectations. You already know them because you drilled into them during the interview, but making assumptions in recruitment kills all deals, as we already know. Let the candidate tell you again. Don't be shocked if they've changed.
- Explain the offered salary range and benefits. Focus on aspects that the candidate has shown interest in. Flexible work arrangements, for example. A bonus based on results, perhaps. Financial support for studies, possibly. Travel opportunities, maybe. Don't oversell. Focus on what you know they want to hear. Ask for feedback and questions. Deal with those.
- If the salary is at the low end of their range, emphasise that there may be flexibility if they perform well during interviews (if that is true – great recruiters do not lie). Also, circle back to the many benefits that meet the candidate's full range of MTA.
- Ask the candidate directly if they want to be represented. But be smart. Don't beg. This is an excellent approach, as an example: 'Ms Candidate, I'm putting together my shortlist for this outstanding role this afternoon. It's highly competitive, but you have a good chance of making the final list. Can I confirm that you're interested in me representing you to this company if you make the final shortlist?'
- Once agreement is obtained, remind the candidate that, at this point, they need to follow through if you can secure them

a meeting. Give them great clarity on the next steps. You will finalise the shortlist by 4 p.m. today. Either way, you will get back to them about whether they are on the shortlist. (In your mind, you're confident they will make the shortlist, but it's not a bad thing if the candidate feels this is a highly sought-after role.)

- Make sure you get back to the candidate that afternoon, celebrate that they are shortlisted for presentation to the client and explain when you expect to hear from your client.
- Confirm the interview as soon as you can.

85 | Gearing the candidate for client interview

Many recruiters seem to feel that their job is 'done' once they have secured their candidate an interview. It's a big win every time you do that, but your effort is only just beginning! You can do compelling work in assisting your candidate to shine at the client interview.

Do not assume that the candidate will always represent themselves well. Nerves, lack of experience, overconfidence, shyness and many other factors can derail an interview, often meaning the best candidate does not get the job. Your role in the 'interview prep' or 'gearing' call is to ensure your candidate is ready to 'put their best foot forward'. You must ensure that your candidate has every legitimate advantage to impress in that meeting. Yes, you guessed it: this is another monumental 'moment of truth', which many recruiters do not manage professionally.

The approach

It may almost seem a little trite, but it is highly influential: exude enthusiasm. Be authentic. You are excited about your candidate getting this role, aren't you? Show it. Use positive words, and ensure your tone and demeanour get the candidate's attention and leave them enthused and wanting the role.

When describing the opportunity, start once again with the *company*, not the job, and highlight all the positive aspects that coincide with the candidate's goals you identified during your interview.

Yes, you did this when you were getting the candidate's permission to represent them to your client, but now they have an interview, so things are getting serious very fast and we need to drill deeper. You don't want the candidate getting cold feet, so remind them that the job and the company match their job-change criteria and tie in with their MTA (chapters 70 and 71).

Reveal your opinion, making it strong and sincere; for example, 'This job has everything you are looking for, with a great company, and it's an excellent opportunity for you to take the next step'.

The gearing

Now we get into the meat of the briefing session. This 'moment of truth' is primarily a *coaching* session to improve your candidate's chances of being offered the role.

Start with a focus on the interview technique. You'll undoubtedly have some generic tips about interviewing, but also tailor them to this candidate. Coach them if they speak too much or too little, for example.

Take the opportunity to coach the candidate on the interviewer. Elaborate on that person's interview style, role, history with the company, demeanour and personality, if you have that information. I remember a Melbourne recruiter who always warned his candidates that the client was a huge St Kilda (AFL football) fan and, even if it went against the grain, to show a fondness for the Saints would do no harm. He made a lot of placements there. This is a true story and a little frivolous, and you must know how passionate football fans in Melbourne are to fully understand it, but it does show how much rapport and common ground can help. It was the recruiter who made that happen.

Trial-run the types of questions the client is likely to ask. You might have excellent visibility to this because some of your other candidates may have been on interviews there already and you will have debriefed them in detail. Help the candidate prepare good answers to the questions. You could even role-play those answers.

Advise the candidate on what the client is looking for. Share with the candidate what the client's hot buttons are. Elaborate on the 'must-haves' in the job description and prepare the candidate to speak to those, including examples and anecdotes from their work history that support their suitability for the role.

Encourage the candidate to prepare questions they should ask and ensure that they are intelligent, meaningful questions that will push the conversation forward and impress the client.

Guide the candidate on research they should do for the interview: on the company, their competitors, products, services, branding and location, and on the travel logistics to get to the interview.

Counsel the candidate on what to wear and take to the interview. For a digital interview, give them videoconference interviewing tips.

Work with the candidate on turning a shortfall in their experience or weakness in their suitability into a positive. For example, the candidate is not particularly strong on XYZ software, but they are going to take a course to improve their skills.

If there are any gaps or unusual features in the candidate's background, discuss those and prepare honest, positive explanations.

The pre-close

You have worked through every aspect of the interview with your candidate, coached, advised, informed and ensured they have every possible advantage to shine that you can glean. Now, you need to remind your candidate why this job is one they should seriously consider taking. Ask the candidate to remind you of their reasons for seeking a change and match those with what this job offers. You need them going into the meeting really wanting this job!

Once again, pre-close on the salary level they would accept if the job *were* right, making sure this falls below what the client is likely to offer. (You will be managing this on the client side, too – see Part V).

Raise the possibility of an offer and lead that into a discussion about a potential resignation from where they are now. Again, this raises the likelihood of a counteroffer; again, go through your counteroffer communications plan (chapter 74).

The wrap-up

You've done a great job, but you're not finished yet.

Ask the candidate *not* to initiate a salary conversation in the interview. Instead, if they are asked what they are looking for, encourage the candidate to simply reply that they are open to the client's best offer, and refer them back to you, their agent.

Encourage the candidate to express enthusiasm at the interview and explicitly tell the client they are interested in the role before they leave the interview (if they are legitimately interested, of course).

Remind the candidate to call you back directly after the interview, and even set up a time with a calendar invite.

Finally, express your confidence in the candidate, and reiterate that they are suitable for the role and have an excellent opportunity to secure it.

*

The difference between the candidate who gets the job and the one who comes second can be minuscule.

Whether or not your candidate receives an offer can hinge on the flimsiest factors. You have worked hard to secure the client's role and find, interview and prepare this candidate. Don't stumble at the final hurdle. Make sure your candidate walks into that meeting with every possible advantage.

Helping your candidate be 5% better at everything mentioned in this chapter could be why they get the job. Then, you have created an outcome that results in a happy client, candidate and you.

And then you get paid. Fun and money, indeed (chapter 120).

86 | The post-interview debrief

By now, you are clear that recruitment is more art than science. It's a craft requiring nuanced skills. So, here we are at another moment of truth: the post-interview debrief.

Often recruiters look for cursory post-interview feedback: 'Are you keen on the job?' is the gist of it. Some even ask for emailed feedback. What a missed opportunity!

The debrief is a veritable goldmine, allowing you to lead this candidate to a 'yes' or to glean information that will assist with the next candidate:

- Make sure the candidate is in a quiet private space. Get comfortable. This could take a while!
- Start neutral. Assess the vibe: 'Did things go as well as we hoped?' Listen and assess voice and tone. Do you feel enthusiasm and excitement, or negativity and disinterest?
- Ask who they met. 'What did you think of them? Did you get on well? Did you meet any other employees? How long were you there? Are you compatible with the people you met? Can you learn things from the people you met?'
- Ask about the workplace environment: 'What were the offices like? Were the facilities good? Easy to get to?'
- Get specific about the role itself: 'Did they describe the job to you in detail? Did it sound interesting? Can you handle the position? Will you learn new systems and processes? Do you think the role will be challenging?'
- Explore salary and benefits: 'Was money discussed and, if so, who brought it up? What was explicitly said about money? Were benefits discussed? What did they tell you in terms of flexibility and working from home?' Out of this conversation will come further questions and answers, and you will start to form a strong impression of how well the meeting went and how interested the candidate is. Spend extra time on areas that fall into the candidate's MTA. Your goal here is to reinforce the 'fit'.
- Then, gauge the candidates' interest in the role: 'What are your thoughts about this opportunity?'
- Now it is time to initiate a 'trial close'. First, ask if they have any reservations. Then, ask my personal favourite question, which I always used and still do: 'On a scale of one to ten, with ten meaning "I want it", where are you?'
- If the vibe is positive, you should ask the candidate at what salary they think they could accept the role. Any hesitation or resistance to that means there is much work to be done yet.

- Lock in the salary once more: 'So if an offer came in at $100,000, would you be in a position to accept?'
- Leave the candidate upbeat and focusing on the positives. Map out the next steps.

87 | Pre-closing the candidate after the final interview

Now we are getting to the pointy end.

Your candidate has had the second and possibly even a third interview. The client is exceptionally keen and has made very positive noises about making an offer. Your candidate is very enthusiastic, and you have pre-closed on the role and the salary at least once. Things are looking perfect, but you need to influence and pre-close this candidate before they get the offer. This is yet again a critical moment of truth, and you must own it (see figure 14):

Figure 14: Pre-closing the candidate after the final interview

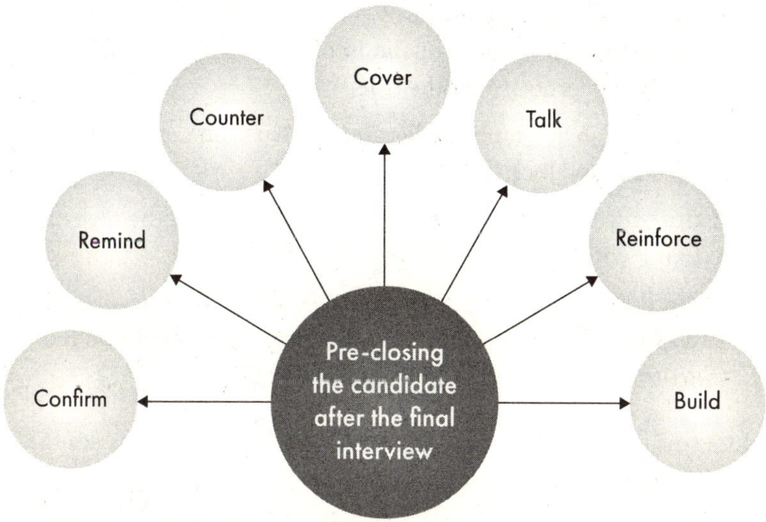

- **Confirm** once again the candidate's thoughts about the job and the company. Build on the positives. Do not assume that, just because they were desperately keen last night, they still are today. 'Has anything changed?' will come up again.
- **Remind** the candidate of their original reasons for making the change. Then, go back to their 'real motivators', but get the candidate to reiterate them where possible. It's tempting to jump in and 'tell' the candidate why the job matches what they are looking for, but the psychology is powerful when the candidate tells *you* that the job meets their goals and can verbalise why. So, ask, probe and uncover. Lead the candidate there.
- **Counter** the fear of change. Remind them that change is good. Change is essential for career advancement: no change, no progress. Careers grow through change. Inertia is what kills you. Staying too long in a job that is 'good' but taking you nowhere could be a disaster career-wise.
- **Cover** prior authority to accept this specific salary; for example, 'Ms Candidate, we have covered why this job is perfect for you and how it meets all your desired criteria. Can I accept on your behalf if we get an offer at $100,000 tonight?' If the answer is 'no' or ambiguous, dig into why. This is an excellent method of unearthing reservations you did not know about or reaffirming the candidate's desire for the role.
- **Talk** through a potential offer and pre-close on terms and salary. Be specific and lock them in.
- **Reinforce** the candidate's enthusiasm: 'You liked the idea of working with X.'
- **Build** the candidate's confidence: 'This would be the perfect move for you. There were many other great candidates on the shortlist. You have done spectacularly well.'

Note this is a pre-close. You do not have the offer. This is sophisticated selling – it's getting a yes before the job is offered.

88 | Delivering the job offer

Delivering an offer to the candidate is the climax of all the work you have done for weeks. It is pivotal to your success, so it is incredible how poorly many recruiters execute the job offer.

Often it is over-exuberance that leads to a lack of preparation and poor delivery, and I understand that to an extent: it's exciting and you have worked so hard to get here. You want to tie it all up! But don't slip at the final step.

Let's start with the golden rule of job offers: do not make an offer unless you *already know* it will be accepted.

Sound crazy? You got a hint of it in the previous chapter with our rigorous pre-close.

When you have the offer, you first clarify all the finer details with the client. Do not go into the offer conversation with the candidate without being able to answer all their questions about the terms of that offer. To wrap this up, you need full details on bonuses, benefits, pensions, superannuation, leave entitlements, reporting lines, work-from-home arrangements and anything else. Predict what the candidate is likely to ask.

Also, if the salary is lower than the candidate is expecting and you have already advised your client of that, *don't* offer it to the candidate. Negotiate with your client first. The deal can blow up if you go to the candidate with an offer that you know is too low. Work with your client to construct an offer your candidate *will* accept. Of course, all this will have been discussed, negotiated and pre-closed with both parties through the process, so it should not be a significant stumbling block (Part V). Having said that, some clients love a last moment low-ball offer!

Once you have a fair offer, message your candidate to ensure they are in a private place to talk. Do not hint at an offer at this stage. Stay calm.

Once you have the candidate face to face – in real life, preferably, or on a videoconference or phone call – you still do not make the offer. Stay calm. (By the way, if you planned to offer by email – don't!)

You ask, 'Has anything changed since we last spoke?'

You ask the candidate to reiterate once again why this role is suitable for them (which will be because it meets their MTA; chapter 71). You listen carefully for any doubt or hesitation. You read their body language and do not offer the job until you have resolved those concerns.

Drill down on their acceptable salary level. Then, move towards getting the candidate to agree to the salary you know you have 'in your pocket' (or an even lower salary), but do not offer the job yet. Ask, 'Is there any reason you can think of that would stop you from accepting this offer if it were made to you today?'

Get a verbal acceptance via a direct pre-close: 'If I were able to offer you this job right now at $100,000, would you accept it?' If you get a 'yes', deliver the offer – which has already been accepted and will be again, for real.

But you are not finished yet. Get a tentative start date and agree on the next steps, which will include reviewing and signing the letter of offer or contract, and planning their resignation.

More on that to come in the next chapter!

89 | Managing the resignation

Let's delve deeper into the crucial skills of managing the resignation, because that is your job and a critical recruiter competency.

When you have offered someone a job and they have accepted it, take the view that the hard work is only beginning. And don't you dare be tempted to pump out a little joyful placement dance because the 'God of Recruitment' loves to stomp on such presumption.

Here are the *bare minimum* steps to manage the resignation. Own them.

Confirm the start date

Confirming the start date is an obvious step, right? But did you do it before the offer? Have you nailed it now that the rubber is hitting the road and your candidate is about to hand in their notice, and her boss will not only try to convince her to stay but, failing that, guilt her into giving a more extended notice period because, you know, she is 'leaving them in the lurch'?

Find out what notice she is obliged to provide and make sure her available start date at the new gig gels with her preferred start date, and that no coercion by her current boss will sway that. Placements go belly-up every day because of this. Nail the start date!

Confirm 'personal allies'

What now? Your candidate is red hot and ready to move, right? But has she spoken to loved ones? To trusted mentors? A partner? Parents, even? You must tread carefully here. Make no assumptions, and don't infringe where you shouldn't.

Say something along the lines of, 'Have you spoken to the important people in your life about this move, and do they support it?' Of course, you don't want to hear, 'I'm a bit nervous about telling my family about my new job tonight. I am not sure they think I should move at this time'. Oh dear.

Agree on the resignation meeting

Don't leave the resignation meeting up to fate! Agree with the candidate on when the meeting is going to be. If necessary, encourage the candidate to set up an appointment with their boss and ensure all the appropriate people who should be there are there. Short version: you need to know the *exact* day and time your candidate is resigning.

Provide the resignation letter

Your candidate needs to attend that resignation meeting with a prepared, professional letter. I used to have several different examples of these letters to provide to candidates. Help them design it, and make sure it categorically states that they are resigning and the date they intend to leave.

Coach on resignation meeting

Some candidates can't wait to resign because they don't like their boss or current job and want to leave immediately. Others have a lot of loyalty and are very tentative and nervous about resigning.

So, you've got to coach them through these feelings, explain that they are normal and reiterate that loyalty is admirable. Still, at the very end, they need to be loyal to their *career*, and if they exit appropriately and with dignity then they betray no one.

Address possible employer reactions

Ask your candidate what reaction she will likely get when she hands in her notice. Will her employer try to guilt-trip her? Will they bring in the heavyweights from head office to try and persuade her?

The critical thing is that you try to ensure that your candidate is not ambushed in the resignation meeting. It's almost certain that her boss has had more resignations than her opportunities to resign, so her employer will already have a game plan ready. Prepare her for the likely responses and help her work through how she will deal with them.

Reiterate why the new job meets the MTA

Your candidate is leaving this job and taking your new role for specific reasons, which, if you are a good recruiter, you would have identified at the beginning of the process. Before she goes into the resignation meeting, get her to reiterate why the new role fulfils all her MTA criteria. This is critical. Don't lecture; work with her to get her to repeat why she's leaving this job. It's far more potent if *she* tells *you* why she should resign rather than you telling her (chapter 71).

Address the counteroffer again

Yes, go through the counteroffer again. Prepare her for its likely occurrence. Get her to remind you why a counteroffer and more money will not solve her problems (chapter 74).

Celebrate the decision

This is a big deal for your candidate. Make sure you celebrate and reiterate that her decision to move is right. Of course, I'm assuming you are an ethical and professional recruiter and it is indeed the proper role for her. That being the case, just make sure that she realises how well she's done to get this offer, what a great move it is and how she should not allow any last-minute hurdles to derail the move.

Set the post-resignation call-back time

So, the candidate has set up a meeting at 11 a.m. on Thursday to resign to her boss, as you agreed. Ask her to call you directly after the meeting. This is big. Reiterate this and get her absolute agreement. If she doesn't contact you by 12.30 p.m., start to worry.

*

Even after you've taken all these steps, though, you're nowhere near finished. Please refer to my 'Valley of Death' template in the next chapter for the 14 steps to take to ensure that your hard-won placement follows through and allows you to shake out those placement dance moves with confidence.

90 | Navigating the Valley of Death

Recruiters must change their inputs if they want to change the outputs. That means doubling down on questioning, relationship-building, avoiding assumptions and managing the key moments of truth.

But now, you need to take it to the *next* level. The Valley of Death just got deeper and far more dangerous than it has ever been.

The 'Valley of Death'? That period between job acceptance and when your candidate puts their delicate derrière in your client's seat: that is the Valley of Death.

You *do* know things can go wrong in that twilight zone?

Sure, I know you do. You are a recruiter, and which recruiter doesn't have a heartbreaking 'Valley of Death' tragedy to tell?

As I write this book, during massive candidate shortages, the Valley of Death is now a veritable minefield of potential missteps, disappointments, disappearing acts and a dozen other pitfalls. You must mitigate the risk by managing this gigantic recruiting moment of truth.

Have a close read of figure 15. Salvation lies within.

These are the minimum 14 steps required to navigate the Valley of Death. Completing each step is crucial to ensure the successful implementation of the next one.

Please read this in conjunction with the previous chapter, 'Managing the resignation', but keep in mind the difference: half of the Valley of Death is after the resignation has successfully happened.

Figure 15: Navigating the Valley of Death!

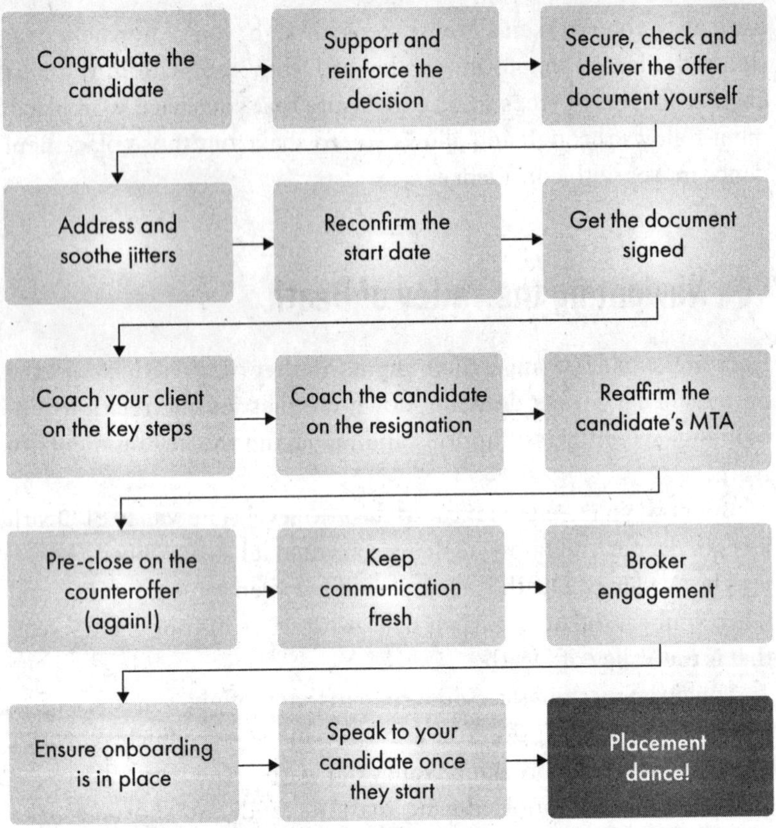

1. **Congratulate the candidate** heartily and sincerely. It's a big day for you because you've made a placement, but it is life-changing for the candidate because it's a career move. So, make the candidate feel great about the decision.

2. **Support and reinforce the decision** by reiterating why it fits with the candidate's MTA and reinforcing how this move is a stepping stone to where the candidate wants to go career-wise.
3. **Secure, check and deliver the offer document yourself,** if possible. Do not allow the client to send a letter of offer or employment contract to the candidate directly: you want to manage that. Get the document sent to you and go through it face to face or via videoconference with the candidate. You do not want the candidate to misunderstand a clause or take exception to a paragraph or before you know it, the deal could be off without your calming influence.
4. **Address and soothe jitters** if there is anything in the contract that the candidate wasn't expecting and that is making them nervous. You can calm their uncertainty and get back to your client to fix it.
5. **Reconfirm the start date** in the new role with your candidate and with the client so there is no possibility of a mismatch or confusion.
6. **Get the document signed.** It is psychologically compelling for the candidate to sign the letter of offer: it's a tangible commitment to proceed. If you detect any reservations or prevarication, there is a problem and you will need to address it fast.
7. **Coach your client on the key steps** to ensure that everything they have promised is delivered. A candidate can become very unsettled if a new employer doesn't follow through on even small commitments, so make sure your client does everything they commit to.
8. **Coach the candidate on the resignation**, as mentioned in the previous chapter. Help them with the resignation letter and coach them on the resignation meeting. Then, manage the resignation day and ensure you get a post-resignation call-back.
9. **Reaffirm the candidate's MTA** so that any last-minute buyer's regret or cold feet are swept away by the excitement of a new job that meets all their goals.

10. **Pre-close on the counteroffer (again!).**
11. **Keep communication fresh** and regular with your candidate throughout the notice period, which could be four weeks or even longer. That is plenty of time for negative things to happen. Meet for a coffee, have a conversation about how the notice period is going or pass on messages from the client. Find a reason to talk often.
12. **Broker engagement** between your candidate and their new employer. This is proven to be very powerful as it shifts the candidate's mindset to the new employer. Perhaps organise a meeting with their new co-workers, a sign-up to the company newsletter or even a walk around the new premises. These are all great examples of how the candidate's commitment to the new role can be cemented.
13. **Ensure onboarding is in place** – that your client has prepared a complete onboarding program and that your candidate's entry into the new role is smooth and welcoming.
14. **Speak to your candidate once they start** in their new role – on days one and five, and monthly after that.

91 | Negotiating the temp pay rate

It is time to change lanes and return to our wonderful profession's temporary and contract side. Let's talk about negotiating the pay rate for the temporary or contract worker.

We want to pay people fairly, but we also want to maintain our margins, and even $1 of margin across a big temp count is a great deal of money.

Where most temp recruiters go wrong when discussing the hourly or daily rate with a temp or contractor is to assume that the only thing at stake for the temp is money. It's not. Money is important, obviously, but so is self-esteem.

Here's how to sell a pay rate to a temp (figure 16):

Figure 16: Selling the temp pay rate

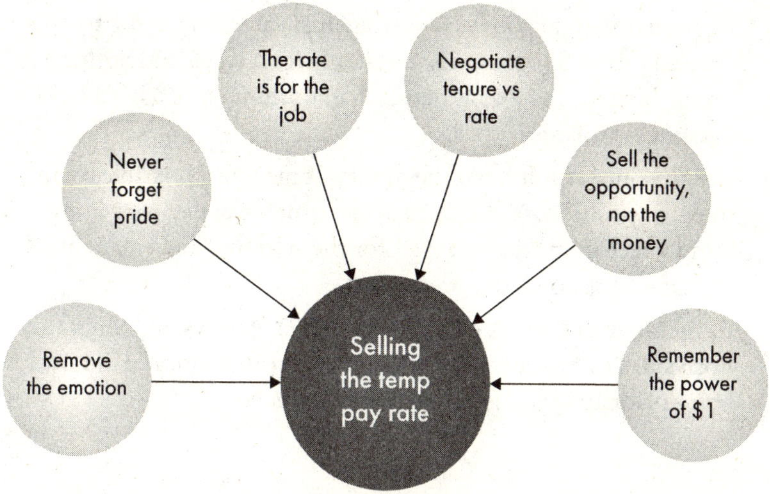

- When talking to a temp about their rate, the first thing to address is to remove the emotion from their point of view. Money is important, but a lower rate also makes a temp feel that they are not *valued* – that their skills are not recognised, that they are misunderstood or misjudged.
- On a similar theme, never forget the temp's pride and their situation. They may be out of work, between perm jobs, so they could be thinking about a rate like a permanent salary; in other words, they feel that they must secure the best rate and lock it in because that is their only chance. This is not true – a lower rate for a short-term temp job does not mean they can't get a higher rate for a higher-skilled job next week. However, it is understandable: people do not want to be exploited or feel demeaned.
- Explain that the rate is for the job, not the temp's overall ability. This is the key to handling both the emotion and the pride issue. You may think that's obvious, but it's not for the temp. 'But I am worth $100 an hour', they may say. Yes, for a financial controller job, they are, but for this reconciliation job the rate is $45.

It's the rate for the job, and it does not mean they are worth less at their core skill.

- Be prepared to negotiate tenure against rate. Maybe the temp's desired rate is $50, but this job is only for a week and nothing is on the horizon, so $45 is better than nothing until a better gig becomes available.
- Sell the opportunity, not the money. It may be a possible temp to perm position, or it may provide valuable experience in the temp's sector, making it easier for them to find a permanent job in that sector down the track.
- Remember the power of $1 (chapter 92). Always be selling to both sides to increase your margin. I am often amazed at how low a priority this is for so many temp recruiters.

92 | The power of one

Many recruitment companies require their temp consultants to operate off a rate sheet, which instructs them what to charge the client and what to pay the temp for a specific skill set or task. The problem with this is that, when the client screws the recruiter down on the rate that they will pay, typically the consultant still pays the temp the rate-sheet amount, which results in the margin being squeezed. Equally, temp rates often rise in a candidate-short market, and consultants without negotiating skills will put the temp rate up without passing on the increase to the client, which has the same effect on the margin.

Companies often don't even notice this and, when they see their percentage margin drop, they blame it on 'the market'. Unfortunately, it's not the market – it's poor recruitment consulting skills.

The temp recruiter knows the margin has dropped in most cases but says, 'It's only a dollar, and it's long-term, so I will make it up'. However, this demonstrates inferior negotiating skills. It demonstrates very shoddy commercial understanding, too, because slowly their margins get eroded, and it costs the business and the consultant a fortune.

For all the temp businesses I have run – and they have been many – the goal has always been to increase the margin by $1 an hour across all our temps. Never gouge clients, never underpay temps, but charge full weight for our excellent service.

It's really not such a big task when you think about it. Over the next six months, can you imagine charging each client 50 cents more per hour and paying each temp 50 cents less? It does not need to be in every case, but if that's the average across your temp count, the dollar difference will be huge.

Let's take, for example, a temp business that is running 150 temps a week. It's not tiny, but it's certainly not huge, and thousands of recruitment companies worldwide are paying many more than that. Have a look at the elementary arithmetic and then decide whether $1 per hour makes a difference:

> 150 temps are paid per week and each temp averages 35 hours of work per week: 150 × 35 = 5250 hours.
>
> If we increase the margin by $1 per hour for every temp placement across all 150 temps, that means the business makes $5250 more dollars per week: $5250 × 52 weeks = $273,000 a year.

Just a lazy *quarter of a million dollars* a year. That's over $1.5 million extra margin in five years. For no extra work. All of that would be profit to the business, except for the part that went to the consultant as a bonus.

Do I have your attention?

That's the power of one.

PART V

CLIENT SKILLS

It is no exaggeration to say that many recruiters provide minimal advice to clients throughout the recruitment process. As for 'controlling the process', that is the domain of a tiny minority.

The truth is that great recruiters know they have the expertise and experience to impact the outcomes at each step.

A recruiter can and must 'make things happen'. But, sadly, most recruiters either just react to what the client suggests or, in some cases, have minimal client interaction, simply acting as the logistics person to set up interviews and message candidates at the client's whim.

Consultative client management is built on credibility, allowing the recruiter to work with the client as an advisor and a real consultant. There is no arrogance built into this point of view, but the experienced recruiter will know more about the nuances of each step and what actions must be taken to get the desired outcome.

Recruiters must get much closer to their clients – close enough to influence their behaviour and their decisions.

93 | Building trust with clients

Throughout this book, I emphasise that the only real road to recruitment success is building consultative relationships based on credibility and respect. I explain that you need 'recruiter equity' (chapter 5) and enlarge on that in the discussion on 'Selling is listening' (Part III), especially concerning credibility, advising, negotiating and believing in your value.

A recruiter who works with clients as partners will build trust and never risk it.

It is so easy to damage trust. Overselling candidates, a lack of transparency, failure to follow through, manipulating salary negotiations, finessing reference feedback to your advantage, betraying confidentiality and, of course, headhunting staff from your clients are just some of the ways recruiters damage relationships. Years of trust-building can be destroyed by one breach.

So, if you want clients to take your advice, keep you informed and treat you fairly, you must actively build trust. There is much you can do, but certain decisive actions will lead to solid, trust-based partnerships over time.

Consistently deliver quality candidates

Self-evident as it sounds, the consistent delivery of quality candidates is the platform upon which trust is built. A track record *counts* – it shows that you are able to do what the client came to you to do. It won't be enough on its own, but trust will never develop without it.

Provide candidates that fit the brief

A candidate mismatch suggests to the client that you don't know what you are doing or are trying to pull the wool over their eyes, neither of which is conducive to building trust. If you have one good candidate and two poor candidates who don't fit the brief, don't send all three, because the other two will sully your outstanding work in finding the top-shelf candidate. Even if the client hires the excellent candidate, they will see it as 'luck' on your part. *It must be,* they will reason; *after all, they also sent those two 'no-hopers'.*

Provide accurate, transparent, balanced reference-checking

Communicate the concerns that emerged from the reference check authentically. Even if it's not to your immediate advantage, this will encourage the client to believe you and trust your judgement.

Never betray client confidentiality

Betraying client confidentiality is easier to do than you think. You visit a client who tells you they have had to let some staff go. A week later, speaking to another client in the same sector, you let that piece of news slip. Your first client will not appreciate that, and it will forever harm your relationship with them.

Be quick to share both good and bad news

It is so easy to let the client know that their preferred candidate is keen on the job, but perhaps you're not so quick to reveal that their preferred candidate is favouring another role. Getting on the front foot with disappointing news will strengthen your relationship with the client, even though they won't enjoy hearing it at the time.

Offer feedback and advice at every stage of the process

Don't just tell the client that the candidate has lost interest and taken another job. It is incredibly powerful to give feedback to the client on why and how the other job differed from theirs (chapter 44). Again, communicating this could be uncomfortable; but, in the end, the client will value your insights as much as anything else you have to offer.

Always do what you say you will do

Deliver on every commitment you make. Even the most minor thing.

Respond well when things go wrong

When things go wrong, even when the fault is yours, it is an opportunity to build trust. A speedy recovery, flexibility in repairing whatever happened, transparency and honesty in accepting your responsibility will likely improve your relationship with the client despite the mishap.

Provide constant updates

Giving accurate feedback and making sure your client *never* has to call you for news are the foundation of a trusting relationship.

94 | 'Does my butt look big in this?'

Stay with me on this one – it starts weirdly but it gets there.

What do you say to a friend who wants your 'real' opinion on a matter of some sensitivity? You know, 'Do you think I should marry them?' or, when showing off a new pair of jeans, 'Does my butt look big in this?' It's a dilemma. You don't want to rock the boat. You certainly don't want to hurt your friend's feelings. On the other hand, being honest, while painful, is almost certainly in their best interests.

To answer these questions satisfactorily takes courage. It takes discretion. It takes a lot of trust between two people.

And, guess what? That is *precisely* the relationship a good recruiter has with clients.

Would you tell your client that they are not securing the best candidates because the interview process is too long and too demeaning for the candidates?

Can you find a way to coach your client on their interview technique, which is turning candidates away? Are you a 'trusted advisor'?

Do you have the 'recruiter equity' to say to a client that they will never hire the calibre of candidate they are looking for unless they offer more flexible work conditions?

Do you have a consultative relationship with your client that enables you to tell them their employer brand is weak and there are negative rumblings in the market about their 'work culture', and that they need to do things to improve their image in the employer marketplace?

These examples are the recruiting equivalent of telling your friend their butt looks huge in those jeans and they had best stop wearing them, or telling your best mate that his new mullet haircut is an embarrassment to men everywhere. It must be done. You are not a friend if you don't. And, as a recruiter, you are not a 'consultant' if you don't.

It takes courage and careful communication. But, mostly, it takes trust with that client (or candidate, for that matter).

They won't necessarily like what you say, but they will deeply value the fact that you can tell them.

95 | The definition of a 'good client'

What defines a client worth partnering with? Where will your best return come from? What *is* a 'good client' for a recruitment agency?

The answers to these questions are crucial but also nuanced, because you have to address the short-term need to fill jobs now – that is our business, after all – but also take a longer view and build trusting client relationships for the future.

The factors defining a good client may change depending on the market. Recruiters must be constantly assessing and evaluating, because the way our profession operates means you simply cannot afford to invest time into clients who are not compatible with your goals.

Let's dig into this and put some meat on the bones of the type of client that will allow you to maximise the placement potential of the suitable candidates you meet.

A *'good client'* will have the following nine characteristics. I am seriously suggesting you evaluate your clients on them. Are you working with threes and fours out of nine? Why?

A 'good client':

1. works hard to attract and hire good people – they have a collaborative talent acquisition team (chapter 60) and do not let 'process' get in the way of outcomes
2. treats recruitment as a corporate differentiator, which means they really *do* believe people are their biggest asset and behave that way
3. works in partnership with you, as proven by their rapid response times, constant updating on job status and exclusive working agreement

4. moves fast – they get back to you on shortlists, interview in a timely manner, give prompt feedback and make an offer when a decision needs to be made
5. takes your advice – on the job description, on salaries, on the market and on the process
6. can sell their company and their vacant roles – not overselling, but understanding that hiring is a two-way process and the best candidates have a choice
7. understands where 'the power' in hiring is right now – writing this in 2022, the power, for the most part, is with candidates, and so employers who want to hire in this environment need to act accordingly
8. pays your fees promptly and without debate, seeing your value and agreeing with your terms
9. is a client candidates want to work for!

All the points are essential, but the last one is the deal-breaker. You get paid for 'acceptances', not 'offers', so work with clients who your candidates want to work for. That means understanding both in-depth candidate motivation (MTA) and what each client really offers in compensation, culture, ethos, training, flexibility and much more.

We are not used to this – 'selecting' clients, that is. We have done it with candidates for years, but clients are somehow sacred. They select us.

Not so much now.

I am not advocating burning bridges or cutting ties. Instead, I advise you to put your energy where the desired outcome is likely (chapter 104).

96 | The magic of a qualified job order

Filling a job does not start with finding suitable candidates for that job brief. Instead, it begins with taking an order that is well qualified in the first place.

That simple truism is readily ignored. Thousands of recruiters worldwide today will blithely take a job – perhaps even received via email – and start looking for candidates, and then bitterly wonder why the client subsequently hired someone through another agent who didn't seem to meet the brief.

The brief presented initially is very rarely the actual brief. It's a starting point!

This chapter outlines the steps to take a qualified order, but you can only take these steps if your interaction with the client is built on a foundation of belief in your role as a recruiter. That starts with you assuming the role of 'advisor', not 'order taker'. You are not there to simply jot down or record what the client says concerning the vacant job or the candidate being sought. You are the expert, after all (chapter 5). You know the market conditions and candidate availability. Indeed, this is a primary opportunity to prove your real value.

Qualifying a job order involves asking many questions and digging into the role's duties, responsibilities and rewards. Critically, it means getting a clear understanding of the outcomes required from the role. Often you will be shocked to discover that these do not align with the experience or qualifications being nominated by the client. This is where you can make a huge difference!

Most job descriptions will have a 10- to 15-point list of all the role's responsibilities and the critical attributes the successful candidate 'must have'. A skilfully qualified job order will prioritise these responsibilities and must-haves so you know what the job is and what the required skills are.

They are often not what the client initially outlines. Qualifying a job order means managing client expectations regarding salary, talent availability, time frames and much more.

A skilled recruiter will stretch the parameters of many of the components initially set out by the client – salary perhaps most obviously, but also qualifications and years of experience. And they will do this with the client's interests in mind, to get the role filled with an appropriate candidate. Does the successful person really need 15 years of payroll experience to run this small company payroll? Almost certainly not. That is your job to advise on.

Qualifying a job order means testing and calibrating the client's assumptions, which are often outdated or flawed. Skilled storytelling from the recruiter can play a big part in this, bringing authentic evidence to the discussion and acquainting the client with the market as it is today. It includes managing and agreeing on the process, and setting time frames and communications parameters.

Taking a job order is perhaps the very best opportunity to prove your worth as an advisor and as a real consultant, to build credibility and trust (chapter 93). Don't miss it!

Figure 17: The pathway to successful job-order qualification

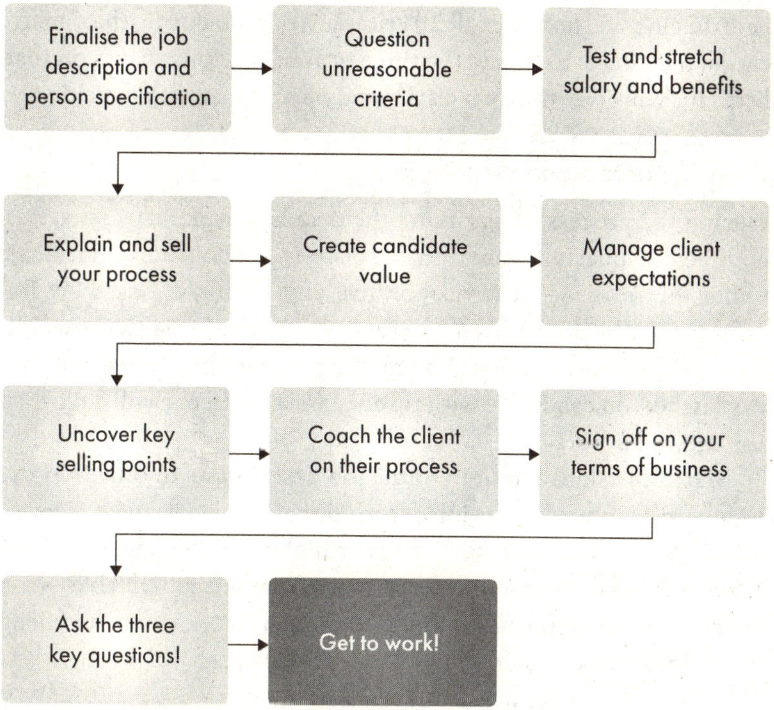

I have summarised the pathway to a successful job-order qualification in figure 17, and you can see how it flows, but let's flesh it out.

Finalise the job description and person specification

Firstly, you need a clear description of the job and the person being sought. Even if you have a 'job description' document in front of you, talk it through. Make no assumptions and take no shortcuts. Even if you have previously filled jobs with this client, get total clarity on the duties, responsibilities, qualifications, experience and outcomes expected of this role.

Weave in questions to gain clarity and detail; sanity-check requirements. You will be amazed how flexible many clients will be on what is stated as 'essential' in the document. For example, a job description document often says, 'The successful candidate must have…' and then lists 20 diverse criteria. I can tell you that the person who gets that job will *not* meet all 20 criteria. Your job during the qualification meeting is to isolate the three or four real must-haves on that list. This will give you great clarity and open the candidate field.

Question unreasonable criteria

During the process of clarifying the details – or perhaps once it is completed – question unreasonable criteria. It's not confrontational. Quite the reverse – it's collaborative and advisory. Ask why; for example: 'Why do we need 15 years of experience on that specific task, Mr Client? Unless I'm missing something, it is routine. A switched-on candidate with three years' experience will have that nailed, won't they?'

Match the skills required to the job description; in other words, if the work outlined in the job description is mundane and low level, question why advanced skills or very high academic qualifications are required. Remember your role is to make this job 'fillable' – for the client, most importantly, but also for you. Work with your client to construct a job requirement that can be filled.

Test and stretch salary and benefits

This will inevitably be the time to test and stretch the salary and benefits offered. This is pivotal, and most recruiters either don't do it or don't go far enough. It's your job to know the *absolute ceiling* the client will go to for the right candidate. Many clients misunderstand this and think we are attempting to get more money out of them for some minuscule increase in our fee. That is not the case at all (and, frankly, it's a giggle-worthy idea). We are trying to understand the client's top benefits package to ensure no candidate slips through the net because of a misunderstanding of what the offer could be. Be prepared to explain exactly that to the client.

Once you've asked the client what the top salary is, they will nominate a figure, and you will say something as simple as, 'Mr Client, if I found an excellent candidate, would there be there any wriggle room? Can you go any higher for the right person?' That may extract an increase right there but, if the client confirms that the nominated figure is their absolute ceiling, you go to the next step: 'If I found the perfect candidate – who has all the skills and qualifications you seek as well as being a perfect cultural fit – but they wanted $100,000, are you instructing me not to refer that person to you?' (This is when the client has nominated $95,000 as the 'absolute top'.) Often the client will reply, 'Well, if the candidate is that good, I would go a little higher'. You lock that in as the ceiling 'for the right candidate', and you might even go one more time. Say it with a smile and explain that you are just trying to ensure accurate parameters.

If you don't do this, you will miss out on suitable candidates. You might have the most unfortunate experience of having one of the candidates you are working with get that same job through another recruiter. If that happens, it's because of one reason and one reason alone: a better recruiter has out-recruited you! Another recruiter managed the moment of truth better than you and has better influencing and advisory skills.

One more thing: suppose the client reaches their absolute salary ceiling and the salary offered is insufficient for the job described. In that case, you need to work with the client to redesign the candidate specification to create a set of experience, qualifications and skills that *do* match the offered salary. What is the point of leaving the client's office or exiting the video call to search for a candidate who you know will want more than is being offered? It will only end in frustration all around.

Explain and sell your process

Now it's time for you to explain and sell your process, which, again, is another massive skills gap among many recruiters. Many recruiters will say, 'Thank you for the job, Ms Client. I'll do my best and come back to you on Friday'. It's precisely that superficial type of explanation that leads clients to give roles to other recruiters or negotiate fees. They don't see what it is we do. A good recruiter will map out exactly what they plan to do to solve the client's problem, including interviewing, research, database review, advertising, headhunting and much more.

The metaphor I like to use in this situation is that you must 'sell the iceberg'. (I used the iceberg metaphor in a different context in chapter 9. So helpful, these icebergs!) If you look at an iceberg, you only see 10% of its total bulk: 90% is below the water. It is the same with how clients perceive the work done by recruitment consultancies: they see 10% of what we do, and most think that's *all* we do. Below the surface are a lot of people doing great work to find those ideal résumés. It would be best if you articulated all of this to the client, detailing the steps you will take, the resources you will employ, the time you will spend and the people involved. Sell the iceberg! You do a considerable amount. Tell them. Create value. Then, arrange a time to talk to them about your shortlist. Make it specific: 'I will contact you at 3 p.m. on Tuesday, Ms Client, to go through my shortlist with you. May I send you a calendar invite to lock that in, please?' You are leading this process – and you should be. You are the expert recruiter, after all.

Create candidate value

You should also take the time to create candidate value at this stage. Don't assume that the client is aware of talent shortages in the marketplace, and don't assume they know the mindset of candidates at a particular time. Tell anecdotes about similar jobs you have handled, explain the screening process and share the market dynamic at that time. You do this to coach the client on the urgency and responsiveness needed to capture the best candidates. Also, make it clear that the candidates you will present on your shortlist will be suitable for the job, will be briefed on the job, will be motivated to move and will be interested in the stated salary level. Create interest and urgency before you have even presented your shortlist.

Manage client expectations

Expanding on the previous point, you need to manage the client's expectations around timelines, candidate availability, potential notice periods and the possibility of counteroffers. You're not explicitly predicting these issues, but you are coaching the client on how they need to operate to capture the best talent. At all times, you couch this advice in terms that make it clear you are acting in their best interest and sharing your insights for their benefit.

Uncover key selling points

A great tip I learned when recruiting was to ask clients why *they* enjoy and appreciate working at their organisation. Why have they been there so long? This can often unearth fantastic selling points, such as training, mentoring or culture, which will be very helpful when you speak to candidates and position the job for them.

Coach the client on their process

It's essential at this stage to coach the client on their process. Who will conduct the interviews? How many interviews will there be? What will the timelines be between interviews? Are there psychological assessments or panel interviews? Who will do the reference-checking? Again, you need to know this information to advise the client on their process and manage the entire exercise to achieve the best outcome.

Sign off on your terms of business

Finally, make sure you then raise and agree your terms of business. Discuss them if necessary, and get a formal agreement signed as soon as possible. My biggest tip to you regarding terms of business is that, if you debate fees with your client, do it *before* you've done any work, not after you've already started – at that point, you have very little leverage and will likely need to concede.

Ask the three key questions!

Ask the three key questions covered in the next chapter!

*

Taking and qualifying the job order is a critical moment of truth in recruitment. The chances of you filling the job will rise exponentially if you can make the dynamic consultative and advisory. The client will be impressed, your relationship will evolve and you will spend your time working on 'fillable' roles, which will lead to improved results, enhanced self-esteem and, without being too dramatic, an extended recruitment career.

It's that important.

97 | Three genius qualifying questions

That previous chapter on qualifying the job order was heavy-duty, I admit – lots to absorb and lots to practice. But we are not finished with this crucial skill yet, so buckle up and come along for the ride.

Every recruiter must ask the three golden questions in this chapter *every* time they take a job order. Must. I cannot imagine a single circumstance in which you should do one minute of work for a client unless you have asked these questions and received a satisfactory reply.

Here they are. *Never* take an order again without asking these three questions. I mean it. It is that important.

1. 'How long has this role been open?'

How anyone could start work on a job without asking how long the role has been open stuns me. But, trust me, they do. It's like driving a bus blindfolded. Okay, it's not as dangerous, but it is nonsensical in the context of recruitment. How can you judge a client's sincerity in hiring? How can you assess whether the job or company is flawed in some way? What if the answer is 'Six months'? What does that imply? What if the answer is, 'My financial controller resigned this morning, and then I called you for help'? What opportunity does that suggest?

You must ask this question and then dig down into the reply, especially if the role has been open for a while. There is a reason. Maybe the salary is too low. Maybe the client is not really committed to hiring. Maybe the company has a poor employer brand. There is something. Why should you jump into that hot mess without finding out what it is? And, once you know what it is, work with the client to ensure the job is 'fillable' and they are committed to hiring before you start work.

2. 'What have you done so far to fill it?'

Again, do not lift a finger to help until you know what the client has already done to fill the role. What if the answer is, 'We have given it to four agencies, we are advertising on three job boards, we have two internal candidates and our TA team is working on it, too'? Is that a job you are likely to fill? Is that client giving you 'equity' (chapter 5)? You need to know the answer to this question to 'triage' the job (chapter 104) and to understand whether selling exclusivity or a retainer is possible in this case (chapters 99 to 103).

3. 'Could we get an offer by morning?'

The question of getting an offer by morning is a bit funkier but can uncover excellent information. The question should be verbalised this way:

> *'Ms Client, if I found a candidate that fits the brief perfectly with all the qualifications, experience and skills, as well as the cultural fit you seek, and I was to present their résumé to you this afternoon, could we get an offer by tomorrow morning?'*

You are not really expecting the client to hire within 24 hours, but the answer can be most revealing. Here are some of the actual answers I've had to this question:

> *'No, Greg, I can't do that because I am only interviewing the internal candidates next week.'*

> *'Sorry, Greg, that's not possible. The CEO hasn't signed off on this appointment, and I'm just testing the market.'*
>
> *'That's not likely, Greg, because we want to assess the response we get from our advertising campaign.'*

How does that make you feel about your commitment to filling this job? In all these and innumerable similar cases, I politely discussed with the client my willingness to start work on his role as soon as he had decided that the internal or job-board candidates were unsuitable or once he had sign-off from the CEO. And, remember, the client never *intended* to reveal this information. They are not going to volunteer it. So, you must ask, and then out it all comes. Alternatively, the client could have said something like, 'Well, I'm not sure we can move that fast, but I'll certainly interview first thing tomorrow'. An answer like that would give you much more confidence that this is a committed client who is prepared to move with urgency.

*

Of course, you can finesse these questions and ask them your way, but these are superb qualifying questions that will clarify how fillable the job is and what additional questions you need to ask to work out the triage level.

98 | Taking and filling the temp job

People often ask me what the difference is between a temp recruiter and a perm recruiter. The truth is that the core skills, competencies and attitudes are very similar. There are definitely nuanced differences, but the most significant contrast is in the core responsibility.

Here it is; read it a few times, please:

- A **perm** recruiter's job is to find candidates, shortlist them and present them to clients for interviews. Then, the *client* decides who gets the job.

- A **temp** recruiter's job is to find the candidates, shortlist them and present them to the client – the same deal. But the big difference is that the *recruiter* should decide who gets the job.

This shocks just about everybody in recruitment. Twenty-five years ago, it would have surprised nobody. But, unfortunately, the temporary placement process has increasingly come to resemble the permanent placement process, which includes shortlisting and interviews all being managed by the client.

I understand that, if it's an eight-month contract at a senior level, there is likely to be an interview. However, it makes no sense for clients to ask for a shortlist, résumés and to do interviews for a two-week payroll job. Unfortunately, many recruiters are going along with this farce, creating unnecessary work and delays and losing candidates.

When you take a temp order, the first thing you need to do is to understand the outcomes the client is expecting for that particular job. They are not the same as for a permanent job, where we need to know whether the role creates a career path for the selected candidate. Even customised cultural fit is less critical. With a temp job, you need to understand the tasks to be executed and the competencies required. Most temp recruiters can do this, and they can also manage the logistics, like the length of the assignment and even the rate discussion (chapter 55).

Where it often falls down is in gearing the client on what to expect in filling the temp job – the process.

Suppose it's a short-term temporary role with obvious responsibilities and outcomes. In that case, you need to tell the client you have candidates that will suit this and that you will call him back in 30 minutes with the right candidate, clarification on the rate and the start date. If the client asks for résumés and interviews, explain that the temp market is fluid and dynamic and the candidate you have in mind will get other offers today. Say, 'I stake my reputation on them doing the job well', or, 'The professional temp I have in mind has completed multiple assignments for me', and, 'If there is a problem with my temp, advise me within a day and I will replace them free of charge'.

Don't agree to a quasi-perm process for a short-term temp job.

Then, call back with one suitable candidate, sell them in and agree on the rate and start date. Yes, a résumé can follow, but you are not providing a shortlist and interviews for short-term temp assignments. This is in no one's interest. It is a first-class test of the temp recruiter's 'recruiter equity' (chapter 5).

Of course, the temp recruiter needs to be skilled at matching and know the candidates' capabilities. But, once you have filled your first temp job this way and all has gone well, you will not need to debate the process with this client again.

I know there are situations in which this cannot work, such as with preferred supplier agreements/lists (PSAs/PSLs), TAs and senior roles. I get it. But the fact is that most temp recruiters default to résumés and interviews. They should default to owning the solution and backing their judgement by nominating the temp to do the job.

It is so much more fun, never mind anything else.

99 | Why do clients multi-list jobs?

The key to successful selling is in understanding the buyer's motivations.

There are several reasons employers multi-list job orders and expect recruiters to compete on the same order with a 'winner takes all' outcome for the agency that fills the role. And I know these reasons because I have asked at least 1000 clients over the years why they behave this way.

Here is what I learned:

- Employers live under the erroneous belief that, by pitting several agencies against each other, they somehow 'keep us honest' and will get better service because we will compete more aggressively. It's an unsophisticated Darwinian 'survival of the fittest' theory that does immeasurable harm to all stakeholders.
- Employers want to give the job to several recruiters because they believe they will 'get a better spread of available candidates'.

- Employers perceive our profession as a résumé-storing warehouse. They have a very shallow understanding of what recruiters do to access candidates.
- They do not understand the cost of recruiting to themselves. As a result, they overestimate their ability to do a good job. After all, 'recruitment is not rocket science' (chapter 1), right? They do not calculate the cost of spending time on work that a good recruiter should do for them. After all, if they are working with four recruiters on the same job, *they* are doing all the screening and logistical management that one good recruiter should handle for them – and then, amusingly, having done a great deal of work, the client pays one agency a *full fee* anyway. It is better to get the agency to do the work but give them time to do it well!
- The final reason is the most damning; this time, it's not the client's fault. Clients multi-list job orders because most recruiters don't have the knowledge or the courage to tell them why it is *not* in their best interest to do so.

This goes to the heart of being a 'consultative' recruiter. Unless you want to be a transactional beast of burden, you must articulate why a client is doing themselves *tremendous harm* by getting recruiters to compete. Let recruiters compete for a client, no problems there – but *not* on the same job. That's just dumb business by all parties.

Let's look at the first two reasons in that list – because they are the 'big ones' most often verbalised by clients – and examine what happens when a client gives a brief to, say, four recruiters.

The first is that the client thinks they get better commitment from each recruiter. Quite the reverse is true. We must be prepared to look a client in the eye and say, 'What you are doing, Mr Client, is inviting us to approach your crucial hiring decision based on speed instead of who can do the best quality job'.

It's a compelling argument: most clients can see the logic when they think it through. Far from getting more commitment when clients get recruiters to compete, they get *less* commitment and *lower quality* service. At best, they can expect a flurry of activity as the recruiters first refer who immediately comes to mind. But when the real work needs to be done in terms of sourcing hard-to-find talent, the recruiters will drop off and focus on clients who *do* give them commitment. (As I write this, in a candidate-tight market, many of my recruitment-agency clients will not take orders in competition at all. Instead, they politely decline if the client will not work exclusively because they have limited candidates and resources, and they choose to work with clients who partner with them and show total commitment.)

Once this is explained to the client, the skilled recruiter will go on to ask the client for a 'window of opportunity' to handle the role exclusively so that they can give the role 100% of their commitment and bring all their resources to bear to ensure the best quality outcome.

The second reason is that they want to get a better spread of candidates. Again, you need the courage to face the client down on this (see chapter 19: 'Ten seconds of courage').

Ask the client what percentage of people who are suitable for their job they think are available to move jobs and are currently registered with any recruiter. The latest research suggests this number is less than 7%. Next, explain the active versus passive job market. Explain that you need time to find the right person and then coax them out of the job they may have now (which involves advertising, networking, social media, headhunting and database-searching). Passive candidates do not respond to advertisements.

The timeless reality is that most people are not looking for a new job, but a high percentage of those people are open to considering an opportunity if it is presented to them (chapter 62). That is where the value is: research, sourcing and candidate outreach and engagement. Do you think recruiters will do *all that* when they have no commitment from the client and are competing with multiple agencies? If the client gives the job to four recruiters, they are just fishing in the same limited active-job-seeker talent pond, and no recruiter will be committed enough to invest time searching beyond that pond.

A great recruiter has the credibility and the confidence to secure the role on a retained basis, or at least exclusively, so they have the time to put in place a full range of appropriate strategies to find the right person.

100 | The contingent multi-listing flaw

The concept of the contingent, multi-listed permanent job order is a fundamental flaw in agency recruitment. This dysfunction is so inherent in most recruiters' business models that they don't even understand the damage it's doing to their business and all the stakeholders. It leads many recruiters to end up doing great work without getting paid. And the irony is that it is clients who often drive sloppy behaviour from recruiters in our profession because recruiters are forced to work based on speed rather than quality.

Would you give a brain surgeon the job of operating on you because they can work the fastest? Would you get three accountants to race to prepare your tax return and only pay the winner? What about a hairdresser? House painter? Ludicrous, isn't it?

Bad outcomes are inevitable if you give a job order to three recruiters in a 'winner takes all' environment in which only one recruiter gets paid for their work. Then, of course, those recruiters are forced into racing to get résumés in front of the client; as a result, they take shortcuts, make mistakes, disrespect candidates and often undermine their self-esteem, confidence and results.

But it's not all the clients' fault. So many recruiters perpetuate this crazy situation by accepting job briefs in competition without a second thought. As a result, we have a dysfunctional situation in which clients call for quality service from recruiters and pay fees according to a 'bounty hunter' mentality.

There is no other reputable profession that works this way, and it's harming everybody.

It's bizarre that highly skilled professionals are willing to work incredibly hard and provide exceptional value to only get paid for 20% of their work. We need agency recruiters to have the confidence, the belief and the skill to explain to clients why it's in the *client's* best interests to give *one* recruiter the job and, therefore, the time to do quality work. Clients will get better service and more commitment, recruiters will have the time to do quality work and look after the candidates, and recruiters will get paid more often for their work.

Recruiters should work fewer, better-qualified jobs (chapter 96). Recruiters should work with fewer, more committed clients (chapter 95). Recruiters should see fewer candidates but look after them better (chapter 79).

Promise your customers more and deliver on it. Raise the entire ethos of what we do. Get paid more often (chapter 95). See your career and earnings grow and your mental health improve. See more of your kids. Play more sport. Take up that hobby you talk about so much but never actually do.

Changing the current dynamic really is that impactful.

So, how does a great recruiter change a client's mindset on this? How do you sell exclusivity?

Read on.

101 | Exclusivity is great for the recruiter

Before we discuss how to sell exclusivity, you must be clear about why it is in the *recruiter's* interests to move away from multi-listed, contingent recruitment and focus on securing client commitment on each order.

Time to focus on quality work

Working exclusively means knowing that no other agency will gazump you, allowing you time to focus on quality work. It reduces the requirement to compete on speed and résumé-racing and will enable you to approach your job methodically and with precision, creating excellent outcomes for everybody.

More repeat business

A welcome by-product of working exclusively is that you automatically secure repeat business. When you work with a client in partnership, they inevitably get a better outcome and have a more positive experience. They see no reason to go anywhere else and come to you willingly with the following order. They will forget other suppliers, have your name in their phone and assume the next order will also be an exclusive arrangement.

A more consultative relationship

The relationship becomes more consultative when you work exclusively or on a retained basis. The client is giving you 'recruiter equity' (chapter 5), and they are looking for you to solve the problem. The client will take your advice, return your calls and follow your lead. It's a seismic shift in the dynamic – for the better!

80% success instead of 80% failure

Perhaps the most apparent benefit of exclusivity is that you will be far more successful. I have seen countless recruiters fill one job out of five for years before learning to gain client commitment, and then that ratio shifts to four out of five. That's 80% success instead of 80% failure. Can you imagine the benefits of repeat business, quality service, improved self-esteem, company profitability and individual earnings?

Better candidate service

One misunderstood benefit of selling exclusivity is that candidates get better service. Recruiters inevitably work on fewer jobs and interview better-targeted candidates when they work exclusively, which means they have the time to get back to candidates and keep them informed (chapter 82).

Increased job satisfaction

The primary benefit of selling exclusivity is not more money, as significant as that is. Instead, it is increased job satisfaction, enhanced self-esteem, improved self-belief, improved relationships and a better reputation. Sure, all this plays into success and more money, but it also means recruiters enjoy their work more (chapter 120).

More money

Having said that it's not all about money, it is about money too. Exclusivity means you will fill more jobs, generate more income and make more commissions.

Longer careers

When recruiters shift from 80% failure in their work to 80% success, they are far more likely to stay connected and engaged with the recruitment profession for much longer.

Working exclusively saves careers.

102 | Exclusivity is great for the client

Not all job orders are equal (chapter 104). Many recruiters are working harder and harder for less return. Plenty of recruiters 'live comfortably' with the fact that they fill one job order out of every five they take.

We must work with clients who partner with us. We need time to do quality work. We need client commitment.

However, selling exclusivity starts with a clear understanding of why working with one quality recruiter on a specific brief is in the *client's* best interests. We need to understand those reasons, believe those reasons and be superbly articulate in explaining those reasons to a client who may be sceptical.

Be ready to engage your clients in this conversation with confidence and conviction. Then, make sure you can deliver when they give you a chance.

Here are 15 reasons why giving a high-quality recruiter exclusivity on each job is excellent for the client:

1. The client is getting the recruiter's total commitment to filling their vacant role. Let's not beat around the bush here. A client may think they get more effort from a recruiter when the role is in competition, but what really happens is a short burst of activity from the recruiter, then waning interest as they realise the client is not committed, and then they put their energy into clients who will work with them as partners.
2. The responsibility for success shifts to the recruiter. If the job is given to one recruiter, retained or exclusive, the recruiter *owns* the problem. The client can focus on whatever it is they do for a living. This is a compelling dynamic and is clearly in the client's

interests. The only sleepless nights I have had in recruitment came when I sold a retainer process to a client and, a week later, I had no candidates. Then, I interviewed candidates on Sunday morning over coffee. No BS. Do you think I (or you) would do that for clients who gave me orders in competition with four other recruiters?

3. The client is taking the focus off speed and back on quality. Why would you want your crucial hiring decision to be based on who can get candidates to you first? Would you hire a brain surgeon because they could do the job fastest? A house painter? A hairdresser? Exclusivity means the recruiter has time to do thorough work.
4. Exclusivity allows the recruiter to bring all their resources to the talent search: not just a quick database search but a thorough, detailed talent search, including networks, communities, searching, advertising and social media.
5. Working exclusively usually means there is time for the recruiter to take a detailed job order. The better the order, the better the match (chapter 96).
6. There is time for the recruiter to complete a comprehensive database search. The client gets the best, not the best we saw that week.
7. The recruiter has time to comb networks (including social media networks) and online resources and tap into the passive talent market (chapter 66).
8. If the recruiter works for a regional, national or global business, exclusivity allows them time to access candidates through their broader reach.
9. Exclusivity means more time to screen thoroughly, saving the clients time and frustration.
10. There is time for thorough candidate interviews, including a full assessment of skills, experience and attitude.
11. The recruiter is able to fully qualify the candidate in terms of start date and salary, once again saving the client much time and frustration.

12. The client saves time by dealing with *one* competent recruiter – no multiple agency briefings and contacts to deal with.
13. The client's confidentiality is preserved as the role is not being touted around town by five or six recruiters each speaking to nine or ten candidates about the position.
14. The client's brand and image are improved by using one recruiter because their job is not devalued in the eyes of candidates, who will be suspicious if multiple recruiters represent the position to them.
15. Exclusivity means avoiding the issue of different recruiters referring the same candidate to the same client, which can be very sordid.

This is an impressive and compelling list of reasons to work exclusively! Of course, you will rarely need to wheel all of them out to convince a client, but it's excellent to confidently enter a conversation believing that what you are selling is truly in the customer's best interests.

103 | Selling job-order exclusivity

It's much easier to sell exclusivity face to face. Success is based on credibility and trust. You can do it via videoconference, and maybe even via a phone call, but it is challenging to suggest this to a client for the first time digitally.

The pitch for explaining to the client why exclusivity is in their best interest happens after you've taken a qualified job order (chapter 96). You've listened carefully and understood the client's needs for this role. In addition, you've ascertained that no one else is recruiting for the position yet.

And then, it's time.

Selling exclusively starts with your demeanour, the confidence with which you deliver the solution to the client. You need to explain it as the way you always tackle roles of this nature. I would deliver it like this: 'Thank you for allowing me to work on this role for you, Ms Client. The way I'm going to solve this problem is…' Then, I would explain my entire process and include a request for a period of exclusivity so that I could apply 'all my resources and commit to focusing on this role'.

It is crucial to sell the entire process to the client. Sell the iceberg. They don't know about all the work you do behind the scenes to secure those two good, shortlisted candidates. You are asking the client to put this problem in your hands to solve. For the client to feel confident, they need to understand that you have a systematic, detailed, thorough approach. Explain precisely what you are going to do. What resources will you bring to bear and how will you go about it? You are building the client's confidence that you can deliver.

Then, wrap it up with one, two or, at the most, three benefits of exclusivity to the client (see the previous chapter). Of course, you will have already learned what's important to them. I found that the three big benefits typically were 'my full commitment', 'quality over speed' and me 'taking the recruiting headache off your plate and leaving it squarely on mine' – they were almost always successful in securing the exclusivity agreement.

A client who hasn't done this before may likely offer an objection. A common one is, 'Wouldn't I get a better candidate spread if I went to several recruiters?' Don't let this faze you; it's normal. You are educating the client on a better way of working. So, explain why time and commitment from you will result in a better shortlist than a superficial, rushed search by several agencies.

The final close is to ask for a specific period of exclusivity. You mustn't make the mistake of asking for an undefined or long period of exclusivity. That will scare the client and make them feel they are potentially locked into an unsuccessful solution.

If you're discussing a relatively junior role, you might say, 'Ms Client, this is how I'm going solve this for you. [Sell the iceberg.] To do this, I need five days' exclusivity, during which you leave the role with me so I can provide the commitment and resources required to solve this problem'. If you're discussing a more senior role that requires a complex and expansive search, such as a CFO, you might require six weeks' exclusivity or even longer.

Use terms like 'partnership' and 'dual commitment'. Try to communicate that you will do most of the work to get the best outcome, but you need a 'window of opportunity' (five days, in this case) to provide a quality solution.

Here are a few sentences I have used thousands of times that really clicked with clients – but, of course, you need to use them carefully and ensure they don't sound cocky, so they are best said with a smile:

> *'Ms Client, if you give a job order to four recruiters, you are, by definition, giving each recruiter 25% of your commitment. What makes you think that any one of those recruiters will give you more than 25% of their commitment in return?'*

Tie up the agreed time frame. Outline exactly what you are going to do. Confirm the client's role and responsibilities in return. Agree on a date and time for the next contact. Agree on the terms of business.

Then, get to work!

It's not just this order at stake. If you fill the role smoothly, the client will be converted to 'exclusivity' and you will not need to sell it again. Filling the first exclusive order could mean 50 exclusive orders over the lifetime of your relationship with this client.

104 | Job-order triage

A recruiter with twelve open orders does not spend one-twelfth of their time on each order. We understand that, right?

Not all job orders are created equal. Some are far more 'fillable' than others. Many are not even real: approval to hire has not been given, you are in competition with four other agencies or the process is just to benchmark already highly regarded internal candidates.

A savvy recruiter will 'triage' (prioritise) their job orders. To do that, you must know each job's 'fillability factor'. The fillability factor is the sum of the criteria by which you judge one job as more 'fillable' than another.

Every job should be continuously reviewed for fillability because it's a dynamic assessment. For example, today's 'low-fillability job' escalates overnight to 'high fillability' when the client raises the salary from $80,000 to $100,000 or drops the requirement for a degree in Mongolian throat singing.

This is not obvious enough to prevent thousands of recruiters worldwide from filling 2 jobs out of the 12 they are working instead of 8 or 9 because they do not home in on the low-hanging fruit.

Savvy recruiters understand that managing and massaging the client's expectations of the current hiring market is an essential skill in any market. That means coaching the client to work harder to appeal to candidates, and to finesse the job description and criteria in the first place.

And that skill requires credibility. The recruiter is an advisor, not a résumé donkey. That's your opportunity to work in partnership with your client to make the job 'fillable' so the client gets an outcome, the candidate gets the job and you get your just rewards.

You assess the fillability factor when you take the order and recalibrate through the order-filling process (see figure 18):

Figure 18: Assessing job-order fillability

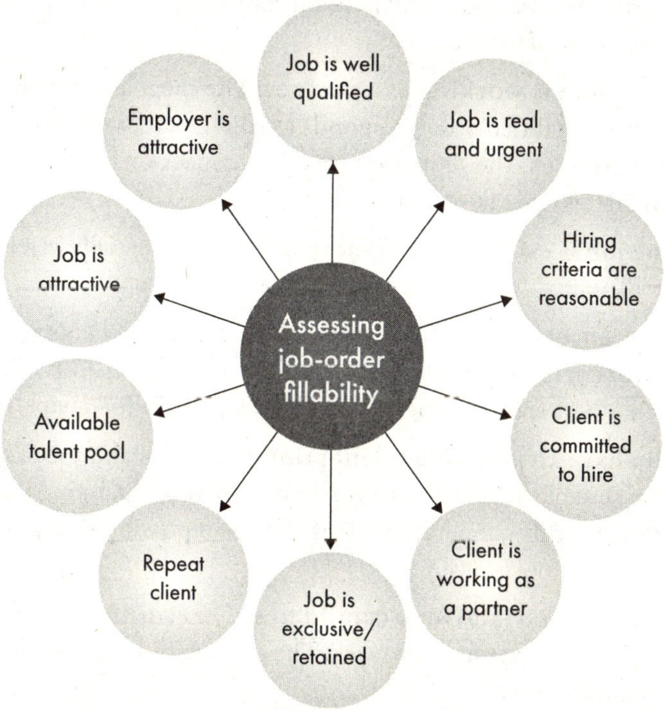

- **The job is well qualified:** The client has allowed you to ask critical questions, understand priorities and manage and massage the job and person specifications (chapter 96) to find a dynamic, fluid solution to a fast-changing market: 'Yes, Mr Client, you can't get what you got two years ago, and certainly not at that salary'. Also, you must have asked the 'three key questions' (chapter 97)!
- **The job is real and urgent:** A client in pain is excellent (chapter 38) – they will move with urgency and consider this hire to be a priority.
- **The hiring criteria are reasonable:** The aforementioned degree in Mongolian throat singing is not a requirement, and nor is some arbitrary '15 years of experience'. You know the drill.
- **The client is committed to hiring:** You have tested and asked the right questions, not to mention confirmed that they actually have approval to hire.
- **The client is working as a partner:** The client allows you to take a qualified order, responds to your emails, takes your calls to discuss the shortlist, provides feedback on interviewed candidates and takes your advice!
- **The job is exclusive or retained:** This exponentially increases its 'fillability' (see the previous four chapters).
- **You're working with a repeat client:** Ongoing clients tend to work in tandem with you. You both have a track record with each other. Trust escalates, along with job fillability (chapter 93).
- **You have an available talent pool:** You can fill this job. You have suitable candidates, or you know where you can find them. (Even a highly cooperative client may be impossible to assist if the talent pool is dire.)
- **The job is attractive to candidates:** The actual role. The duties. The learning. The tasks. The mentorship. The career potential.

- **The employer is attractive to candidates:** Of course, 'fillability' explodes if you are working with a hot company in a fabulous location with a strong employee value propositon, excellent benefits, a track record of fairness, equity and loyalty to staff and a shiny employer brand. Offers will be accepted, and that is when we get paid.

Constantly triage and evaluate your orders for fillability. Of course, you will not fill every order, but your hit rate will increase exponentially if you develop the skills to assess fillability in real time and spend most of your time on the most fillable jobs.

105 | Pitching the shortlist

I talk elsewhere in this book about the critical importance of 'volume of activity' in recruitment success (chapter 23). I homed in on candidate-client interviews as the key metric for increasing placement numbers (chapter 30). Yet, many recruiters concede the opportunity to increase the conversion of submitted candidates to interviews, reducing the likelihood of consistent success. In addition, many recruiters ignore my advice on connectivity and consultation (chapters 24 and 25), attach their shortlisted candidates to an email, send them off to a client and… hope.

A quality recruiter does not leave the possibility of interviews to chance or client whim. They understand that submitting the shortlist is a 'moment of truth' and will set up a time to talk the client through the shortlisted candidates. Yes, it's understood that résumés will be sent, but the recruiter has just interviewed these candidates and is perfectly positioned to advise the client on their strengths, weaknesses and overall suitability.

I am very aware that there are situations in which this is not possible. With PSAs/PSLs and RPO, speaking to the actual client is nigh on impossible. However, the issue is that many recruiters default to just sending résumés. You need to consistently move clients to work in this consultative fashion, as everyone gets better outcomes this way.

Presenting the shortlist – the recruiter mindset

As with almost every instance of interpersonal communication, mindset and confidence play a huge role in the outcome. Many recruiters default to increasing the volume of résumés submitted to clients to compensate for their lack of ability to manage the 'presentation' moment of truth. The mindset of a skilful recruiter is 'quality over quantity'. They want quantity, too, but never at the expense of an appropriate match. One candidate might be superior to the other two on the recruiter's shortlist, but the recruiter will work hard to get all three suitable candidates interviews. The number of times my least preferred candidate was offered the job over the candidate I was sure would get the offer are too many to count!

The mindset starts with the recruiter believing they are not a keyword-matching résumé-spammer. They know that their shortlisted candidates fit the brief. They understand that they bring value and that they consult in this process. They believe they have insights to offer that may not be on the résumé and can advise the client accordingly. They also believe in their value and want to get paid more often for their work. They know that more client-candidate interviews result in more placements, which means more fun and money (chapter 120). For these reasons, they want to present the candidates face to face or over the phone and get client agreement on interviews, and then send the résumés as backup collateral.

Plan your call. What are the client's 'hot buttons' regarding this role? What does the candidate have that the client seeks? What can the candidate bring that makes the client's life easier? Focus on these points.

How to present shortlisted candidates

Before you speak to your client about the candidates on your shortlist, remind yourself of your goal: *to get your preferred candidates interviews*. That's it. So, make sure you only present candidates who fit the brief. For this conversation, face to face is best; but, if that's not possible, a videoconference or phone call works well.

Here is a big tip: pre-empt the conversation by clarifying that you have 'two ideal candidates' and are calling to 'set up interview times'.

Tell the client that you will first highlight why the candidates are suitable, then send follow-up résumés. But, first, can we find an ideal time for the client to interview? So, the reason for the call is set early.

Don't oversell your candidates. Be authentic and transparent about shortcomings or weaknesses, but have explanations and the counterbalancing strengths close at hand. Only highlight the two to five competencies, skills or qualifications you know the client wants to hear. Don't start at the top of the candidate's résumé and simply read all the way through: you will lose the client quickly and they will ask you to send the résumés.

Less is more when selling the candidate shortlist.

The skill is to match the candidates crisply and convincingly to the job's key must-haves – another reason taking a qualified job order is so critical (chapter 96). Anticipate any client objections, and construct and rehearse your arguments to overcome them. If you need to get the decision over the line, have one big 'wow' factor up your sleeve: a massive and relevant achievement, a compelling quote from a referee or a relevant and exceptional qualification. Once you have presented your candidates and proven that they fit the brief, move the client towards an agreement to interview. This is the 'presenting shortlist close':

> *'So, Ms Client, X is an exceptional candidate and is actively on the market, and we do not want to lose her to a competitor. She fits the criteria, I have prepped her for your role and she is excited to meet you. You mentioned next Tuesday works for you. How does 9 a.m. suit you to meet X?'*

The rationale for this entire conversation is that you have understood the brief and interviewed the candidates, and you know the match; therefore, you are the best person to explain it. The résumés will be sent and the client can dig into more detail later, but these are the best candidates on the market. They are considering other options, and so we need to set up the interviews *now* to keep them engaged.

However, even the best shortlist presenters sometimes hear the fateful words, 'They sound interesting. Can you please send me the résumé so I can review it?'

Dive into the next chapter for tactics on how to respond.

106 | 'Send me the résumé'

Many recruiters will buckle and comply if the client says, 'send me the résumés'.

The problem with that is you haven't achieved your goal, which is to set up the interviews, and there is an increased chance of your candidates going rogue and dropping off. It also teaches the client that you don't have confidence in your shortlist or your process and that you need the client to assess and screen the shortlist before agreeing to interview. That is a poor outcome: you lack 'recruiter equity'.

If the client says, 'Send me the résumé', stay calm and ensure that you respond along the lines of these two examples, which worked exceptionally well for me:

> *'Of course, I will send you the résumés well before the interview, Mr Client. However, these candidates are the best on the market and in demand. What is there on the résumé, Mr Client, that I cannot tell you in far more detail now? Getting these candidates locked in is our immediate goal.'*

Or:

> *'I will send you a résumé, Mr Client, in due course. However, she fits your role well and is worth your meeting very soon. So, we should lock that in. In fact, I will stake my reputation on the fact that you will not waste your time seeing her. She is a prime candidate and I want you to secure seeing her before she goes to one of your competitors.'*

You only do this if you know your candidates are high calibre. Everything said must be true. You are acting in the client's interests because they *do* risk losing the candidates.

107 | What it means if a client rejects your shortlist

Let me share a familiar tale.

You send a client a shortlist of three candidates for a specific job order. By your estimation, they are all worthy of close consideration. They should be interviewed.

The client does not embrace your 'shortlist pitch' (chapter 105) – or, more likely, you do not have the credibility or influencing skills to get them to hear it in the first place (chapter 24).

You wait for the client to respond to your shortlist. When they do, it is in the form of a short note saying, 'We will interview Lee, but not the other two candidates. They are too light on experience.'

That's it. No further correspondence will be entered into.

I see recruiters celebrating in the face of this scenario. 'I got an interview', is the cry.

Do you accept that your client rejects candidates you present on your shortlist? This is no celebration moment. You have *failed*. You lack 'recruiter equity'.

Recruiter equity is the trust, buy-in and belief your clients have in your ability and judgement. It combines your experience and knowledge, giving you the power to advise clients and truly impact the outcomes of your interaction with them (chapter 5). Most recruiters lack this altogether. The client's rejection of their advice and candidates when they present a shortlist for a permanent brief is a classic example of how this can be exposed.

If a client rejects or will not interview any of your shortlisted candidates, it can mean only one of two things:

1. You misunderstood the brief. You got it wrong.
2. The client does not trust your judgement.

It can mean *nothing* else.

Both of those outcomes are a disaster. They mean you did not achieve equity in the relationship with this client.

Equity means ownership, or a share of ownership: in this case, joint ownership of the problem *and the solution*. You are the expert. In your judgement, these candidates fit the brief. However, once the client rejects your considered referrals, it illustrates that you are not trusted. The client is taking ownership of the solution.

You have become a transactional referrer of résumés.

I understand it's hard. I know clients often try to dominate or will not communicate through the process. I know TA often gets in the way (chapter 60). But that's no reason for you to concede your role as an objective expert advisor.

Building recruiter equity starts with taking the job order, at which point you will map out your process and sell the quality of your screening and matching. It continues with the 'shortlist pitch', where you will overcome objectives and 'sell your candidate in' confidently and authentically. Finally, it requires you to challenge the client on their decision to reject your shortlist. You recommend those candidates for a reason. Stand by those reasons.

Tell the client you stake your reputation on these candidates. They are worth seeing. (Of course, this assumes you really believe in your shortlist and have not padded it!)

If you do this well, the short-term reward will be that the client sees your candidates for this role. But, more importantly, the client learns to respect your belief in your process and recommendations and is unlikely to question future referrals. Instead, the client will perceive you differently and take you more seriously, and the dynamic will change forever – infinitely for the better.

108 | Gearing the client for the interview

While some recruiters invest time in preparing candidates for the interview with the client (chapter 85), it's much less common for recruiters to counsel and coach the *client* on creating a desirable outcome. This is a mistake because many clients have only cursory interviewing skills, and every recruiter knows how a poor client interview can turn off good candidates.

So, as with every 'moment of truth', a great recruiter has a plan to 'gear' or prepare the client to ensure the best possible outcome.

Firstly, before discussing the candidates being interviewed, check with the client if there have been any changes since the last time you spoke. Making assumptions in recruitment can be a disaster (chapter 27). Have the criteria changed? Have new candidates from another source entered the frame?

Then, contextualise the screening and selection process. You need to create an image for your client of the candidates they are about to interview as the 'cream of the crop'. It is best if you hint at the fact that the client is in competition to secure these candidates, which is always true. Without using these words, your advice is that the client needs to be 'on their game' because the candidate is assessing the employer as much as the other way around.

Remind the client that candidates have a choice. If they are interviewing elsewhere, don't be afraid to mention that.

And now, the big one: coach the client on specific 'candidate sell' points. In other words, communicate to the client the candidate's key objectives, and help the client plan to cover these as positively and as thoroughly as possible: 'Here are three things the candidate is looking for. It will help if you cover these during the discussion. Feel free to note them down'.

Examples might include:

- learning and mentoring environment
- some flexibility in work arrangements, including two days a week working from home
- exposure to new technology, 'especially the XYZ system that your company runs'.

Coaching the client on the candidate's salary goals is also essential. If necessary, justify those goals and give examples. Counsel the client on the timing of the salary and benefits conversation.

Agree on the candidate feedback timeline and manage the client's expectations.

Set a time for the client to discuss candidate feedback after the interview with you. Explain how critically important this is to keep momentum in the hiring process.

Finally, pre-close the client on the next steps, which might include second interviews, a reference-check process or psychological testing. Confirming with the client prior to the interview what will happen after the interview ensures that you're not met with any surprises.

Gearing the client for the candidate interview is a 'moment of truth'. Prepare and practice the small influencing dynamics that might give you a 5% advantage.

That might be all you need to create the right outcome.

109 | Debriefing the client after the interview

Your candidate has been for an interview and it's time now to debrief with the client. Please remember that these client moments of truth are happening in parallel with candidate moments of truth, and you will also debrief the candidates your client has interviewed (chapter 86).

Once again, avoid making assumptions and start the conversation by checking in with the client and asking if any changes have occurred.

It's imperative to get the client's feedback first before revealing to the client what the candidate thought. It's common for the client to ask you what the candidate thought of the interview, so you should get in early by asking an open-ended question like, 'How did the meeting with the candidate go from your point of view?'

Take notes on what the client says because you will use these points in follow-up conversations with the client and the candidate. Don't wing it. Try to stay calm and somewhat impassive regardless of whether the client is highly enthusiastic or negative about the interview. You want to maintain your status as a professional advisor, not a self-interested bystander.

Sometimes the client will wax lyrical about the interview, and you just let them talk. Sometimes it's like getting blood from a stone. You need to drill down either way. Can the candidate do the job under consideration? It's obvious, but getting the client to say this is a big step forward. Do they have the technical skills required? Were any strengths and weaknesses identified during the meeting?

Then, explore cultural fit. Will the candidate fit into the team? Do you have any comments on their interpersonal skills?

Explore whether the client feels they can personally relate to the candidate. Did they build some rapport? Will the candidate respond to the client's management style?

Getting the client to verbalise why this candidate suits the role and the environment is a compelling dynamic.

If the feedback is generally positive, subtly reinforce what the client says. For example, mention that you also found the candidate very friendly and collaborative throughout the process, or that a referee said something similar to the client's feelings. Don't overdo this, but gentle affirmation can be compelling. It must be true. Great recruiters do not lie.

Ask how long the meeting lasted and how it ended. How did the client leave things with the candidate, and what did the candidate say at the end of the meeting? Did the candidate express an interest in the role? How were things left? What is the next step?

Ask your client whether salary and benefits were raised, who raised them and how the conversation went.

Now, it's time to move towards a pre-close. Ask the client whether anything else is needed before we can move to the offer stage. This is a powerful question; it sometimes moves things forward very fast, either directly to an offer (occasionally) or to the client saying the candidate is a definite 'no go'. Either outcome is good because it provides clarity. At the very least, this will lead to a conversation about a second interview, reference-checking or a need for additional candidates to consider.

Thank the client and, depending on what was discussed, list and agree on the next steps you will be taking to move things forward.

110 | What if the interview goes badly?

Sometimes the interview won't go well. It is going to happen.

Of course, that is disappointing and possibly damaging to your relationship with the client. Still, it would be best if you turned it into an opportunity to recalibrate and get things back on track.

The interview usually goes badly for one of three reasons:

- The candidate was off form or had lost interest.
- You misjudged the candidate's skills and personality fit for the role.
- The client changed their mind or defined the job incorrectly in the first place.

It's also true that, on some occasions, the client does a shocking job of running the interview, but they are very unlikely to acknowledge that.

If the client is expressing negativity about the interview, don't leap into justification mode or try to sweep things under the carpet. This is your opportunity to identify exactly what went wrong. If a candidate was weak in certain areas where you thought they were strong, that's important news for you to consider moving forward.

Usually, this situation is an excellent opportunity to recalibrate the role's requirements. Often the candidate interviewing process prompts the client to clarify what they are really looking for. This can irritate the recruiter as it feels like a moving target, but see it as a chance to refine and reset.

If necessary, reconstruct the job description and the person specification based on the client's feedback. Once you've done that, move fast to sell the client a new recruitment plan based on the reconstructed job description, and set up a process for a new sourcing strategy or a fresh shortlist.

Recruitment is not an exact science. People behave in interviews in ways you cannot predict. Both clients and candidates can change their minds midstream, and the recruiters who win in the end are agile and nimble enough to recalibrate, provide new advice and then move forward fast.

111 | Negotiating the job offer

Throughout the interview process, you will have been pre-closing the client on their preferred candidate, or perhaps the top two candidates. This means asking questions such as, 'What more will we need to do or know, Mr Client, before you could make an offer?' You will have discussed salary after the first and second interviews, just as you will have had equivalent conversations on the candidate side. As a result, you will calibrate the client's salary expectations against what you know the candidate will accept. This is a core recruitment consulting skill and a pivotal 'moment of truth'. I've seen many recruiters celebrating an offer that, on questioning, they admit they think is unlikely to be accepted at the offered salary level.

This is precisely where recruiters with influencing and consultative skills shine. Please don't wait until the client nominates their offer amount and try to convince them to raise it. Instead, negotiate an appropriate potential salary amount before an offer is made.

When the client indicates they want to make an offer to your candidate, be pleased and optimistic, but remain calm. Overexcitement will unsettle the client because it sounds as though you are desperate.

On the other hand, reinforce the correct decision you believe your client is making. For example, 'This is a good appointment, Ms Client. This candidate is exceptional and fulfils all requirements for the role, and I'm sure they will make an outstanding addition to your team'.

In a considered way, work through all the details of the offer – for example, the salary, bonus, superannuation and pension allowance – and finalise information on all benefits and leave entitlements. Consider what a candidate will need to know before they can say yes to the offer.

Despite the pre-closing you've done on salary throughout the process, it's not uncommon for the client to surprise you by making an offer lower than you know your candidate is expecting. Therefore, you must stand your ground and act as a trusted advisor. Making an offer to the candidate at a lower level than they're expecting or are likely to accept will not provoke a favourable outcome. At best, it will lead to an unseemly haggle; more likely, it will lead to an offer rejection.

If the salary is too low, you need to negotiate with the client before making the offer to the candidate. It shouldn't surprise the client because you will have been advising the client of the appropriate salary level all the way through. However, clients can be fond of making a last-minute low-ball offer, and you are acting in *their* interests if you push back, consult with them and get the offer up to a number that the candidate is likely to accept before making your initial offer.

Clarify the preferred start date, which, of course, you've been negotiating with the candidate as well. Build in flexibility if you can. For example, 'Ms Client, we will aim for 24 March as the start date, but if it must be a week later, can that work, too?'

Discuss the potential induction process with the client so you can communicate this to the candidate. This will increase the candidate's confidence level and the likelihood of a positive response to your offer.

Agree that the client will send the letter of offer or employment contract to you and that you will work through it with the candidate. Managing this process is essential. If you allow the client and the candidates to deal directly over this, minor issues can flare up and lead to a negative outcome.

Map out the process going forward, including the timing of receiving the contract or offer letter, your anticipated feedback from the candidate and any other details that will keep things running smoothly.

112 | Post-acceptance client management

You've gained acceptance of your job offer from the candidate and tied up all the details with your client. Finally, the start date has been agreed upon and the contract is signed.

Time to celebrate? Perhaps crack out a little placement dance?

Not yet. Feel good, certainly, but there is work still to be done. Just as you need to closely manage the candidate (chapters 89 and 90), you must keep close to your client between the offer being accepted and the candidate starting the new role.

Firstly, ensure that the client delivers on all their commitments to the candidate – preparing and sending the contract letter, first and foremost, but other documentation or procedural matters must also be handled promptly and efficiently. You do not want your candidate to find any reason to reconsider their acceptance, especially as they are likely to be still receiving offers or opportunities from other sources.

Recently, I found that an excellent strategy is to work with your client to broker engagement with the candidate before their start date. This could include arranging a casual coffee meeting with prospective new co-workers, signing them up for the company newsletter or organising a tour of the facilities. This is wise because it shifts the candidate's engagement to the new employer and makes the new job feel very real, making the candidate less likely to reconsider or rescind their acceptance of the offer.

113 | Are you 'client fit' or 'client flabby'?

Recruitment became more 'remote' because of COVID-19. There was no alternative. But now, for many recruiters, it remains that way because, *'It suits me!'* (chapter 25).

In the current (at the time of writing) candidate-tight market, many recruiters have developed a one-sided skill set focusing only on candidate activities. As a result, we have an unhealthy situation where clients are being ignored or, at best, under-serviced. A generation of recruiters is evolving who can't even find their 'BD muscle', let alone flex it.

Even in 'normal' times, there is a tendency to be complacent about client relationships. I bet you have seen and heard it, too:

- 'That's my client.'
- 'Oh, don't worry about that client. She only uses me.'
- 'I get all their work.'
- 'I don't need to take this job in person. I know this client well and he is 100% loyal to me.'

Sound familiar?

No matter the vagaries of the market, it is always time to get 'client fit'. That means honing every aspect of the client relationship and keeping it oiled, supple, vigorous and healthy.

Take this little quiz to check your 'client fitness' (and note that I am talking about good, regular clients, not one-hit wonders or prospects):

1. Have you seen your client contact face to face in the last three months?
2. Do you see that person at least four times a year?
3. Do you take every permanent or search order in person (or at least via videoconference) if possible?
4. Have you met every line manager in the client business who could potentially be a hiring manager for you?
5. Have you met your client's boss?

6. If your client is a line manager, have you asked to meet the HR/ Talent team, gone to see them and asked, 'What can I do to make your job easier?' (Lots more information on this crucial relationship can be found in chapter 60.)
7. Have you studied your clients' websites closely recently?
8. Do you subscribe to your client's blog, LinkedIn page, news-letters, Instagram, Twitter feed and business Facebook page?
9. Have you tried, and do you try to use, your client's products and services?
10. Are you connected to every client on LinkedIn? (Laugh not, here is the truth: most recruiters are *not*.)
11. Do you massage your clients' 'social ego' by sharing their LinkedIn updates, commenting on their blog and 'liking' their (work) Facebook page?
12. Have you asked, 'What is there about my service that I could do better, or what could I add?'
13. Have you found a good reason to get your client into your office (e.g. a quick sandwich lunch in the board room to meet your CEO)?
14. Have you built up your recruitment 'chat' (chapters 44 and 45) and developed a series of insights, advice and market intel that you can tailor to any client and use to differentiate yourself from the inbox-spamming, résumé-flicking, transactional recruiting hacks? (Ouch!)
15. Have you followed up with every placement you have ever made at your client company, and do you do so every six months?
16. Suppose you have temps on long-term contracts at your client's site. Do you 'make yourself big' by going to see them, handing out holiday gifts, running onsite training, bringing in morning tea, celebrating temp longevity and generally making sure you are 'visible'?
17. Do you know who your clients' clients are? And do you know lots about them?
18. Do you keep up to speed with your clients' professions or industries, especially their competitors, and know the key issues and trends?

19. Have you done an annual or biannual 'business review' with your client – like a mini-performance review, in which your work is summarised and assessed and communication occurs to improve the relationship?
20. Do you know each client's three most significant staffing/HR issues, and do you discuss them often to assist?
21. Do you keep up to date with each client's benefits structure, vacation allowance, social media policy, flexible work policy, salary review schedule and any other factors that could influence the interest of a future hire?
22. Do you regularly provide your clients with value-adds that you don't charge for, like salary surveys, events, webinars and market updates?
23. Have you agreed to 'standing briefs' with your client? These are mapped out and defined skill sets that your client is always interested in, even if there is no specific role available. Most companies are open to hearing about 'that special someone'. You need to know who that is and float them in (chapter 48).
24. Are your most current business terms up to date and signed off by the client? Or are you still operating off the business terms they signed in 2009?
25. Have you introduced your clients to another recruiter on your team, or your manager, so that clients 'feel the love' and know they can call on someone else if you are out or away?
26. Have you specifically thanked your client for their business, maybe over lunch, with a small gift, or even just with a visit with the sole purpose of thanking them?

Okay, are you feeling exhausted from your fitness test? Score yourself now:

- **0–13:** You are unfit. You are totally out of shape and unworthy of keeping your clients. Commit to getting fit or accept that you will die a young recruiting death!
- **14–18:** Lift your game. You have some things right but you have a long way to go.

- **19–22:** You are a 'client fit' amateur athlete. You're working hard and looking pretty good, but you still have not yet nailed it.
- **23–26:** You are a superbly honed, 'client fit', Olympic-level superstar. Nice job!

114 | Signs your clients don't rate you

You call them 'clients' and you think they see you as a business partner. But what do they think of you? More to the point, do they *ever* think of you?

I know I am hammering this point but seeing how shallow so many recruiter–client relationships are distresses me. So much angst stems from that.

Take this quick test and tick each statement that does *not* apply to you, then add up your 'client cred' score:

1. Your clients won't meet you to provide a new job brief. It's emailed or given over the phone, or maybe it's just a few lines in an email. In the post-COVID-19 world, even a Zoom meeting is too hard for them. 'Just send me candidates' is the message.
2. They give you jobs in competition with other agencies. And you are not even first.
3. When you eventually arrange a meeting or a videoconference, they keep you waiting or even stand you up altogether.
4. They don't return your calls, even though the job was 'really, really urgent'.
5. They routinely don't interview the candidates you present.
6. They won't give you sound reasons for rejecting candidates they have declined to interview.
7. They demand urgency from you every step of the way but are slow to come back to you in a timely fashion themselves.
8. They don't give you feedback on the candidates they interview from you.
9. They arrange second interviews with preferred candidates directly.

10. They ignore your advice on salary and conditions, flexibility, the recruitment process and… pretty much everything, actually!
11. They raise issues and information critical to the candidate's hire (that they have never told you) with the candidate directly.
12. They make an offer directly to your candidate without going through you or telling you.
13. They haggle your fee after the deal is done.
14. They offer perm jobs to your temps without telling you.
15. They take forever to pay your invoice, despite promises that they are 'following up right now and it will be paid today'.

Score yourself here:

- **0–7:** You don't have clients, you have tyre-kickers.
- **8–11:** More work is needed to elevate your status to 'trusted advisor'.
- **12–15:** Nice job! Your clients are treating you as a partner.

115 | Fire unprofitable clients

In most of the recruitment businesses I have run, and many I now advise, 70% of the business comes from the top 20% of clients. As a result, over 50% of your gross profit (net fee income, or NFI) will often be generated from fewer than ten client companies. Even on an individual consultant desk, you will find that a high proportion of fees will come from three to five clients.

Maybe you know this already. So, why spread your marketing dollars, personal delivery and business development efforts across all clients and prospects equally? You will not thrive by spreading yourself so thin. It's transactional. It's superficial. It's dangerous for your financial health. So, what you want to focus on now is 'share of wallet', not market share.

Target long-term clients with fee-generation growth potential. Work with companies that will use your services regularly; partner with growing companies. The best client is a client that needs all or most of your service offerings.

We must understand that the best business is often the hardest to win but the most profitable once you have it. Therefore, we must invest time, resources and brainpower into developing, nurturing and retaining these key clients.

The most significant stress in recruitment comes from working with dickheads. Not colleagues – although that can happen, too – but irrational, uncooperative, unethical clients.

Here is the irony: as recruiters push ever harder to win business, they become more superficial in their work, more transactional in their approach and less discerning about who they do business with. Why? Why work with clients who treat you like mud and jerk you around consistently? It's crazy! In an environment of chronic and sustained talent shortages, you need to head in the other direction!

I get resistance to this from some recruiters. They say the transactional model is 'just the way the market is'. They acknowledge it is mud against the wall but claim it's what clients want, and to win you need to throw more dirt. If that is true, God save us all.

However, thankfully, it is not. These recruiters have caved. They have capitulated to the transactional-recruiting tsunami and joined the shallow mob of hard-selling, résumé-pumping, cold-calling, candidate-burning, price-cutting recruiters willing to play that dirty, cheap game.

I don't buy it. There is a market for quality recruiting. So, you must be brave enough to fire those clients who won't work with you and give more time to suitable clients who want a partnership.

Who exactly should you fire as a client? Start with the following:

- Clients who jerk you around with sketchy job specs, demand the world from you and give nothing in return
- Clients who pull jobs halfway through assignments or fail to return your calls
- Clients who use three other agencies in competition with you (on the same job)
- Inflexible clients who take no advice and ignore your feedback
- Clients who consistently try to negotiate fees, especially after you have gone to the ends of the earth to fill their job

- Clients who see no value in service or quality but only want to talk about price
- Clients who show no respect for what you do or say, abuse your guarantee and refuse to pay the bill in the end.

You recognise your client here, don't you? You are smiling as you read this! Yet you still work with these people. Why? They absorb your time and torpedo your self-esteem. They take your focus away from where it should be: on your targeted clients and prospects who can offer you long-term, sustainable, profitable business.

116 | How to fire a deadbeat client

Before you sit a deadbeat client down for a good firing, you must decide whether there are any circumstances in which you *would* do business with this client again. Usually, that is the case. That being so, it's crucial to leave the communication door open for the relationship to be picked up again if the circumstances are right.

Occasionally, when a client has been obnoxious or dishonest, you may decide never to do business with them again. (It's a liberating feeling, I promise!) In this case, you can kill the relationship there and then. However, still do it politely. Nobody needs extra enemies.

Here are my steps to firing a deadbeat client:

1. If possible, sit down with your client face to face. If that's not possible, then over videoconference or the phone is the next best thing. Email? That never works. It always gets ugly. Don't go there.
2. Remember to use a collaborative tone of voice. Avoid revealing any anger, bitterness, hate or frustration you really feel. Be polite. Be respectful.
3. Then, it's your time to explain to the client that you really do want to work with them and you do want to help them acquire great talent, but the status quo does not allow you to do that.
4. Next, go over the prevailing market conditions and the difficulties in finding talent, and spell out everything you will

do to assist this client in getting what they need. Explain your process, quality commitments and everything else that makes up your service, and what you need to do to get the client's desired results. This might seem strange, as you are about to sever the relationship, but you are laying the path for the client to be rehabilitated – either during this conversation (unlikely) or sometime in the future when they realise they really do need your help (slightly more likely).

5. Follow this by shifting the conversation to what the client needs to do to make the partnership work for their benefit. Do you see what this does? 'I want to help you. This is what I can do to help you. However, this is what *you* need to do to help you.'
6. Then say, 'So, this is how we can get the result you want. Can you commit to working this way with me?' (This essentially says, 'It's my way or the highway', but nicely.)
7. If the answer to that question is a flat 'no', be upfront: 'Working the way we currently do, Mr Client, does not achieve the results you or I want. But, of course, it is your choice how you work, so when you are ready to come back and work with me in a partnership model, as I have described today, I will be delighted to start working with you again'.

Bang! That is a fired client! But the door is still open, and no one has been rude or insulted or humiliated. Remain polite and collaborative, and say you want his business – but on specific terms.

Truthfully, how often does the client 'come back into the fold' once fired?

About one time in five is my experience.

PART VI

YOUR RECRUITMENT CAREER

Companies around the world spent US$550 billion on staffing and recruitment agency fees in the year I wrote this book (2022), and it was growing at 14% a year at that time.

In my five decades in this profession, I have seen it evolve and mature, and I now believe it offers a real career path for the right people.

The National College of Ireland now offers a BA (Honours) in Recruitment Practice. (*The Savage Truth*, my first book, is mandatory reading for that degree, I am delighted to report.)

Deakin University in Australia is taking registrations (at the time of writing) for the 2023 intake of the new Graduate Certificate of Recruitment and Talent Acquisition. The minimum admission requirements are a bachelor's degree or higher, two years of relevant work experience in recruitment or the recruitment industry, or evidence of academic capability judged to be equivalent.

These are tangible signs of the 'professionalisation' of recruitment and how it is now being recognised as a legitimate career choice.

The quality of training and development within recruitment companies continues to evolve. You can follow a path of specialist recruiting excellence, which is terrific for many. My friend Graham Whelan is an excellent example of that (chapter 2). You can move into management and leadership, or focus on business development, or support functions like marketing or learning and development. The opportunity to start your own business is very real if you have the right temperament, experience and plan.

You will need the attitudes and mindset I spelled out in Part I to thrive as a recruiter long-term, and you will also need to deliver the behaviours and activities covered in Part II to have a fruitful recruiting career.

People who succeed in recruitment come from various backgrounds and have widely disparate personalities, but the core competencies are almost always universal, I have found.

Let's explore that.

117 | You own your career

Many people are advised to look for a company that 'provides a career'. Often, I hear candidates say they want to leave a job because their current employer is not 'looking after my career'.

Sure, it's essential to work for a company where you can thrive and which offers opportunities, but you must, above all, understand this: the person who will always care most about your career is *you*!

The biggest mistake you can make in your work life is to leave your career to your employer or anyone else. Instead, you must work at your career goal, plan it and drive it where you want it to go. Don't outsource your career!

Ponder this: success in your career will never be just a matter of qualifications or skills. It will always be a matter of *motivation*.

As I write these lines, there is a global skills shortage. That will change, but getting a job now is not a problem for most.

But a job is not a career. No one is going to serve you a career on a silver platter. Your career will be what you make it – no more, no less.

And so, as clichéd as it sounds, the starting point is to find what you like doing. A career without passion and enthusiasm will have no meaning, no joy and little hope of long-term success (chapter 120).

Does your career goal keep you awake at night? If not, maybe you need to start worrying. You likely have many more years at work ahead of you and, trust me on this, no one else is having sleepless nights about what happens to your career (except maybe your mum). So, that means no one is steering your career ship.

Are you okay with that?

118 | Three career paths

This could be another uncomfortable read. I make no apologies, because I can help you immensely with the 'Savage Truth' and not at all with a liberal sugar-coating.

Do you think you are a 'good recruiter' when you are only average? It's easy to fool yourself. You are billing more than most in your team, so, surely, you are a 'gun', right?

It doesn't matter where you work – if you recruit in an agency, you will end up with a future that looks like one of these three.

1. You are superb at it

You learn the skills and you earn the relationships. You are an influencer who can manage the moments of truth in recruitment for the greater good. You have mastered the 'craft' of recruitment. You enjoy high self-esteem and respect from your customers, and reap fun and money (chapter 120). Your job is exhilarating and it feels like a vocation and a hobby, not work at all, because you tackle it with passion, believe in what you do and are intrinsically happy to place people in work.

That is recruiting nirvana. It also describes *less than 10%* of all recruiters working right now.

2. You are no good at it

You just don't get it, or you work at a place where you will never get it. You suffer rejection, depression, humiliation and failure. You fight against the tide for a while. You even see flickers of success, but it's a losing battle and you end up hating every day. You fill one job out of five and, although you are not reflective enough to see it, that means you fail 80% of the time at work. And the percentage of candidates you see who you place is even worse!

Soon you will leave the industry entirely, shaking your head in disbelief that anyone could stick at such a relentless job. That's unfortunate; you failed as a recruiter, but it is not the end of the world. You gave it a go and it was wrong for you, and maybe now you will thrive at something else.

3. You are mediocre at it

This is the worst fate of all. You don't have the intuitive love of listening, understanding and making the match. You can't connect with clients or candidates at a level that resonates with them. You don't have the urgency, the negotiating skills or the drive to make things happen. You don't own the moments of truth through sophisticated influencing skills, the hallmark of all successful recruiters. You are just good enough to keep your job and follow a process well enough, but the extreme highs never cancel out the massive lows of this business because you just don't get enough of them. It's a life of bad months followed by the odd average one. You resent what you do and spend a lot of time blaming clients, candidates, colleagues and your employer.

That fate is career purgatory! It is a worse outcome than being no good at recruitment and getting out early.

I am not suggesting everyone must be a superstar. That's not realistic, and that's not life. But you cannot plod as a recruiter. I mean it. This is one job you cannot be average at. Step up! Challenge yourself! Learn new skills. Move up the value chain.

Hear me on this: it is better to fail at this job and get out than be poor at it and stay.

119 | You must be a huge drinker

If you are a drinker, you will likely succeed as a recruiter. Yes, you read that right.

Oh, wait, slight typo!

I mean, You need to be a DRIINCKAE. This is what a DRIINCKAE looks like.

Digital fluidity

People who 'get digital' are comfortable with social media, can build an online brand, are great e-sourcers, can find people on the web and can build relationships online. They maximise the applicant tracking system (ATS) and leap on any new tech brought in to automate the mundane. But they are not one-trick digital ponies. They know when to pivot to real-life communication, when to move offline to face to face or on the phone. They know that the real value in recruitment is in managing the moments of truth, where human influencing skills make all the difference.

Reach

'Reach' means a network. Immense value comes from accessing candidates that others can't. In recruitment, good managers look to hire people who *know* people: people who are 'connected' and known in a niche, or at the very least have the competencies and skill set to build a community and a network. They may not know 'everyone', but they know the right people who know other right people. They know where to find the right people, and they have *instant* credibility once they do.

Intelligence

Intelligence is hugely underestimated in recruitment, I have found. Everyone says recruitment is 'not rocket science' (chapter 1), which is true, but it's not easy, either. Over the long term, recruitment requires an incredible mix of street smarts, commercial nous, interpersonal intelligence and much more. In the modern era, clients and candidates just will not accept mediocrity. In recruitment, you need intellectual prowess, which earns credibility, and emotional intelligence – knowing when to shut up and when to speak, what to say and what not to say.

Influencing skills

Influencing skills is the big one. Huge. Good recruiting managers look for people who have these skills already or have the potential to develop them. Questioning skills. Listening skills. Storytelling. Authenticity. The ability to gain trust through credibility and impact the key moments to create better outcomes for the greater good. These are *must-haves*! So many recruiters are transactors, good at logistics. This is not enough anymore!

No dickheads

Sure, you can bill, but you are not nice to have around. You lack respect for clients, candidates and colleagues. You do more damage than good. You create unrest and tension. You gossip and undermine. Everyone who has been in recruitment for a while is thinking of someone like this right now! No matter how much you bill, I won't hire you. Ever.

Content

Yes, you need the ability to write. Not email so much, but that's a bonus; I mean blogs, status updates, compelling profiles, and InMails to open a candidate outreach conversation.

Knowledge and niche

Specialisation is the future of recruitment. Credibility through expertise: a mile deep and an inch wide. That's the way.

Attitude over résumé

Always prioritise your attitude over your résumé. A good employer can fill the gaps in your experience and skills if you have the right attitude (Part I). Of course, you need a certain amount of proven competence to make a start, but attitude and trajectory also count.

Empathy

I know, 'empathy' might seem like a crazy word when talking about recruiters. But the days of the arrogant, showy, pushy, superficial recruiter are over. Do you want great candidates to work with you? You have to feel their pain and understand their hot buttons. That is the only way to build an offline brand and become a 'talent magnet'.

*

So, there it is. Great recruiters are DRIINCKAEs.

You won't have all of these attributes. You won't hire people who have all of them. But look for the best mix you can find and then work at acquiring the missing ones.

120 | Fun and money

There are only two reasons to come to work: fun and money.

And you must have *both*. Unfortunately, one of them will not be enough. Not if you want to love what you do. A job that gives you just one or the other can often seduce you into thinking you have found your dream job. But, in most cases, that dream fades like a mirage as you realise a crucial ingredient of 'job love' is missing.

For recruiters, who have such a complex job with so many disappointments, you *must* have them both for it all to be worth it. Fun *and* money.

Let's dig into what I mean by 'fun' and 'money'.

At work, 'fun' is much more than just having a giggle. Fun begins with working in a business where you believe in the vision and the ethos. To do a challenging job well every day, it has to have meaning for you. Fun on the job means working with people you like and respect. Fun at work includes collaboration, mutual support and a strong bond forged by shared goals. Fun means winning more than losing, continuous learning, constantly growing as a businessperson and doing something you know impacts people positively. That's fun. And it includes traditional fun, too: being able to laugh, socialise easily, enjoy each other's company and celebrate group and individual success. A job that enhances your self-esteem and sense of worth: that is fun.

If you are going to thrive as a recruiter in any role, you need to have 'fun' the way I define it here.

But what about 'money'?

I don't simply mean the amount you get paid, as crucial as that may be. I mean working in a financially successful business, for a start. You will thrive if you work for a business that has a great product or service and you deliver it well. 'Profit' is not a dirty word. Profit is like oxygen: we don't wake up daily with 'profit' as our only goal, but we sure notice when it's not there!

Making money means being able to invest in people, learning, marketing and technology. And that is fun! 'Money' also means getting a fair reward for the effort put in and the results achieved. So, a heavy compensation element for results is a good thing: that means, if you are good at your job, you get extra-well rewarded. And financial success is important in only one way: it gives you more choices in life.

And that leads us back to fun!

So, there it is. Want to love what you do? Work with the 'twin sisters of the holy grail': fun and money.

121 | Tips for the rookie recruiter

A generation of recruiters left the industry because of the COVID-19 pandemic. However, the industry has bounced back and continues to thrive, so many new recruiters are being hired and trained. And that is a great thing.

But looming in the background is the reality that a massive percentage of rookies don't last. Most won't make a career out of recruiting.

Here is my best road map for somebody starting in agency recruitment for the first time. Of course, it's not a guaranteed formula for success, but follow these guidelines and you give yourself every chance of getting through the first six months – which, frankly, most don't manage!

Do the small things well

First and foremost, do the small things well. For example, turn up to work on time – or, in a remote world, never let a Zoom meeting wait for you. Wear the appropriate clothes for the environment you are joining. Get to every appointment on time. Return messages fast. Meet mini deadlines set for you. Do what you say you will do. Never allow yourself to be 'chased' for a task you committed to.

Be a willing learner

It is critical to be a willing learner. 'Coachability' is a crucial recruiter requirement. Poor listeners, know-it-alls and those who just can't focus on learning different ways in their new environment are likely to fail long-term. Your goal is small steps of incremental improvement every week. You will feel the exhilaration of 'getting better', and you can be sure that your employer will notice.

Keep your head down

I don't mean that you should be a shrinking violet, but don't be too cocky too early. Resist the temptation, on day two, to tell a hilarious story about your holiday in Bali and how drunk you all got. Listen far more than you talk. Of course, engage and be responsive, but know your place… until you know your place.

Don't join a tribe

Alliances, cliques, factions: every office has them. It's tempting to 'join' one as, when you are new, you feel alone. But don't. Treat everyone with respect and be open to help and guidance from everywhere.

Be brave

It might sound strange to talk about courage in a desk job, but you do need to be fearless in recruitment. Make that cold call when it's time to do so. Interview that candidate for the first time. Negotiate a fee if you must. I have noticed that new recruiters show their 'courage colours' early. A good employer will not throw you in the deep end too soon, but they will be delighted to see your willingness to tackle the task head-on. You learn faster doing that, too (chapter 19).

Treat candidates like gold

Treat candidates like gold… actually, no, treat them like human beings with feelings (Part IV). Develop your own 'candidate response charter'. Responsiveness, respect and empathy should be your go-to ethos.

Build your digital online brand from day one

Learn about LinkedIn as a branding platform, blog and build an online community of fans (chapters 58 and 59).

Compete with yourself

Don't get caught up in office ego fights. Your biggest competition is not your 'competitor', your clients, technology, the recruiter sitting next to you or anything else. Your competition is you. You must be better than you were yesterday. Make that your daily goal (chapter 7).

Never stop learning

You are never 'done' as a recruiter. Read articles and blogs ('The Savage Truth' blog, every day, for a start: www.gregsavage.com.au.

Also, visit the Savage Recruitment Academy, for sure. What, you thought this book would be commercial-free?). Attend seminars. Learn from others. Add new skills always (chapter 18).

Look for mentors

Your company will have some great operators (hopefully). Of course, some will be more helpful than others, but all will enjoy an ego stroke when you ask, 'Can I learn from you, please?'

Ask

Listen, learn and try new things, but don't suffer in silence. If you don't understand, ask. Be polite; ensure the person you ask is not in the middle of a critical call. Ask if they have time. Then, ask your question. The answer will be in the business.

Take notes

You are not so smart that you can remember it all. In training, when being coached, when your mentor gives you a tip, write it down. Review it later and implement it. I have conducted 1000 'newbie' training sessions – no exaggeration at all. Seeing a one-week-in recruiter sitting there for 90 minutes and not writing down a single word amazes me. Decades of experience being shared with you in your first week; tangible, actionable tactics and tips – do you think it's going to just 'sink in'? I know right then, they won't make it. And they don't.

Get on the phone

No matter what others do in the office, your mantra will be 'get on the phone'. Think about the outcome you want: is it better achieved via email or over the phone? Usually, it's the latter. Defy your generational instinct to avoid the phone call and swim against what others do. Pick. It. Up.

Don't take it personally

Here is the news: people are going to let you down. Things will go wrong. Clients and candidates will be rude and ungrateful. It's not a popular thing to say, but too bad: toughen the fuck up (chapters 10 and 13)!

Never get drunk at a work function

Don't drink too much at your first work function. Or your second. Or your third. In fact, never drink too much at a work function. Plenty will, but I have never seen anyone enhance their career, reputation or credibility by drinking too much at a work event, and I have been to infinitely more of those than you have.

Develop an ethos of networking from day one

Your first candidate interview went well? Ask the candidate who else they know who may be looking to move. Always be ferreting out new contacts and expanding your network.

Do quality activity with the right people

From the beginning, follow the golden secret that even many experienced recruiters don't know: success comes from quality activity with the right people (chapter 23).

Never assume anything

Even if the 'wise' ones around you make assumptions, don't. Ask. Check in. Recalibrate. Be sure you know your client or candidate's thoughts before you act or advise (chapter 27).

Engage

From day one, build relationships based on equality. Engage. Take the long-term view. Do what you say you are going to do. Never leave anyone wondering (chapter 25).

Don't mess with your reputation

Your reputation is the only thing you will take with you when you leave. Every contact with candidates, clients or colleague is a moment of truth. Ask yourself after every interaction, *Did what I just did or said enhance or damage my reputation?* Remember, it's not only about the candidates you help – it's also about the ones you don't help. Treat people with respect, do what you say you're going to do and never screw anyone over and, in the long run, your reputation will get you there (chapter 128).

122 | AI, automation and your career

In my first book, *The Savage Truth*, I covered the topic of artificial intelligence (AI) and automation, and little has changed since then. I am very confident about our industry. I am investing in recruitment companies and recruitment tech.

Our industry is rapidly evolving, but it will not die anytime soon. Recruiter jobs won't disappear altogether, but the job of the recruiter will most definitely change because of AI. If you don't adapt accordingly, you will not survive as a recruiter.

The recruiter role is not over, nor will it soon be. But you must consider where you actually remain of value. What do you need to be good at to 'beat the machine'?

Let the technology take from recruiters what technology does *better* than humans, because now there is a great deal that machines can do better and will do better soon. Understanding that you won't beat technology at what it does well is critical because it shows you where you must excel.

Let's have a look at what computers do well.

Sourcing

Talent identification – finding people – will become easier and easier. Everyone is online, and most people are online more than ever before. Privacy is disappearing as a concept, and the search tools available now are getting more and more powerful. Soon, finding candidates – that job that sourcers thought was such an arcane art – will be done by an algorithm. AI will be easily programmed to find skill sets across digital databases, and it will do it better than people can.

So, the 'finding people' part of sourcing becomes less complicated, but the contacting and engaging is more complex than ever.

Screening

Innovative technology can easily and quickly assess candidate CV suitability against the job description and automatically parse résumés in a database. There will no longer be a need for human screening at the first contact.

This might be good because most recruiters do not read résumés in full. They make gut decisions about résumés, don't review social profiles and do not talk to every candidate. Robots may well do the screening job better. Faster, for sure, but better as well.

Automation of logistics

Already fully functioning chatbots handle logistics now, such as arranging interviews, saving the recruiter vast chunks of clerical time. Reference-checking, while not 'logistics', is another part of the process that is becoming increasingly automated.

Matching

At first pass, machines will match résumés to a job description faster and better than humans. But, of course, when it comes to nuance, reading between the lines, assessing potential and trajectory, then things are different.

Chatbots

Increasingly pervasive and sophisticated, chatbots are everywhere online already. They can ask predetermined questions to screen a candidate, answer questions or update a candidate about where they are in the hiring process. Some chatbots can also generate and place ads on job boards and push appropriate job listings to candidates automatically.

Research suggests that chatbots are improving the candidate experience and generating a higher percentage of candidates who follow through on applications. Consider the amount of time recruiters save here if this is all done by automation.

Late in 2022, we saw the emergence of the next generation of chatbots with advanced conversational capabilities, such as ChatGPT. They can answer questions and perform tasks such as writing essays, blogs, emails and even code. Early feedback is that they are highly effective, and there are implications for recruiters in that these tools may well be able to write better candidate outreach emails, job descriptions and marketing content than recruiters can. We will see, but there is no doubt that this is all part of the evolving role of tech in recruitment.

*

So, all *that* leads us to the elephant in the room, a huge question that must be addressed. AI will handle sourcing, screening, matching, logistics, reference-checking and even early assessment. So, if automation is going to do such significant parts of recruiters' jobs, what is left for recruiters to do?

This is what I believe: any task that takes no time to think about will be automated. Where potential answers can be predicted and predefined, an algorithm can be written and a computer can predict outcomes with scary accuracy through machine learning. But tasks that take thought, planning and opinion are much harder for AI to replicate. Where there are shades of grey and nuance, and influencing is possible, AI is unlikely to help.

A good example of this is what most recruiters call 'sourcing'. An algorithm can find people; for example, if you key in 'Melbourne, UX designer', your computer can scour LinkedIn, Twitter, Facebook and a thousand other digital storage houses and find people. Well, actually, it won't find people – it will find their profiles! And that's the point. Machines can find the profiles, but the *people* are harder to reach.

Approaching people takes skill and finesse. It requires tailored, sophisticated, bespoke outreach (chapter 66). That takes thought, planning and market knowledge. It needs credibility and insight, as well as articulation and listening skills. It's a seduction. It's a sell.

When is AI going to do that?

This is how we must face the future that will be hard upon us soon: AI, and technology generally, frees you up to do much better that which only you can do. This is critical to grasp and act on. You need to be very, very good at that part of recruitment that machines cannot do, because that is the sweet spot.

Ironically, this means that the actual value of a recruiter will now be in their selling skills. The real value is in the 'craft' of recruitment. That is the bit of your job that will be left once the machines march in. The part of recruitment that is left for recruiters to do is the human part.

When I use the word 'selling', I need you to understand sales differently. I don't mean cold calling, handing out business cards at an event or spamming candidates around town. I use 'selling' to mean influencing, persuading, advising, consulting, listening, storytelling, networking and building reputation and brand. Yes, I use the word 'selling' in a much more modern, holistic and consultative way.

This raises two fundamental truths:

1. The recruiter can act as a real *strategy advisor* to clients: credible enough to work as a talent consultant, a sharer of knowledge, an influencer of tactics and a creator of outcomes. This will be true of both agency and in-house recruiters.
2. The agency recruiter will shift to acting as an *agent* for the best talent, which is a much bigger statement than it first sounds because it involves trust and exclusivity.

Your value as a recruiter is in your knowledge, your advice, your influencing, your consulting, your networks, your brand, your influencing and your problem-solving skills.

Embrace the technology and automate as much as you can so you can add value where it counts. That will be your competitive advantage.

123 | The 'C' word will kill your career

Much of recruitment is changing fast. We may not like it, but that is a fact. Technology is the most obvious part, but candidate behaviour and client expectations are also changing.

Most recruiters respond to this change in one of three ways, all of which will hold you back and may even signal your demise:

1. **The ostrich:** You bury your head in the sand and do absolutely nothing. You convince yourself and those around you that 'it will all be okay' and 'the old ways still work best'. You have your card-and-sticky-note system. You have your 'loyal clients'. 'It is a people business, nothing more', you cry. 'Recruitment is still recruitment' is your mantra, and you are sticking to it!
2. **The worker bee:** You can feel the change affecting your results and you are concerned, but you are uncertain how to respond. So, you work even harder at the things that are not working, trying to replace quality with quantity: more untargeted cold calls, more mindless scrolling through LinkedIn, more spam emails and InMails, and more poorly worded job ads that bring tons of irrelevant candidates – which you then vigorously screen because it's good to feel busy! Right?
3. **The puppy dog:** You know you must evolve and you are trying, but, mostly, you are making small, ineffectual changes at the periphery, like advertising on different job boards or writing the odd blog. There's lots of activity, but none of it is forward or effective. There's no plan. There's no structure.

None of these options is anywhere near good enough. Agency recruitment is not dying, but your career might.

So, there is the fourth way, the one you must follow: embrace the change like a long-lost brother and use it to make you more effective. *Reject* the 'C' word: *complacency*. Test your paradigms of the recruiting world daily. Everything is changing; so, inevitably, you must change, too. AI is not a threat if you use it to soak up all the drudgery so you can become better at selling, consulting and creating outcomes.

Here is how you can reject complacency:

- Get specific about incremental change – slight shifts to the way you have always worked. It is a recruitment truth that getting 5% better at the critical moments of truth means you will become 50% more productive (chapter 18).
- Undertake a self-managed 'nanodegree'. Give yourself three months to upskill or learn about something you know is a weak

spot for you. It is not your company's job to do this; it is your job. After all, it is your career, right (chapter 117)?

- Take on a mentor to challenge and stretch you. I have had countless recruiters sit opposite me and proudly trumpet, 'I have five years of recruitment experience!' They are wrong: they have *one* year's recruitment experience *repeated five times over*. They are no better now than they were after 12 months. They are stagnant. They are stale. They rinse and repeat.

Today's recruiter is never 'done'. You are never 'trained', 'expert' or 'finished with learning'. It's a constant process of renewal, upskilling and starting again.

I like the concept of 'living on the edge' because it suggests being alert, dexterous and nimble. From today, I encourage you to adopt as your mantra that you will live on the edge. The word 'edge' means 'sharp', which is what modern recruiters must be if they are to be future-fit – which is hard for many of us who are very set in our ways. That needs to change.

Past success as a recruiter is no longer a reliable indicator of future success. Think about that, please. You cannot rely on your track record, your history.

The more experienced you are, the more danger you are in. Inertia, resistance, complacency: they will kill your career.

Be 'edgy'. You must reinvent yourself and become a better version of what you already are. Now.

124 | 'Now' is never 'normal'

I went to school on a bus reserved for 'whites only'. That referred to people, if you are confused.

This was normal. And it was just the tiny tip of the racist apartheid iceberg designed to secure white privilege and deny fundamental freedoms and opportunities to most of the population of South Africa.

When I turned 18 and ventured down to the pub in Cape Town, I had a choice of the 'Men's Bar' or the 'Ladies' Bar'. The Men's Bar was not a euphemism: it was a bar reserved solely for those of the male gender. The Ladies' Bar was not for women only but was so called because it allowed women to join men for a drink.

This was normal.

Of course, I refer to white men and women in both cases, because other races were not admitted. Totally normal.

I came to Australia at age 21 and didn't suffer from culture shock on these matters. After all, we were only seven years on from allowing people of First Nations descent to be counted in the census as *human beings* resident in this country.

This was normal.

If I slid into the local pub in Adelaide for a quiet one – and I assure you, I did – I found a similar situation to that in Cape Town. I might choose the 'Public Bar' for my imbibing, but this was an ironic misnomer as, until the mid-1970s, *only men* were permitted to drink in public bars. Most pubs included a Ladies' Lounge with chairs and tables where women and men could drink together, but women were usually not admitted to the Ladies' Lounge unless accompanied by a man, and were usually not permitted to buy their own drinks. Of course, no bars were available for First Nations citizens, but they were generously allowed to buy 'grog' in paper bags through a door at the back of the pub.

This was normal.

Five years into my recruiting career, and after two years in London, I came to Sydney in 1985. This was pre-internet, so there were no job boards, and classified advertising in the newspapers ruled the day when it came to job-search. *The Sydney Morning Herald* had a massive lift-out of jobs called 'The Classifieds', and it was 100 pages thick and full of job ads, all paid for by recruiting agencies and direct-hiring companies. These were the 'rivers of gold' that drove the fortunes of the mighty Fairfax Media (although nowadays those rivers of gold have been diverted and flow to Seek).

But when you opened the lift-out, it was broken into two sections. So, prepare yourselves for what is to come.

The first section was called 'Men and Boys' and the second section was called 'Women and Girls'.

Please reflect on what I'm telling you. When I was six years into my recruiting career, people placed ads in the paper according to the gender they thought those jobs fit. Indeed, if somebody were looking for a nurse's job, they would go to 'Women and Girls', while an accountant would peruse 'Men and Boys'. Because, you know, men couldn't be wasted on a girl's job like nursing, could they? And a woman couldn't be trusted with important, 'smart' jobs like handling numbers, could they? Obviously not!

This was normal.

In Sydney and London in the 1980s, every job we took started with the specification of the gender sought. Also, I'm sure it was probably against the law, but I can assure you that it was commonplace to specify your preferred (or *required*) racial profile, too.

This was normal.

In South Africa, the UK and Australia at that time, it was commonplace to refer to those who were not heterosexual with what we would describe today as horrific homophobic slurs. There were dozens of words used, but in Australia the most popular started with a 'P', in South Africa the most used descriptor began with an 'M' (you won't get it unless you have lived there) and in the UK it probably started with an 'F' or a 'B'. I am not talking about late-night bar-room bigotry – these words were used in board rooms, schools, workplaces, sports fields and on the bus by men and women alike (and children too, consequently).

This was normal. No one blinked at this – except perhaps the people who were, in fact, being referred to! But few knew because the closet was jam-packed at that time.

If this shocks you, I am pleased, because it serves my point.

So, what do we learn from this very recent history?

Firstly, be slow to smirk at my examples and write them off as failings of the three countries I have referred to. Every country has its dirty past (and some of them have a pretty grubby present). The problem is that, at the time, we mainly did not think it was 'dirty' at all.

It was *normal.*

Secondly, there is little we regard now as 'normal' that we can take for granted and consider permanent. The emergence of specifying personal pronouns to clarify your gender identity for everyone is not something many of us would have predicted only a few years ago.

The fanatical Twitterati and social media ranters who bang on about the 'new normal' and how working from home (WFH) is here to stay are good examples of those who have no grasp of historical precedent. I am not arguing for or against WFH, but it's not unlikely that after one deep, prolonged recession, people will work where they are told to work.

Pretty much nothing is forever. That is both scary and exhilarating. We can drive change, and we can improve our lot and that of others. But we also need to be nimble!

The pace of change has accelerated exponentially. Therefore, we must be dexterous and prepared to make informed predictions and change course accordingly.

There is no such thing as the 'new normal'. Stop saying it. There is only the 'now normal', which is about to be replaced by the next 'now normal'.

Savvy recruiters adapt accordingly.

125 | Wasted emotion

Don't get me wrong, being emotional about placing people in jobs is expected. In fact, it's essential. I love the passion of a recruiter on a mission to fill a role or place a candidate. I am relaxed about screams of joy or moans of despair. I love a placement dance!

That is healthy emotion. It's *wasted* emotion you have to curb and eliminate.

The days of moping because a placement fell through. The bitterness and angst over a temp who bombed out. The tears and recriminations over some meaningless in-office spat. The self-pity and 'woe is me' because a candidate got a counteroffer. The slumped shoulders and defeatist language that follows a bad month or quarter. All that is wasted emotion.

It's dragging you down. It's wearing out your battery. It's eating away at your self-esteem. Also, it's dragging those around you down.

You have chosen a challenging career. In this job, people will let you down. People will lie to you. People will back out of commitments. People will be rude and ungrateful. 'Certainties' will crumble (chapter 10).

So, there – now you know.

I don't expect you to be a recruiting robot. Have a quick cry. Kick the desk. Have a few beers. Then, leave it there! Move on. Don't waste your emotion on stuff that's dead and gone (chapter 13).

Save the emotion for the next placement dance!

126 | You can recruit worldwide

My recruitment career has allowed me to run and own recruitment businesses worldwide. Literally. At Aquent, we had 30 offices in 17 countries (from 2001 to 2010). With Firebrand, I owned a company with 10 offices in 8 countries. My speaking gigs have taken me to dozens of cities across five continents. My 320,000 LinkedIn followers and 1 million blog readers a year engage with me consistently.

So, I have had the privilege of seeing recruitment and recruiters worldwide close up. It has been a privilege and I have learned so much, but especially this: great recruiting is great recruiting – anywhere! The core tactics and competencies that make for a great recruiter are the same everywhere.

If only I had a dollar for every time I have been told, 'Oh, but that won't work here, Greg!' or 'Things are different here'. You don't even have to cross borders to hear it. Try going to Brisbane in Australia with an idea born 'down south'. Tell someone in Manchester, 'This is how the London office does things'. Tell a Capetonian that 'the okes (dudes/guys) in Joburg do things this way'. Open a conversation in Christchurch with the line, 'Hey, in Auckland, what they do is…' and see how that flies – the word 'JAFA' (just another effing Aucklander) will come up early and often. In Osaka, they don't even trust the udon from Tokyo, let alone the recruiting!

Everyone believes where they are is 'different', usually harder and somehow more complex – in a word, special.

At a certain level, of course, they are right. A client visit in Japan follows a different path in terms of manners and protocol to the free-flowing style of Australia, for example. Yes, every country has its traditions, etiquette, habits and nuances.

However, the core aspects of recruiting? The ability to sell? The crucial need to focus on activity? The importance of prioritising, qualifying and talent-picking? The need to know and deliver on critical metrics? The deep understanding of your clients? The need for continuous learning? The ability to manage stress? The ability to plan? Recruiter equity? Listening and influencing skills? A candidate-care ethos? Winning exclusivity? The resilience required to survive? Managing the 'craft'?

These elements are universal.

127 | Are you a 'recruiting tragic'?

If recruitment takes hold and becomes your career, it will become your life, too. When that happens, you will be a 'recruiting tragic'.

What is a recruiting tragic? Someone who can't help bringing most things in life back to recruiting, or recruitment, or recruiters.

I admit to being guilty. I know many others in the club. We did not plan to be like this. We don't speak of our affliction; it's just in our DNA.

Think you may be a recruitment tragic? How many of these have you been guilty of?

1. You see two people – smartly dressed, folders by their sides – talking earnestly at a café. You are immediately convinced it's a job interview and you try to work out who is doing the hiring.
2. When you meet someone new socially, it starts to get interesting only when they talk about their job.
3. In any new town, your eye automatically finds recruitment agency shopfronts or signs that suggest a recruiter occupies the building. In extreme cases, you take photos of recruitment offices in strange places. (Confession: I have pictures from Myanmar, Kathmandu, Darwin, Santiago, Cape Town and a

dozen other places. I know, I know! But, remember, I admitted guilt already. Recruiting tragic!)

4. The weatherman on TV says, 'Temps tomorrow will go up to the high 30s', and you think, 'Not a bad temp count this week. Wonder what the margin is?' Or, you see a poster like this one I snapped on my phone (see figure 19). It was in a car park, talking about parking, but I immediately thought, 'Cheap Perm Placements'.

Figure 19: Cheap perms

5. You don't mean to do it, you can't help doing it, but within a few minutes of meeting a new person you have decided whether they would make a good recruiter or not. (Usually not.)
6. Just chatting with friends and acquaintances, talking about why they might leave their current job, you want to drill down on a potential counteroffer – right there, right now!
7. The 'employment statistics' put out by the government (any government) just make you laugh as they are so at odds with the reality on the ground as you see it.
8. You know there are many hopeless recruiters out there, and you criticise them yourself, but you still feel very offended when recruiters are demonised as a group. When confronted by a pompous 'anti-recruiter' type, you think to yourself, *Well, you are a lawyer and defend criminals for a living! And you are a*

banker and probably a criminal! All I do is find people jobs and help companies grow. Or, if you are beyond redemption, like me, you say those things aloud. Very liberating, I find.

9. Any interview scene on TV or in a movie – indeed, any hiring scenario – gets you on the edge of your seat and is often much more interesting to you than finding out who committed the murder. (Oh, and you also consider most of these scenes to be 'unrealistic' and not the way it would *actually* happen.)
10. A drive in an unfamiliar part of town has you mentally taking notes of company names you see on signs because 'they look like they have lots of staff needs'. Sometimes, you stop and write company names down or dictate them into your phone.
11. Sitting on a train or a bus, you start fantasising that the 'perfect' candidate for the crucial, hard-to-fill role you are working on is sitting just across from you. Or maybe next to you. Or by the door. They are definitely on this train or bus!
12. You read random job ads and mentally edit them as they 'should have been worded'. Then, you read between the clichés to decipher what is really going on!
13. When you travel, you study the local job ads as closely as anything else, as I did in Dubai one time and was richly rewarded with this incredible job advert that would get you in big trouble in other countries (see figure 20)!

Figure 20: A job ad in Dubai

14. When a friend is battling to decide between potential partners in a relationship situation, you offer advice using terms like 'shortlisting', 'reference-checking', 'second interviews' and, sometimes, 'performance on the job'.

15. You will never admit it, you are ashamed to admit it, but I am admitting it: you sometimes dream about candidates and clients! Not in a creepy way; they just seep into your unconscious mind because… well, because you are a recruiting tragic!
16. Someone you hardly know mentions they have secured a new job. Then, even though you know better, you make the fatal social faux pas of asking what the salary is. You know it's wrong. It's just that the words tumble out before you can stop them, and you have to check if it's 'market rate'.
17. When a friend comes back from a first date, you debrief them like you would a candidate reporting back on a first interview, asking if they 'pre-closed' a second date and occasionally asking what it would take for them to 'have a follow-up meeting'.
18. A friend or acquaintance asks you to help her 16-year-old daughter with her résumé for her first part-time job application. You produce a five-page masterpiece that might well get the CEO of BHP their next job! And, if they ask you to give her some tips, God help her! She is given a gearing, role-play interview, and tutoring on grooming and etiquette, is asked to prepare 20 questions and is told to buy new shoes for the interview!
19. In the toughest of times, you plan to leave recruitment. You even look up job ads and bookmark them. You are definitely leaving recruitment! But you don't. Ever. (Except for the few tragics who actually do quit… and then come back, quick smart!

So tragic! But we are happy, right? And proud, too (chapter 3).

128 | Treasure your reputation

As I said in chapter 121, your reputation is the only thing you will take with you throughout your career when you leave a role. Every contact with candidates, clients and colleagues is a moment of truth for you and your career.

Ask yourself after every interaction, 'Did what I just did or said enhance or damage my reputation?'

Remember, it's not only about the candidates you help – it's also about the ones you don't help. That goes for clients, too, and colleagues and suppliers.

The phone call not returned. The borderline lie. The snappy response. The shoddy piece of work. The poor service. All of these and much more will impact your reputation.

Treat people with respect, do what you say you're going to do and never screw anyone over, and your reputation will get you there in the long run.

Your reputation is your elixir of eternal recruitment-career life. Protect it and burnish it through your actions.

Acknowledgements

Thank you, Lesley Williams of Major Street Publishing, who jumped on my musing about a second book and ensured it got done.

I have had the most exhilarating ride across five decades of recruitment and I am deeply grateful for all I encountered on the journey: recruiters, clients, candidates, business partners, suppliers and all who have supported my events, social channels, Academy, 'The Savage Truth' blog and my first book, *The Savage Truth*. Thanks, too, to the recruiting associations who have been so supportive over the years – in particular, the RCSA and APSCo in Australia, and REC in the UK.

I am so fortunate to receive regular, tangible affirmation of my speaking and writing efforts, and it is that feedback that prompted me to write this book.

I am also acutely aware that what success I have had over the years in recruitment has been supported by many people in many different ways. So, thank you, everyone. I am very grateful.

To Bronwyn: thank you, as always, for everything.

Acknowledgements

Afterword

I first met Greg Savage sometime in the late 1990s in his capacity as one of the founding Directors of Recruitment Solutions; I was writing at the time and went along to interview him for a story on the business. I instantly liked him, not least because he was refreshingly direct, but also because he made my job incredibly easy. His willingness to share his experience, mistakes and successes in equal measure, without a need to dress up the facts or always frame a positive response, made for a compelling story.

Decades on, Greg continues to lean into the concept of sharing his knowledge. In fact, there are few people I can think of in the recruitment profession who have been as giving as he has. It's been, as the cliché says, a win-win formula: our profession has gained tremendous insight and learnings while Greg has built an outstanding career as a trainer, speaker, advisor and, not least, successful author.

I was privileged to have some input into his first book, *The Savage Truth*, a biography of Greg's personal and professional life that is a must-read if you haven't already. Naturally, I'm delighted to see that, true to his trademark style, Greg has turned his hand to yet another invaluable resource in this, his second publishing venture, this time a practical how-to on all aspects of recruitment.

RECRUIT – The Savage Way is the perfect training ground for all staff – both new and established – and will be a brilliant check-in for leaders to ensure they're covering all bases when it comes to developing their teams. As Managing Director of APSCo, the Association for professional firms in Australia, I applaud Greg for all that he has – and continues to – contribute to the development and professionalism of this wonderful industry.

Consider this book as a significant leg up for your career as this will undoubtedly be your roadmap for a successful career in recruitment.

Lesley Horsburgh
Managing Director, APSCo Australia

The Savage Recruitment Academy

The Savage Recruitment Academy is an e-learning platform for recruitment-specific training presented by Greg Savage and hand-picked industry colleagues.

Every recruitment leader agrees that ongoing training and development are integral to your agency's productivity and staff retention. Unfortunately, it is the first thing to fall by the wayside when business starts heating up.

The Savage Recruitment Academy offers a solution to this problem by providing world-class training on demand. Individuals or agencies can subscribe to the platform on a quarterly basis to gain ongoing access to Greg's critically acclaimed masterclasses, along with Sixty Savage Seconds microlearning videos and regular webinars.

The Academy has the full range of competencies covered:

- A comprehensive 15-module 'Rookie Programme' to fast-track your newbies
- An extensive range of development material for experienced recruiters covering candidate and client skills, selling and much more
- 'Team Leader' and 'Billing Managers' masterclasses
- Owner-level and director-level material, including strategy and growth
- Marketing, social media, branding and use of LinkedIn.

There are currently over 60 hours of recruitment-training video content, with new material added regularly.

From February 2023, the Savage Recruitment Academy is powered by a state-of-the-art learning management system (LMS), allowing users to easily navigate the 60+ hours of recruitment-training content.

New features for the Savage Recruitment Academy include:

- A new Netflix-style layout, allowing you to browse through courses based on category and skill level easily
- Unpacked versions of every Savage Masterclass, allowing you to quickly navigate to content relevant to your training needs (growing the Academy to over 180 courses!)
- Tracking of your learning history, allowing you to pick up from where you left off with any in-progress courses
- Full reporting for team leaders, allowing you to track your organisation's utilisation of the academy platform.

Subscribe today to have 40 years of recruitment experience at your fingertips!

The Savage Truth

Lessons on leadership, business and life from 40 years in recruitment

The Savage Truth is the story of Greg Savage, his stellar career in recruitment and the lessons he has learned on leadership, business and life over a career spanning four decades. *The Savage Truth* is a must-read for recruiters, next-generation leaders and lovers of business biography.

It is a book in two parts. The first part covers Greg's early life – the people and events that shaped him – and follows his career path, which took him from his hometown of Cape Town around the world before settling in Sydney. He gives an honest, open, often humorous account of his experiences, which reflect how much recruitment and business have changed.

In the second part of the book, Greg distils his learnings into guidance and advice for his successors in the recruitment industry and, more broadly, to anyone working in the business. Topics he covers include recipes for business success; scaling a start-up; taking a company to IPO; making successful acquisitions; growing a cross-border global business; preparing for, surviving and managing a recession; building a personal brand; recruitment marketing; negotiating fees and margins; hiring great people; the attitudes that shape success; people leverage; performance management; 'Savage' leadership skills; and preparing your business for your exit – and, of course, great recruitment skills.

All this is liberally sprinkled with amusing anecdotes and historical facts, as well as painful admissions of mistakes made and lessons learned.

Throughout his fascinating career, Greg has learned countless lessons in leadership, business and life. One of his greatest achievements is his success as a communicator. Greg is one of the most highly respected voices across the global recruitment and professional services industries, speaking regularly to audiences around the world. An early adopter of social media for recruiters, Greg's industry blog, 'The Savage Truth', is a must-read in the recruitment industry. In November 2018, he was named one of LinkedIn's 'Top Voices'.

The Savage Truth has surpassed 10,000 copies sold globally. In 2022, *The Savage Truth* was included in the curriculum as required reading for the National College of Ireland's Bachelor of Arts (Honours) Degree in Recruitment Practice.